This Thing Called Trust

This Thing Called Trust

Civic Society in Britain

Paul Stoneman
Researcher, Institute for Social and Technical Research
University of Essex, UK

palgrave
macmillan

First published 2008 by
PALGRAVE MACMILLAN

Palgrave Macmillan in the UK is an imprint of Macmillan Publishers Limited, registered in England, company number 785998, of Houndmills, Basingstoke, Hampshire RG21 6XS.

Palgrave Macmillan in the US is a division of St Martin's Press LLC, 175 Fifth Avenue, New York, NY 10010.

Palgrave Macmillan is the global academic imprint of the above companies and has companies and representatives throughout the world.

Palgrave® and Macmillan® are registered trademarks in the United States, the United Kingdom, Europe and other countries.

ISBN-13: 978–0–230–54267–9 hardback
ISBN-10: 0–230–54267–0 hardback

This book is printed on paper suitable for recycling and made from fully managed and sustained forest sources. Logging, pulping and manufacturing processes are expected to conform to the environmental regulations of the country of origin.

A catalogue record for this book is available from the British Library.

Library of Congress Cataloging-in-Publication Data

Stoneman, Paul, 1978–
This thing called trust : civic society in Britain / Paul Stoneman.
p. cm.
Includes bibliographical references and index.
ISBN 978–0–230–54267–9
1. Political participation – Great Britain. 2. Civil society – Great Britain. 3. Trust – Political aspects – Great Britain. I. Title.

JN900.S76 2008
300.941—dc22 2008030651

10 9 8 7 6 5 4 3 2 1
17 16 15 14 13 12 11 10 09 08

Printed and bound in Great Britain by
CPI Antony Rowe, Chippenham and Eastbourne

Contents

Tables

Figures

Preface

We all know that politicians lie, or at the very least hold back the full truth. We also know that they make mistakes; they are after all human. But there is a fine line between a critical public demanding more trustworthy political elites and a cynical public unwilling to entertain politics at all. In Britain and across many western democracies there is a growing feeling that politics doesn't matter and that politicians are generally all the same. Political cynicism is beginning to crowd out political activism. With it comes declining participation rates in 'conventional' politics like voting in a general election, and when votes are registered, they are less predictable than they have ever been. Since the turn of the millennium, pollsters have never had it so hard.

This is why trust is *the* buzz word in today's civil societies. Academics and politicians are increasingly realising that by ignoring the issue, generations of potentially active citizens could be lost to the realm of cynicism. Some individuals initially helped me to recognise this. In particular Andy Wroe first brought the trust literature alive for me and Paul Whiteley was a constant source of encouragement and all round knowledge and guidance, while Albert Weale, David Sanders and John Bartle also offered much needed advice. My thanks to all of them.

Introduction

Between 1997 and 2005, the Labour Party in Britain had governed for two successive terms for the first time in its history. Throughout this period, one word seemed to dominate the political landscape: *Trust*. The word was central to New Labour's electoral campaign after political scandals of Tory sleaze and corruption, and upon election in 1997, Blair stated, 'the British people have put their trust in us. It is a moving and it is a humbling experience, and the size of our likely majority imposes a special sort of responsibility on us'. Within months, however, Tony Blair was forced to ask the British public for its trust again in the wake of the 'cash for favours' row involving Bernie Ecclestone.[1] He then pleaded for the public's trust once more over public service reforms upon election victory in 2001. 'We earned the trust of the people in 1997 ... and we know also that though we have striven at all times for your trust, there have [been] times of difficulty too.'[2] In 2003, the Prime Minister was then perhaps faced with the most serious question of trust any British leader has ever encountered – lying about intelligence and hiding his real motive behind the invasion of Iraq.[3] Ironically, and as an attempt to reduce the intensity of the debate, Blair argued that the decision to go to war with Iraq was 'not a matter of trust but of judgement'.[4] He recognised that a lapse of judgement is perhaps forgivable; duping others to misplace their trust is not. This marks a fundamental change in how the public evaluates government and politicians. No longer is British politics dominated by ideology; it is dominated by concerns of *integrity*.

Arguing for trust or not for trust, New Labour's time in office under Tony Blair illuminated trust's pivotal role between the governed and government in Britain and perhaps any Western Democracy. Acknowledged as a crucial moral resource, no government's or politician's stock of political capital can endure without it. The concern is that recent survey data demonstrates that government in Britain is perceived as the least trustworthy public authority. This book seeks to understand why.

Scope of the book

Despite being a popular word in everyday discourse, particularly for politicians, this thing called trust is actually quite allusive. It is notoriously hard to make but easy to break. It is also allusive in terms of its meaning, in terms of measuring it, and finally, in terms of explaining it. It is this triumvirate of concerns that represent the initial focus of the forthcoming chapters:

- What does the concept of trust mean?
- How can we measure it?
- What factors explain different levels of trust?

Establishing a clear conceptual and theoretical framework for trust provides the basis for exploring it empirically. While trust in society and trust in government are both considered throughout, it is the latter that is of primary concern, especially trust of government in Britain.

Background

In Britain in 2004, the Audit Commission concerned by the lack of faith in public authorities commissioned a report, *Trust in Public Institutions*.[5] The concern also extends to many other nations (see Norris 1999 and Pharr and Putnam 2000 for example). At stake, it is argued, is the efficacy of democratic government and its ability to represent interests and solve social and economic problems (Nye et al. 1997; Norris 1999; Pharr and Putnam 2000; Hetherington 2004).

But the literature on trust doesn't start and end with politics and the political process. Whether it is choosing a partner, a simple economic transaction between two people, or forming a treaty between nations, trust plays its part by enabling the belief that all parties involved will carry out their promises. As Hollis notes,

> Everyday is an adventure in trusting thousands of others, seen and unseen, to act reliably. Would you exchange your old car for my pile of banknotes if you thought I might have printed the notes in my

> cellar? You might risk it if you knew your old car was all rust under the new paint. Fraud is a fact of life too. But fraud depends on honesty in general and we readily grant the overall need for banknotes to be genuine and second-hand cars what they seem. (Hollis 1998: 10)

Put simply, trust pervades all walks of life, and to a certain extent it is taken for granted. For example, when was the last time you did actually check the authenticity of the banknotes you carry? It is fortunate we don't always have to, as the costs to an economy would be very serious if continually checking banknotes instead of planning how to spend them was the norm. This is why Putnam (1993, 2000) believes trust 'lubricates life'; it allows us to go about our daily business without the need to monitor others' intentions and actions. And it does so in many hidden ways that trust is often taken for granted.

Ulrich Beck's (1992) vision of Western societies as risk societies captures the uncertain nature of the environments that surround us. In the face of uncertainty, we undertake decisions of risk; and with risk, the question of who to trust and why becomes a central concern. The outcomes that we commonly identify as risks – such as crime, pollution, food hygiene, and bad government – are more or less a risk depending on the action of others (Coleman 1990: 91). And if we can trust the relevant others, then uncertain environments can be negotiated without harm. For example, communities in which social trust is widespread, crime is less of a risk (Putnam 2000: 67); where business magnates can be trusted to run ethical companies, pollution and food are less of a risk to our health; and when politicians make sincere and realistic promises, government is less of a risk to our political interests.

The concern with trust in government

Much of the impetus for the current wave of research on political trust stems from the declining trust index in America. Between 1960 and 1994, the number of survey respondents believing that Government in Washington 'will do the right thing' fell from 73 per cent to just 22. This spawned a host of comparative research that attempted to corroborate the findings in the US with many other Western democracies (for example Norris 1999; Pharr and Putnam 2000). One factor soon became clear; falling trust in government was not unique to America, it was happening simultaneously across many different countries that have different political systems and different cultures (see Dalton 1999: 63–4; Inglehart 1999: 250–3; Newton 1999b: 175–6 for the relevant data).

Noticing that trust indices had fallen across Western democracies, political scientists became concerned. A clear shift in the role and perception of government had occurred in the latter half of the twentieth century. In the aftermath of the Second World War, government was viewed as benign. In 1945, for example, Clement Attlee's Labour government embarked on a political project that marked a new beginning for the relationship between British governments and the citizenry: the establishment of a welfare state. No longer would government let the underprivileged fend for themselves; from the cradle to the grave, it would attempt to make sure that no individual suffered in abject poverty. In the United States, a similar vision for government was emerging. By the 1960s, Lyndon Johnson's goal of the 'Great Society' meant government initiated multi-million dollar programmes promising to eradicate racial conflict, inner-city decay, crime, poor housing and poverty. On both sides of the Atlantic, buoyed by two decades of peace and rising prosperity, office holders – and more importantly the public – believed that government would improve the quality of life for all.

But how circumstances changed. Survey research now suggests that public scepticism towards government is currently the norm. Political party membership levels have fallen dramatically across Western democracies (Dalton 1999), unconventional elite-challenging activities are on the increase (Inglehart 1999), and publics no longer believe their governments and politicians to tell the truth and act for a greater good (Nye et al. 1997; Pattie and Johnston 2001). Paradoxically, the scepticism doesn't flow one way. Office holders and seekers also reflect the changing perceptions of government. In the US for example, it is prudent to run *against* government. Despite the recent Democratic Party belief in a proactive role for government, Bill Clinton in his State of the Union Address (1995) declared that 'the era of big government is over ...' reminiscent of Ronald Reagan's claim that 'government is not the solution to our problems; government *is* the problem' (1981 Inaugural Address). This captures a sentiment that is no longer uniquely partisan in origin, that is, unique to parties of 'the right' who believe in a 'minimal state'. In Europe, the anti-government rhetoric is neither as stark nor as widespread, but the policy response has been very similar: to limit, and in some cases reduce the role of government. In Germany, the 'Agenda 2010' policy programme initiated tax cuts and reduced public spending in an attempt to revive the German economy. In Britain, the Labour Party ditched its long-standing commitment to the state ownership of national services and industries in order to present itself as a viable electoral option.[6]

It is this 'fall from grace' (Nye et al. 1997: 6) that has alarmed political scientists. The institution of government held in high esteem in the 1950s and much of the 1960s is now an object of general scorn and derision. And furthermore, there doesn't seem an obvious reason why. Western democracies have enjoyed a democratic peace, witnessed the end of the Cold War, and are more prosperous than ever. Yet faith in public institutions has dwindled. The shift in public mood has been stark and anomalous, and surely losing faith in government is not a good thing. Or perhaps it is.

Why worry?

Russell Hardin (1998, 2002) argues a crucial point: trust is only desirable when the relevant other is trustworthy. Without trustworthiness, trust is misplaced. But Hardin fails to note that the opposite is also undesirable. Individuals who fail to trust when the relevant other *is* trustworthy waste opportunities for fruitful cooperation.[7] In terms of declining political trust, this opens up three possibilities:

1. A lack of trust in government is desirable as government in untrustworthy;
2. Government is trustworthy, it's just that citizens are highly critical of public authorities; or
3. Government is trustworthy, it's just that citizens are apathetic/cynical about public authorities.

The first possibility involves a scenario where government performance on valence issues is perceived to be incompetent. The second involves a disgruntled public in terms of government's policy agenda and perhaps more general features of the political system. The third possibility also involves a disgruntled public but in this instance characterised by a sense of indifference or hopelessness. What this demonstrates is that research on trust in government doesn't have to assume that falling trust or low levels of trust are indicative of something 'bad' in democratic politics for the research to be relevant. This research neither assumes increasingly bad government, more critical citizens, or more cynical citizens. These are claims that should be dependent upon empirical examinations of political trust, not assumed prior to.

Given the three possibilities one could still perhaps rightfully ask 'so what?' Trust is a word with benign connotations, but it shouldn't be merely assumed to play an important role in democratic politics.

Fortunately, political scientists seldom make this assumption. Since Almond and Verba's (1963) seminal study of political cultures, two concerns have preoccupied scholars of beliefs in government.

- As trust in politicians and institutions decline, so to could support for democracy itself (Easton 1965; Crozier, Huntington and Watanuki 1975).
- Even if the future of democracy is secure, the efficacy of government is not (Norris 1999; Pharr and Putnam 2000; Hetherington 2004).

Of course, the first concern is more troubling than the second, and fortunately the recent trend is for support of democratic governance to increase (Norris 1999: 7f). Nonetheless, it will be demonstrated that there are signs that dissatisfaction in Britain is extending to more general features of the democratic system, as opposed to only being directed towards political actors. This does not necessarily mean that the very foundations of democratic government will be questioned. It is, however, indicative of changing beliefs towards how government and politicians are legitimised in the eyes of publics. It perhaps also indicates that the political institutions are failing to adapt to the changing political culture of Britain.

Establishing the principles of democracy

According to Held (1996: 195) the grounds upon which democratic governments are legitimised can be separated into seven different analytical distinctions. We express government to be legitimate when

1. There is no choice in the matter (*coercion*);
2. Little or no thought has ever been given to existing political circumstances and we do as we have always done (*tradition*);
3. We cannot be bothered one way or another (*apathy*);
4. Although we do not like a situation (it is not satisfactory and far from ideal), we cannot imagine things being really different so we accept what seems like fate (*pragmatic acquiescence*);
5. We are dissatisfied with things as they are but nevertheless go along with them in order to secure another end; we acquiesce because it is in the long run to our advantage (*instrumental acceptance or conditional agreement*);
6. In the circumstances before us, and with information available to us at the moment, we conclude it is 'right', 'correct', 'proper' for each of

us as an individual or member of a collectivity: it is what we genuinely ought to or should do (*normative agreement*); and

7. It is what in ideal circumstances – with, for instance, all the knowledge we would like, all the opportunity to discover the circumstances and requirements of others – we would have agreed to do (*ideal normative government*).

Empirically, we can think of these analytical distinctions as a continuum running from dictatorship (1) to utopia (7). Western democracies and emerging democracies are of course found somewhere in between. What can be said for Western democracies of late is that characterisation 2 does not apply. Part of the reason why there is dissatisfaction with government in such countries is because 'traditional' attitudes and life-styles no longer exist (Dalton 1996; Inglehart 1999). Almond and Verba (1963) outline a 'traditional' political culture in Mexico, for example, which is characterised by low support for democracy and a relatively high support for non-democratic government. This creates a strong emphasis on deference to public authorities, a key indication of any political culture based on tradition. The trend in question for scholars analysing the 'tri-lateral' nations, however, is a shift from traditional attitudes and an increasing *lack* of deference; it is a move away from traditional political cultures to less stable and predictable ones. In Britain, this is evident through the possible decline in class voting and an increase in voter volatility.[8]

But a lack of deference towards public authorities is not always accompanied with widespread dissent. A term increasingly used to characterise politics in Western democracies is *apathy* (Di Palma 1970), along with its synonyms 'disillusionment' (Mishler and Rose 1996) and 'disaffection' (Pharr and Putnam 2000). So increasing dissatisfaction with politics and the political process contains a paradox: a consequence might be increasing political protests, but so is increasing political alienation. This implies a lack of 'normative agreement' with regards to the role of government, which leaves Western democracies – according to Held's analytical distinctions above – caught between apathy and instrumental acceptance. Indeed, Held (1996: 253) himself notes on the current uncertainty within Western democracies:

> There is widespread scepticism about conventional democratic politics. There is [also] uncertainty not only about what kinds of [new] institution[s] might be created but also about what general political directions should be taken. Thus, as possibilities for antagonistic

> stances against the state are realised, so too are the germs of a variety of other kinds of political movement, e.g. movements of the New Right. It is in this context that renewed concern about the direction of liberal democracy has given way to fresh consideration of the very essence of democracy.

But the movement from thinking about political institutions and its actors to the very essence of democracy amongst a citizenry is a long process. As Norris observes, publics can and do "distinguish between different levels of the regime, often believing strongly in democratic values, for example, while proving critical of the way democratic governments work in practice" (1999: 9). As such, and following on from Easton's (1965) classification for political support, Norris (1999: 10f) outlines the objects of political trust, that is, the political ideals, institutions, and actors that individuals within democracies will support or reject. These objects can either be specific or generalised, where specific refers to particular political actors and institutions (such as politicians, parliament and the police) while generalised refers to satisfaction with the political system as a whole and the values and principles it is governed upon.

The lack of normative agreement on the role of Western governments might mean that the current cynicism towards politics and the political process could indicate governments failing to accord with democratic values, as opposed to merely reflecting a lack of concern for such values amongst citizenries. But the long-sighted and perhaps pessimistic concerns voiced by the tri-lateral commission (1975) is that continual disaffection with politicians and the institutions of government might lead to the legitimacy of the overall system being questioned, and ultimately to the regime principles and the basis of the political community. Political *dis*trust specific to political actors and institutions could, across time, 'spill-over' to the more diffuse objects of political trust that relate to the system as a whole.

The efficacy of democratic governance

While we can be confident of the future of democratic governance based on the nation-state (although not confident of its exact nature), we are less certain of its ability to provide us with the collective benefits democracy should bring (viz. Weale 2002). A mass of comparative evidence testifies that the *efficacy* of democratic governance is a problem with public institutions struggling to represent citizen interests and solve social and economic problems (Nye et al. 1997; Norris 1999; Pharr and Putnam 2000;

Hetherington 2004). In 2005, global dissatisfaction with 'the government' was found to be 65 per cent in Western Europe, 73 per cent in Eastern and Central Europe, 60 per cent in North America, 61 per cent in Africa, 65 per cent in Asia Pacific and 69 per cent in Latin America (Gallup International 2005). Individual countries have commissioned their own studies. In Britain in 2004, the Audit Commission concerned by the lack of faith in public authorities published a report, *Trust in Public Institutions*.[9] The *Democracy and Power* studies (1997–2003) concluded for Norway that 'democracy was in decline' with increasing voter apathy and declines in party membership, a pattern replicated across many Western Democracies (Dalton 2002). With such concerns over the participatory nature of democracies, the concept of trust and the civic culture thesis started by Almond and Verba (1963) lives on, with more recent works (Putnam 2000; Hetherington 2004) seeking to understand how citizen representation can be improved and institutional performance enhanced.

The issue of institutional performance is heightened at a time when the demands of democratic citizens are as fierce as ever: better homeland security; more efficient transport services; a vastly improved national health system; more funding for education; more police; a reduction in poverty home and abroad; bigger state pensions; more housing. The list is endless. The irony is that such demands require citizens to place greater trust in the individuals and institutions of government as they often necessitate increased public expenditure and greater government intervention. Occasionally they require greater trust on government policy inventions. But as citizen expectations shift towards more quality of life concerns (see Rapley 2003 for an overview) there is increasing confusion as to which parties are best to govern on such issues, and indeed whether government alone is capable of effectively tackling them. So as Pharr and Putnam (2000: 2) state, 'while the sky is not about to fall in, all is not well in [most] democracies'.

The case of Britain

The empirical analyses that precede the theoretical chapters will cover two areas. First, using the European Social Survey 2005, a set of competing explanatory models are tested for a host of West European countries. While illuminating some aspects of the nature of trust and differences between countries, it will be argued that the lack of localised, contextual data often characteristic of comparative datasets restricts a deeper understanding. As such, the second set of analyses benefit from utilising the more in-depth British Election Studies (1987 to 2005) where factors closer to leaders and the party system are considered.

The evidence provided from this last set of analyses will lend support to at least one of three specific claims in relation to declining government trustworthiness in Britain:

1. A recent report by the Hansard Society and the Electoral Commission (2004) argues that politics in the UK is a 'minority activity' and is becoming a 'minority interest'. But at the same time the report highlights the fact that 75 per cent 'want to have a say in how the country is run'. This suggests that the problem is not necessarily apathy but rather people want to be politically aware and participate but feel it is not worth the effort (Government is untrustworthy).
2. Falling trust in government might reflect nothing more than a healthy increase of critical citizens. Networks of secondary associations still flourish in this country despite downward trends in the US (Hall 1999) and increasing prosperity has led to the development of post-materialistic attitudes that are less deferential to authorities (Inglehart 1999) indicated by increasing tendencies to engage in more unconventional activities such as protesting (citizens are critical).
3. Falling trust in government might be within the context of general political apathy, perhaps a product of decreasing social interactions (Putnam 2000). Persistently low local and European election turnouts coupled with falling turnout at general elections suggest a wider malaise (Norris 2002; citizens are more cynical).

Explaining why government is no longer viewed as trustworthy will shed light on which of the descriptions best fits recent trends in British politics. Such an understanding is essential in uncovering which social, economic or institutional remedies are required to foster greater trust between government and governed.

A guide for the reader

For those of you who are not are not familiar with social scientific research, a few guidance notes will be helpful. When tackling the issues of trust, be that in other people in general (social trust) or government, the first concern must always be conceptual; what does this thing called trust actually mean? As such, the first two chapters (Part I) concentrate on untangling a lot of the confusion surrounding trust as a concept and how it plays a role in daily life. Along the way it is often illustrative to talk in terms of a hypothetical individual deciding whether or not he/she can trust another hypothetical person. Throughout, those deciding whether to trust or not will be referred to as a *truster* and the relevant other being evaluated in terms of how trustworthy they are will be referred to as a *trusted*.

When it comes to understanding trust from an empirical point of view, that is as a thing to be measured and explained, the analyses will present a wide range of statistics generated from social surveys. Ultimately, when evaluating which factors best explain different levels of social and political trust, the answers that individuals give in these surveys will be treated as a set of variables. This allows researchers to identify any statistical relationship between these variables, for example, whether individuals saying they are currently dissatisfied with the economy are also more likely to say that they find government mostly untrustworthy. By employing a technique called *regression analysis*, it is possible to present this as a correlation, with the advantage that this correlation represents the strength of the relationship after 'controlling' for any statistical relationships with other possible factors. For example, finding government untrustworthy might also be statistically related with coming from a poor background. Regression analysis simply provides social researchers with a way of evaluating which is more important, if either is important at all.

A final statistical technique used is that of *clustering*. Principally, this technique is used to understand the structure behind a set of variables to see whether or not they can be reduced to a smaller set of variables. A good example is in terms of political ideologies. A 'socialist', for example, would probably believe in (1) greater redistribution of wealth towards poorer people; (2) more public expenditure on the welfare system; and (3) the re-nationalising of former publicly owned companies. Clustering allows researchers to see whether there is a high degree of consistency across these beliefs, that is, that people tend to completely agree with all three beliefs *and* tend to completely disagree with all three. If this is the case then researchers can be confident that the answers given in relation to these three aspects of public policy are being driven by an underlying attitude of socialism. In a similar fashion, I will use this technique to see whether trust in government and trust in people can also be treated as attitudes.

Part I

The Nature of Trust

Thomas Hobbes originally and most sombrely demonstrated the problem of collective action, in which the binding of rational individuals to cooperation for the good of all could only be achieved through external constraint (the *Leviathan*). It is an attempt to move from a situation where cooperation is individually irrational (with the opportunity cost being a beneficial outcome for all), to a position in which it becomes rational to cooperate. The actual 'problem' of collective action, that is, coordinating actors to cooperate, can be characterised as a failure to make credible promises, and this is where trust plays a crucial role.

Despite the popularity of the concept of trust in social scientific research and in everyday life, little consensus exists on what it actually means. The aim of **Chapter 1** is to review and resolve such confusion establishing the basis upon which the antecedent conditions of trust can be explored. **Chapter 2** moves on to the concerns of functions and maintenance – what role does trust play in society and what maintains perceptions of trustworthiness between individuals?

1
The Meaning of Trust

1.1 Introduction

Trust is a word that we are increasingly using in our social and political lives: 'I trust you will find these shoes comfortable madam'; 'I trust the postman to deliver the mail on time'; 'I (mistakenly) trust the trains to run on time'; 'I trust Bush and Blair over Iraq'. Just from these examples, we can see that trust has an evaluative property – it predicts instances of 'good' people or outcomes. But what exactly is trust? When we say that word, what are we actually conveying?

A relationship based on trust is a particular type of relationship, and it is distinct from all other types. Some argue that it is more than distinct; it is a superior type of relationship (Hollis 1998). The trouble with trust is that we know why we need it, when it is possible, and we know when we benefit from it – but we often don't know what it means. Trust relationships are rarely formalised, often leading to ad-hoc definitions and haphazard usages of the word. A review of the relevant social scientific literature only points to more confusion. Some envisage the nature of trust as selfish, others see it as altruistic. Furthermore, some argue it is to behave in a certain way, while others claim that to trust is to share a common moral framework. For example, trust has been defined as an inductive expectation (Gambetta 1988), as risk-taking behaviour (Luhmann 1979) and as morality (Fukuyama 1995).

The goal of this chapter is to clarify this thing called trust. In attempting to uncover what trust is it seems scholars conflate its meaning with the reasons why we need trust and the factors that make others trustworthy. It will be argued that trust is not a feeling or emotion, but a belief (Hardin 1999), separating it from closely related concepts such as faith. It is also a belief that is not merely concerned with satisfying self-interest. Trust has a moral dimension. It is not that someone is trustworthy because they happen to satisfy you in some way. An individual is evaluated as potentially trustworthy because the context of the relationship dictates that a relevant other *ought* to satisfy your interests. Without an underpinning obligation for the relevant other to fulfil a duty, relationships cannot be in the realm of trust. With reference to trust in society and government, this chapter will also cover the role of information in the formation of beliefs of trust.

1.2 What trust is

Conceptually speaking, trust has many cousins, and it is often the case that our usage of the word is misplaced. As Hardin (2001: 7–8) argues, the use of trust on the streets and in the social sciences suffers from 'conceptual slippages', with the most frequent slippage between trust and trustworthiness (see also Levi 1998: 80). But trust is also closely related to and confused with other terms, most notably 'confidence' (for example Gambetta 1988: 7) and 'respect'.[1] If we take basic dictionary definitions of these terms, we can see why confusion exists. According to the Oxford English Dictionary, faith is defined as 'trust or confidence'; confidence is defined as a 'firm trust or belief'; and trust itself is defined as 'confidence in the truth of anything; resting on the integrity of another; faith; hope'.

Not surprisingly, little consensus exists within social and political theory as to what trust actually means. As Barber (1983: 7) identifies, 'in both serious social thought and everyday discourse, it is assumed that the meaning of trust and of its many apparent synonyms is so well known that it can be left undefined or to contextual implications'. Baier (1986: 10), for example, defines trust as 'accepted vulnerability to another's possible but not expected ill will (or lack of good will) towards one'. Warren similarly defines trust as 'a judgment, however tacit or habitual, to accept vulnerability to the potential ill will of others by granting them discretionary power over some good' (Warren 1999: 311). Both scholars stress the vulnerability to ill will that is an effect of trust, but others have stressed the positive assumptions of shared values that under-gird trusting relationships. For example, Fukuyama defines trust as 'the expectation that arises within a community of regular, honest, and cooperative behavior, based on commonly shared norms, on the part of other members of the community' (Fukuyama 1995: 26). Likewise, Elster (1989) posits trust as the 'ability to make credible promises' when an individual is 'part of a code of honour' (1989: 274–5).

In addition to reflecting faith in another's character, trust may also reflect a belief in the correctness of general principles. According to Giddens, trust refers to 'confidence in the reliability of a person or system, regarding a given set of outcomes or events, where that confidence expresses a faith in the probity or love of another, or in the correctness of abstract principles (technical knowledge)' (Giddens 1990: 34). Rational choice approaches echo Blau's position that we trust one another only to the degree that our own interest is served (Blau 1964). For example, Hardin (1999) argues that 'to say that I trust you means I have reason to expect you to act for your own reasons as my agent with respect to the relevant matter. Your interest encapsulates my interest' (Hardin 1999: 26).

Ostensibly, Hardin's (1999) definition seems the most useful. The other definitions confuse the conditions under which trust is required (when we are vulnerable and confronted with risk), or make conceptual slippages between related but distinct concepts (most notably confidence). Nonetheless, I will argue that Hardin's definition is not without its limitations. But first, some of the definitions can be knocked aside by understanding the reasons why we need something like trust in our lives.

1.3 Why we need trust

A trusting life is often equated with a 'good' life, a sentiment that finds expression in contemporary arguments for trust as a precondition of cooperation (see Fukuyama 1995: vii). When we form relationships with others we need to believe that the relationship will be beneficial. Of course, if an individual decides to use another purely as a means to an end, the chances are the one being used will not benefit from the relationship at all. Being manipulated and used not only loses individuals material benefits – it also means being treated without dignity. A consequence is that the victim feels stupid for allowing themselves to be used. We all want to be treated with dignity, we all want to retain an element of self-esteem, and, to put it in rational choice terms, none of us wants to be duped into being a sucker in a prisoner's dilemma game and lose material benefits. This is why the path to cooperation is not so straightforward, and why trust can play a protective role in getting us there.

1.3.1 Vulnerability

The fact that we can be exploited points to an important characteristic about all social and political environments – that we are vulnerable to others. The underlying reason for such vulnerability is that others are not always motivated with your interests specifically in mind. More problematic, is that some are motivated by the desire to fulfil self-interest to such an extent that they are even willing to cause you harm in the process. Such behaviour is characterised as opportunism – one individual gaining at another's expense. Opportunistic behaviour arises when an actor adopts an 'I' rationality as opposed to a 'we' rationality (Hollis 1998). In doing so, they reject the claim that by 'free-riding' and harming the interests of others they effectively harm themselves – a denial of what is in the interest of all is also in the interest of each (a 'we' rationality). Instead, they are motivated by a potential net benefit in exploiting the vulnerable position of others ('I' rationality).[2] I expect that most students living in halls of residence have been victims of the midnight food thief. Such acts of opportunism inevitably lead to food being withdrawn and cupboards being locked. The consequence is that the free exchange of food items based on the principle of generalised reciprocity is undermined, and the benefits of convenience, variety and the utilisation of food resources are lost. Once we are aware of an opportunist in our vicinity, we act to protect our vulnerability, despite the fact that collective benefits are sometimes forfeited.

1.3.2 Uncertainty

In theory, certainty would circumvent the problem of vulnerability. Knowing the exact motives of individuals and how they will behave allows hazardous situations to be avoided. But of course, certainty presupposes perfect information, an idealised and unattainable state of affairs. We need to look no further than Allison's (1971) analysis of the Cuban missile crisis to demonstrate that reality is in fact the complete opposite, not to mention the Invasion of Iraq and Weapons of Mass Destruction. As we can never be definite about our judgements and predictions, the best we can do is think in terms of probabilities. The result is that imperfect information is taken as given for all individuals as human cooperation and conflict exist in the context of bounded rationality (Simon 1983: 17–23). This is to acknowledge that no one person or organisation is able to comprehend all the important aspects of politics and society.

> To say that human rationality is bounded is to say that there are pervasive and ineliminable information asymmetries in a society, so that some individuals will always know more about some particular facet of social life than any other individuals could. This in turn leads to pervasive problems of trust. (Weale 1999: 11)

Having greater access to human resources, particularly better quality education, will privilege some groups in society over others. And this is precisely why some will feel and actually be more vulnerable than others – lacking the knowledge and understanding of politics, society and the workings of economy, means they are more likely to be duped into a subordinate role.

> We know that wealthy, more highly educated people take a greater role in civic life. They have greater stakes in what government does. They understand political and social life better. They are more likely to be interested in politics, to know whom to contact, and perhaps most critically, to know how to make their voices known. (Uslaner 2002: 4)

But even the privileged are only less vulnerable as problems of trust arise from uncertainty about the intentions of others and their capability to perform given tasks. And no one individual can escape that uncertainty. This is why game theory has become the paradigmatic analysis of individual decision-making within the social sciences (see Ward 2002: 84–5). Many rational choice theorists follow the approach of von Neumann and Morgenstern (1944) by presenting a set of axioms of individual preferences, which are then used to derive utility functions characterising individual decision-making in an environment of uncertainty (see Morrow 1994: 308–11 for a review). Game theory assumes that we are all vulnerable as self-interest is assumed to be an irreducible motive for all actors. A further assumption is that all the actors involved possess imperfect knowledge, that is, possess a degree of uncertainty. And all such analyses that combine vulnerability and uncertainty operate under the rubric of risk.[3]

1.3.3 Risk

The concept of risk has become pervasive in the social sciences because of its ability to pull together older categories such as sin, danger, cleanliness, purity and pollution (Douglas 1992: 3). It is generally understood as a situation in which an outcome is unknown, but has known probabilities, which can be contrasted with uncertainty where an outcome is simply unknown. A fruitful area of risk research is in relation to social welfare and social policy, particularly focusing on citizen evaluations of health and environmental hazards and associated risk-taking or risk-aversive behaviours (see Weale (ed.) 2002 for example). Recent concerns include whether the British public trusts the government in relation to the risks surrounding food safety,[4] as well as the risks surrounding the security of personal data stored by government.[5]

Risk's close relationship with trust hasn't gone unnoticed. Paul Slovic argues that relationships involving risk management rely heavily on trust:

> [M]uch of the contentiousness that has been observed in the risk-management arena has been attributed to a climate of distrust that exists between the public, the industry, and risk-management professionals. The limited effectiveness of risk communication efforts can be attributed to a lack of trust. If you trust the risk manager, communication is relatively easy. If trust is lacking, no form or process of communication will be satisfactory. (Slovic 2000: 697)

Research on trust in the social sciences has not only overlapped with research on risk, but has also been conflated with risk by defining trust as risk-taking behaviour (Luhmann 1979: 24). However, an obvious problem exists with this definition – it defines a cognitive variable with reference to behaviour only. Furthermore, acting in a trusting manner (cooperating) in a risky situation might not be done out of trust; blind faith, ruthless self-interest and sometimes sheer stupidity are also reasons why people cooperate with each other.

While not providing a definition of trust, the concept of risk captures why we need it. It is the potential for opportunistic behaviour that essentially determines the need for trust, as it gets to the heart of what is motivating a potential trusted (see Hollis 1998). A lack of credible information, on the other hand, relates to what Bacharach and Gambetta (2001: 148–9) call the 'secondary-problem of trust', which begs the question of whether we can trust our own judgements about the trustworthiness of others.

> The presence of trustworthy-making qualities is not sufficient to induce trust...as trust has two enemies: bad character and poor information. The incidence of good character sets an upper bound on the amount of trust in a community. Actual trust, however, may fall below that threshold because of the difficulties incurred communicating the presence of these qualities. (Bacharach and Gambetta 2001: 150)

So, if everyone in a community possessed the quality that makes trust possible (that is, all have a good character/will) then, in theory, there is no limit to every individual trusting one another. However, in practice, conveying that individuals possess the appropriate quality requires reliable and effective communication, something not always possible.

1.4 Formalising trust

When formalising trust, that is, presenting a series of reasonable conditions that need to be satisfied in order for trust relationships to attain, it is initially useful to outline the different forms of trust relationships. In essence, there are two types of trust relationships.

1.4.1 Contractual and paternalistic trust

Thinking about the types of relationships that we commonly ascribe trust to, the basis of trust relationships seems to have two origins: (1) because of a verbal or non-verbal promise; (2) because one of the individuals involved has a duty to protect the interests of another (for example, parent–child or citizen–government relationships). We can therefore think of trust relationships as being either contractual or paternalistic.

This distinction neatly categorises the two most common types of trust under empirical investigation – social trust and political trust. Outside of family life, social trust represents a form of social contract (Bellah 1985) governed by the principle of generalised reciprocity (Yamagishi and Kiyonari 2000). Its contractual nature arises from the fact that individuals are pressured into accepting the principle of reciprocity on account of maintaining a trustworthy reputation which secures the future cooperation of others and mutual gains (Putnam 2000: 53). Political trust on the other hand is paternalistic in nature. Public authorities are relied upon to protect the interests and lives of citizens by minimising risks in public life. By holding the status of citizens, institutions such as government are obligated to carry out these public duties to the best of their abilities, the crux of Locke's notion of trust in government (Locke 1988: 426–7).

In both types of trust, the person who is trusting is doing so because they hold reasonable expectations regarding the future actions of another. As the next section will argue, the unique aspect of relationships of trust is that a relevant other forms their intentions with a truster's interests in mind.

1.4.2 The conditions of trustworthiness

Contrary to research in social-psychology, trust is neither a feeling or emotion, but a cognitive belief.[6] It is a belief that captures the presence of a good will in a relevant other, that they are cooperative in nature. As such, the formation of the belief requires trusters to hold two pieces of information: information of the intention of a possible trusted, and information of the actual behaviour of the same individual. Such knowledge allows an individual to assess the trustworthiness of another. This is a pre-requisite for a trust relationship to attain, but does not capture the conditions under which we can talk of a relationship of trust actually attaining. A relationship of trust will only attain if a person believes that another

> Intends to promote their interests;
> Promotes their interests qua their interests;[7]
> Has the ability to fulfil the intended action.
> (Ullmann-Margalit 2002: 3)

This is to specify more clearly the definition Misztal (1996: 9) offers which states that 'to trust is to believe that the results of somebody's intended action will be appropriate from our point of view'. This definition implies a belief that the action of a possible trusted is 'intended'; that it overlaps with our interests ('appropriate from our point of view'); and that the intended 'result' of an action attains.

The intentional condition (condition number 1) relates to our common understanding of accountability. For someone to be praised or scorned for their actions they must have actively decided to pursue those actions in the first place. The fact that they chose to form a specific intention relays information to others about the qualities of that person's character. Only with such information can a judgement be made as to whether someone possesses a 'good' or 'bad' character, which dictates whether or not they can be trusted (Bacharach and Gambetta 2001: 150).

Condition number 2 formalises what an 'appropriate action' is for trust relationships to attain. Defining appropriate action in terms of interests is to accept the premise of Hardin's (1998) encapsulated interest account of trust. A person can only ever be trusted when they have an incentive to fulfil the trust, that is, your trust in them encapsulates an interest in fulfilling that trust (Hardin 1998: 12). What Misztal's definition does not state is that the trusted's intention is formed with the truster's interests in mind. This forms the second premise of Hardin's encapsulated interest account: 'I trust you with respect to some action if your reason for doing it is to take me into account in some relevant way' (Hardin 1998: 12). The crux for trust relationships is not that an action satisfies your interests, but rather an action is taken because it satisfies your interests (promotes your interests qua your interests).[8]

The final condition (number 3) relates to what Ullmann-Margalit (2002: 2) refers to as competence. An individual's intention, it could be argued, is only as good as their behaviour. To demonstrate a 'good' intention most of us will look for the corresponding behaviour as proof of that intention existing. That someone says or even promises to perform a task might not be good enough, for words can be meaningless, 'cheap-talk'. So, for example, the fact that someone says 'I love you' might not be sufficient for a completely trusting relationship until they actually act as if they do. You might want to believe them, and they might actually believe themselves when they say it. But without demonstrating that it exists within the relationship through their behaviour, we are probably best to refrain from trusting our partner on the matter.

The nature of the three antecedent conditions means that trust overlaps with two of its conceptual cousins, namely respect and confidence. When we respect others, we treat them with consideration. We can understand why they believe in and pursue the interests they do, without necessarily adopting the same outlook on life as them. Respect then requires a certain amount of empathy but it doesn't commit us to identify with the other. Confidence is also conflated with trust.[9] It is a belief that reflects how likely we think it is an outcome will attain. Through repeated observations, we derive such a judgement inductively and use it to predict the future. For example, everyday of my life the sun has risen. I am therefore very confident – almost 100 per cent confident – that it will rise again tomorrow. However, I am only 50 per cent confident that the 8:42 train to London Liverpool Street will depart on-time, as 4 out of the past 8 times I have used the service, it has departed late.

1.4.3 Trust, distrust and agnosticism

As trust denotes an action being taken because it satisfies the truster's interests, distrust denotes an action being taken because it violates the distruster's interests. But while the concepts are mutually exclusive, they are not mutually exhaustive (Ullmann-Margalit 2002: 2).

By this it is meant that even if an individual doesn't find another trustworthy, this is not the same as finding them untrustworthy. Similarly, if an individual doesn't find another untrustworthy, this is not the same as finding them trustworthy. There are two reasons why this is so. First, because of an intermediary stage of agnosticism between trust and distrust (passive indifference), and second, because of active indifference. Ceteris paribus, individuals lacking credible information regarding a relevant other will be inclined to remain indifferent as will they if they possess information but are not sufficiently interested in forming a trusting or hostile relationship with this person. However, it cannot be assumed that more information always leads to greater trust – that information could potentially reveal an opportunist. What this means is that increased levels of information only make the possibility of agnosticism less. Increased information will either reinforce or develop positions of trust, distrust or indifference.

1.5 How trust works: information, media and the presumption of distrust

Trust is a belief, and beliefs feed off information. But beliefs are not always matters of choice – socialisation processes and human psychology have something to say about that.

1.5.1 How trust works: psychology and the presumption of distrust

Before someone can trust, that person needs information regarding the intention and capabilities of the relevant other. This is to state an obvious point – that before we trust, we must have reasons to believe the other is trustworthy. But what if we have limited or no information? What if the trustworthiness of the other is relatively unknown? In such circumstances, a great deal of uncertainty arises. Do we then automatically assume that it is better to be safe than sorry and turn to distrust? Or do we proceed effectively blindfolded and act in a trusting manner? It is argued that in the absence of credible information individuals will fall back on a 'default' position of distrust, that is, placing a presumption of distrust over a presumption of trust (see for example Levi 1999). The presumption of distrust is seen as a natural tendency within humans as it supported by a psychological mechanism known as the 'asymmetry principle':

> When it comes to winning trust, the playing field is not level. It is tilted towards distrust as ... negative events are more visible than positive events ... negative events carry much greater weight than positive events ... [and] bad news tends to be more credible than good news. (Slovic 2000: 698)

Empirically, it can be explored whether such a tendency exists. The diagrams below (Parts (a)–(d) of Figure 1.1) demonstrate the logically possible relationships information could have with decisions of trust. Amount of information runs from zero to complete information on the

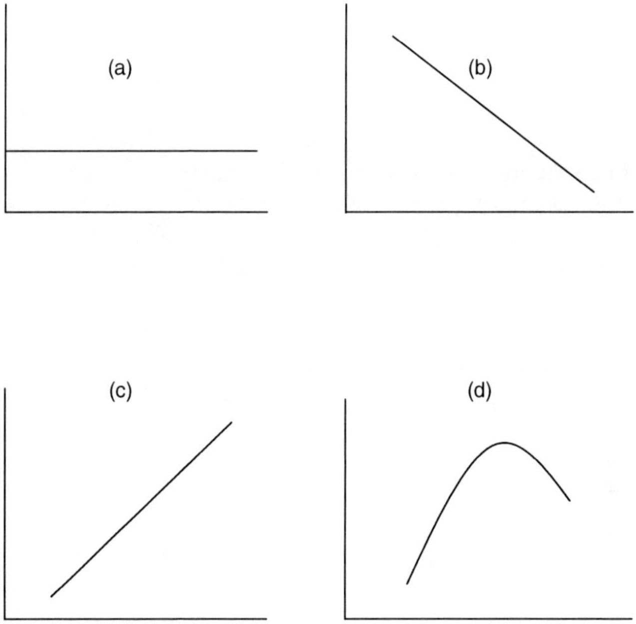

Figure 1.1 Trust and information

X axis, level of trust on the Y axis. Part (a) demonstrates a situation where amount of information has no effect at all on beliefs of trust. Part (b) represents a population that presumes trust, but becomes increasingly cynical or critical as they receive more information. For example,

> many discussions presume that declining trust in doctors reflects some general and pernicious process in the society at large. Perhaps this is so. But perhaps doctors have simply become less trustworthy, or, more likely, they were never so trustworthy but now we know more about them. (Guinnane 2005: 6)

Part (c) of Figure 1.1 suggests that people presume distrust in the absence of information but increases in information promote indifference and eventually complete trust. Part (d) reflects a situation where individuals presume distrust, become trusting with a certain amount of information, but become less trusting (more critical) with higher levels.

Using the European Social Survey, these diagrams can be tested against the relationship between media use for public information and (1) trust in people, and (2) trust in government. Dividing the working sample of all countries into sub-groups by their level of media usage from zero to 4 or more hours a day, variation in trust in government can be charted across these different groups. Three different types of media usage in question are television, radio and newspapers.

The first chart below (Figure 1.2) demonstrates that diagram (d) (above) is the most accurate characterisation of the relationship between information and social trust. Regardless of which media format used, the group of individuals who never use that particular type of media are the least trusting of other people in general, suggesting that an absence of information does promote a presumption of distrust. Also note that beyond 3 hours of media usage per day, people seem to become more critical of others.

Performing the same analysis but replacing social trust with trust in government yields exactly the same result. Figure 1.3 demonstrates that an absence of information is associated with a higher level of distrust, but each additional unit of media usage promotes greater trust in government until 3 hours of usage and over where increasing criticism begins to set in.

These results suggest that distrust, not trust, is normally employed as a 'default strategy'.[10] Citizens without information on people and

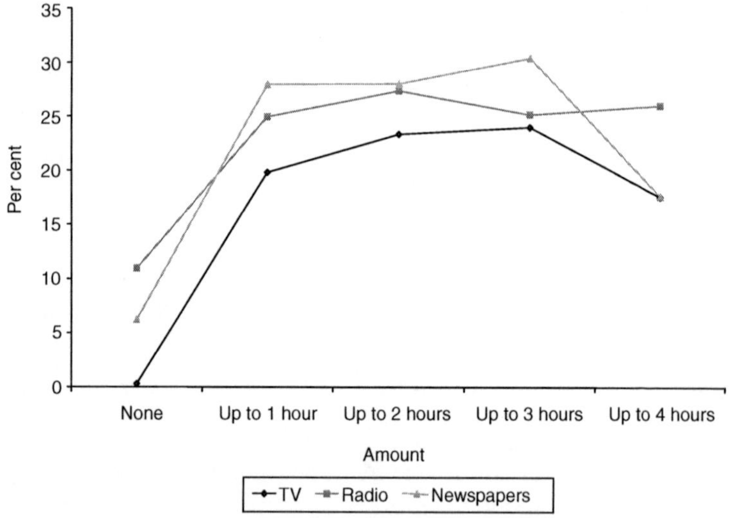

Figure 1.2 Media use and social trust

Note: Percentages are based on respondents answering 7, 8, 9 or 10 on a combined 10 point scale of how trustworthy they think people are ('most people can be trusted' + 'most people are fair').

Source: ESS round 3, 2006.

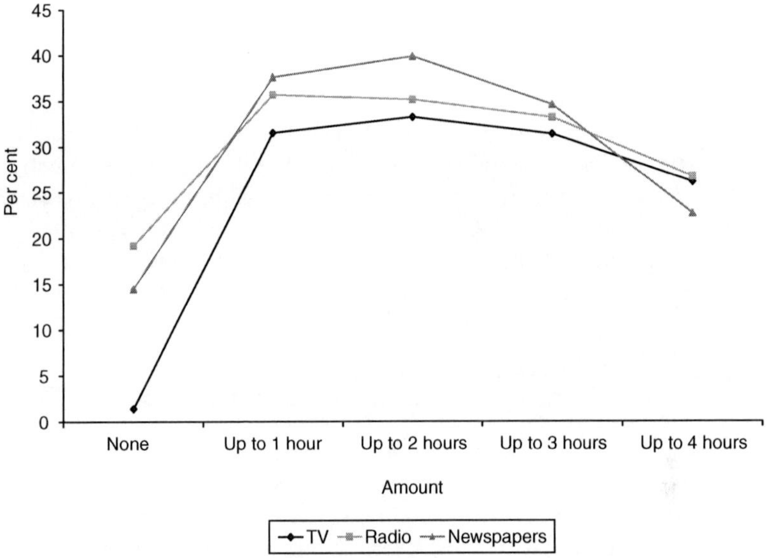

Figure 1.3 Media use and trust in government

Note: Percentages are based on respondents answering 7, 8, 9 or 10 on a combined 10 point scale of how trustworthy they think parliament and politicians are.

Source: ESS round 3, 2006.

government will think the worst – the playing field is not level, and our automatic tendencies are to presume distrust of others. In the context of trust in government, the media seems to mobilise people into thinking more about public issues, and crucially, in a way that doesn't promote cynicism, but does eventually promote critical thinking.

1.5.2 Why distrust?

The tendency to remember and emphasise the negative aspects of life means that when it has come to designing systems of government and political constitutions, they are often designed to prevent the abuse of power. For example, the belief in the primacy of distrust over trust is implicit within political systems built on Madisonian principles, exemplified by a constitutional design with a separation of powers and many legislative veto points.

> This line of reasoning accepts that instrumental rationality and opportunistic behaviour are ineradicable features of political interaction and seeks to provide constitutional protection to political

> actors in the hope that, protection having been provided, actors will have more confidence in seeking out the potential for measures of common gain when it is there. (Weale 2002: 8)

The central notion behind such thinking is that 'strong fences make for good neighbours'. One interpretation is that this leads to the institutionalisation of mistrust, that is, 'mistrust breed[ing] mistrust' (Weale 2002: 9. See also Hollis 1998, especially chapter 5). The institutionalisation of mistrust can lead individuals and whole societies applying the presumption of distrust to situations where there might be no good reason to do so, a major concern for normative jurisprudence (Hursthouse 1999: intro).

As argued, our vulnerability to others and our uncertainty regarding their intentions forms the basis of such trust dilemmas. But individuals can manipulate vulnerability and uncertainty to solve problems of trust. The rule of thumb of human psychology seems to be 'minimise vulnerability, and then worry about uncertainty'. Think of the common piece of advice 'it is better to be safe than sorry'. It asks us to remove ourselves from situations in which we can be taken advantage of thereby minimising vulnerability. Perhaps it is understandable as no-one wants to be taken advantage of, even to the point that possible future gains are forfeited for immediate security. Such distrusting strategies work by reducing vulnerability; less common trusting strategies work by reducing uncertainty.[11]

1.5.3 The difficulty in overcoming distrust

If a presumption of distrust commonly prevails, it would then represent an entrenched psychological trait. A common feature of traits is that they are difficult to remove. One way of demonstrating this empirically is to analyse the stability of trust beliefs. With the use of panel data from Britain (British Election Panel Studies), it is possible to track the same group of individual's level of trust in government across a given time frame. This allows for change in trust in government to be captured. Analysing whether those individuals who start from a position of distrust are more likely to maintain a position of distrust than those who start from a position of trust isolates presumptions of distrust towards government. The data is utilised by separating respondents into two extreme groups of government trusters and government distrusters. Percentages are calculated to reflect the number in both groups whose beliefs are stable or variable. If there is a presumption of distrust present towards government, then we would expect to find a larger number of distrusters maintaining their position of distrust across time in comparison to trusters. The sample is restricted to medium and high users of the media for information to 'control' for any possible media effects.

As Figure 1.4 demonstrates, distrusters were twice as likely to maintain their position of distrust towards government than trusters (34 per cent compared to 17). While not conclusive proof of the asymmetry principle, it does suggest that the playing field towards government is indeed not level; on average over a third of the electorate who distrust government still distrust the institution over four years later, compared to only 17 per cent who maintain a trustful position over the same time period.

The fact that trust is difficult to make but easily broken (Newton 1999b: 169), is another way of demonstrating a psychological tendency to distrust first, and maybe trust later. Given this, we usually have to work hard to make ourselves trustworthy to others, a concern for the next chapter.

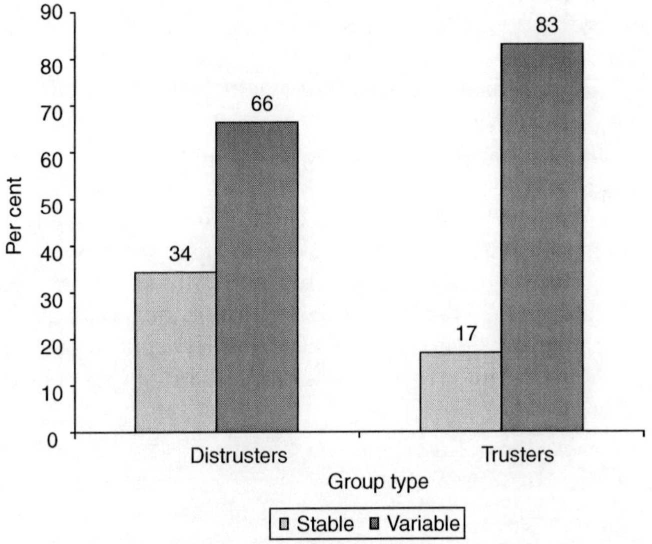

Figure 1.4 Stability of trust beliefs towards government, 1987–2001
Source: BES panel data pooled sample (1987–1992, 1992–1997, 1997–2001).

1.6 Conclusion

I have argued that trust is easily confused with, but related to, other concepts that are used to convey similar meanings. As such, trust has suffered from a lack of conceptual clarity, and scholars have to take great care not to confuse it with its behavioural correlates such as cooperation or risk-taking (Levi 1999: 5; Hardin 2001: 9–12). Nonetheless, risk-taking behaviour identifies an environment of uncertainty, and specifically it is uncertainty that relates to our vulnerability to others. In such an environment the need for trust is great. We can never be certain when another will adopt an 'I' rationality as opposed to a 'we' rationality and take advantage of the trust we place in them (Hollis 1998).

Trust is an emergent property of relationships where at least one of the individuals or parties involved has an underlying obligation to deliberate and act on the interests of another, either because of a promise made or because of a paternalistic relationship. We can only talk of James trusting Richard because the latter made a promise to help the former move house; we can only talk of a child trusting its parents because the latter is supposed to act for the child's interests; likewise, we can only talk of trust in politicians and government because they are supposed to act for the interests of the majority of citizens. In all three examples, it is not that a relationship brings certain benefits that defines trust; it is that a relationship brings benefits *and* the relevant other is obligated to do so.

It was argued that the starting point for any relationship of trust, and indeed any relationship, is information regarding the relevant other. Focusing on trust in people and trust in government, it was demonstrated how certain levels of usage of the media can shape levels of trustworthiness people place in society and government. Absence relevant information, people fall back on a presumption of distrust. Nonetheless, it was demonstrated that although reliable information was necessary for trust to develop, it isn't always sufficient – information can also promote criticism.

2
The Role and Maintenance of Trust

2.1 Introduction

Architects of democratic societies are always faced with one overarching problem: how can individuals be coordinated to act for the common good given that individual self-interest prevails? This conundrum pervades the social sciences. Economists, concerned with deriving effective models of internal relationships within organisations, have emphasised the binding role of formal incentives. Political science imported and developed the economic approach by emphasising the role of sanctioning within collective action and cooperation (see North 1990 and Ostrom 1998 for example). Sociologists, likewise, took the free-rider problem seriously, most notably James S. Coleman (1990). All of these responses reacted against the sometimes unethical and ineffective Hobbesian solution of enforcing collective action through a central authority. But Hobbes' central caveat remains intact in the social sciences – that the wants and desires of individuals have to be taken seriously as self-interest is an irreducible fact of life.

The replacement of enforcement with incentives, while an improvement, still had many shortcomings as a description of events. Economic organisations cannot operate effectively based purely on formal incentives (Arrow 1974); projects of collective action cannot endure based purely on sanctions (Ostrom 1998); and social order cannot ensue with a social system based purely on 'metaphorical' individualistic contractual grounds (see Durkheim 1933: 215 and Bellah 1985: 12–30). Something from the analyses was missing. For many, this missing 'x-factor' is trust. The aim of this chapter is to evaluate the validity of such a claim by outlining the different roles trust plays within society.

Given that trust plays a benign role in politics and society, it could only do so if there are mechanisms that maintained it. The previous chapter highlighted that – in the context of cooperation – individuals will either try to gain short-term advantages by defecting when feigning trustworthiness (opportunists), or will be trustworthy and cooperate unless they believe to be confronted with an opportunist (fidelitists). But what stops fidelitists from becoming opportunists? And how are opportunists actually prevented from getting away with opportunistic acts?

Crucial to answering these questions is the role played by the internalisation of social norms, specifically the norm of reciprocity. Effective social norms make individual behaviour more predictable, reliable and hence more trustworthy by providing implicit rules for individual conduct. However, the nature of these norms, as stated by scholars (e.g., Coleman 1990), is somewhat problematic. The argument is that individuals accord with norms as a strategy to secure the satisfaction of self-interest. What I will demonstrate is that for a group of individuals to hold a bare minimum compliance with a norm we cannot merely offer the satisfaction of self-interest as an explanation. More crucial is that norms such as reciprocity hold an authoritative grip on individuals.

But social norms themselves require certain conditions to be met before they can develop (Axelrod 1997: 31). Prior to any dialogue between individuals or organisations the actors involved must have mutual respect. In order to achieve this, effective communication will signal to both actors that they believe the other to have legitimate goals/interests and that their own personal ends together do not conflict. Upon this basis, a recognition of mutual goals will establish the possibility of cooperation. This cooperation will be dependent on the establishment of mutual confidence through a process of iterated interaction and will only satisfy the antecedent conditions of trust once the principle of reciprocity is internalised by both actors. The logic of the chapter's argument is demonstrated in Figure 2.1.

Working down the decision tree in Figure 2.1 we can see the three processes that foster and maintain trust in bold typing – (1) effective communication; (2) iterated interaction; and (3) the development of a norm of reciprocity. If effective communication is present then such dialogue can earn mutual respect from the parties involved and provide the basis of cooperation if their interests converge. Granting a period of prolonged interaction, a norm of reciprocity will develop where both actors expect the other to cooperate accordingly.

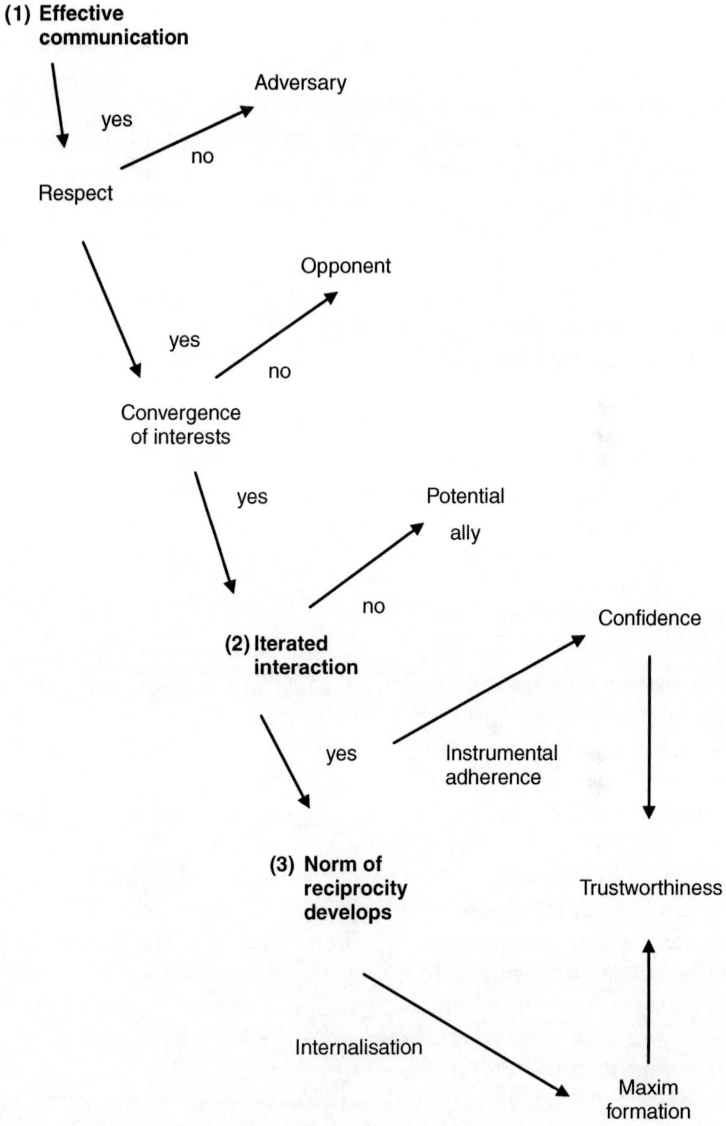

Figure 2.1 Building and maintaining trust

2.2 Effective communication and iterated interactions

Chapter 1 noted that trust is sometimes confused with the concept of respect. But respect is prior to trust in that it allows us to understand why others believe in and pursue the interests they do without necessarily adopting the same outlook on life as them. Subsumed in respect therefore is a certain amount of empathy but also the acceptance of another's autonomy and the right to determine their way life. For respect to be established, the latter need only be a negative right, that is, their way of life can take on any form they choose just so long as it does not infringe upon the autonomy and way of life of others.

Respect, as defined, is the basis of Mill's 'harm principle' in which individual liberty can be pursued free of external constraint until it infringes upon the liberty of others:

> Human liberty requires liberty of tastes and pursuits; of framing the plan of our life to suit our own character; of doing as we like, subject to such consequences as may follow; without impediment from our fellow creatures, so long as what we do does not harm them, even though they should think our conduct foolish, perverse or wrong. (Mill 1859: 13)

Of course, establishing at what point such infringements take place is often highly contentious. Would most European states ever allow an organisation like the Klu-Klux-Klan the freedoms of association and expression granted in the United States? Is a Muslim cleric publicly preaching hatred towards 'the west' a threat to the liberty of others? Likewise, should the United Nations respect Iran's wishes to pursue a nuclear programme? The argument for restricting the freedoms of such individuals and groups is that their motives and intentions are explicitly antithetic to the ideals of Liberal western democracies. Indeed, the argument against communicating with some terrorist organisations like Al-Qaeda and Hamas, propounded by various leaders of European countries and the United States, is that it is naive to communicate with others who at no level can be respected or respectful.

However, it could also be argued that communication is the only way of establishing respect and without someone making the first move, a mutual stand-off will endure. The deeply unpopular concessions made by the British Government as part of the Good Friday Agreement (1998) towards the Republican movement in Northern Ireland is a pertinent example of attempting to move from a position of mutual stand-off to a position of respect and ultimately power-sharing between loyalists and republicans. The road to Stormont and the period thereafter, however, was far from easy. Mutual stand-offs are extremely difficult to overcome and are only done so when both parties involved effectively signal true and cooperative intentions. To recall, the antecedent conditions of trust state that a truster must believe a trusted to be genuinely motivated to remain true to the expressed intention. Effective communication then would involve a trusted offering plausible reasons why they wish to fulfil their promise, perhaps by demonstrating some recognition of a greater good. As this process involves creating a common understanding between two actors, an appreciation of each others' view point, of the conditions they find themselves in, and of the reasons why they wish to pursue certain courses of action needs to develop. This would help to remove any distrust between the actors and both can begin to believe that toleration of each other's positions and ambitions is manageable. Put in other terms, both have earned each others' respect.

But ongoing effective communication is never sufficient for trust and cooperation to develop. Research on trust development demonstrates that an individual's perception of others' trustworthiness and their willingness to engage in trusting behaviour when interacting with them are also largely history-dependent processes (Deutsch 1958: 270; Solomon 1960: 225; Orbell et al. 1994: 113). According to such models, trust between two or more interdependent actors thickens or thins as a function of their cumulative interaction. Interactional histories give decision-makers information that is useful in assessing others' dispositions, intentions and motives principally by allowing trusters to monitor the actions of potential trusteds across time. This information, in turn, provides a basis for drawing inferences regarding their trustworthiness and for making predictions about their future behaviour (see also Axelrod 1997). To relate this back to Northern Ireland, the Good Friday Agreement was successfully implemented only when Provisional IRA decommissioning took place and loyalist paramilitary activities ceased. Despite further problems from 2000 onwards, the acts of decommissioning were an important part in establishing mutual respect and power sharing by signalling true motives and intentions.

Evidence of the importance of interactional histories in judgements about trust comes from a substantial body of experimental research linking specific patterns of behavioural interaction with changes in trust. For example, a number of studies have demonstrated that reciprocity in exchange relations enhances trust, while the absence or violation of reciprocity erodes it (Deutsch 1958: 273–4; Pilisuk and Skolnick 1968: 130; Putnam 2000: 28). Furthermore, if a trusted is more likely to meet you again, they have less of an incentive to lie, promoting a pre-requisite for encountering trustworthy individuals emphasised by Lupia and McCubbins (1998: 24). The implication is that individualistic contractual theories of politics and society remove individuals from the processes that determine their propensity to trust and cooperate.

> One can understand the logic of the war of all against all in a Hobbesian state of nature, since in being subject to the predation of others, all individuals have to be ultra-cautious about their interactions. However, within an established and on-going political community, it is more reasonable to think that the willingness of individuals to cooperate with one another will depend upon their past experience of cooperation, and in that sense will rest upon a principle of reciprocity rather than selfishness. (Weale 1999: 12)

But direct past experience is not the only information that individuals depend on, if only because cooperation can occur with others we have no such knowledge of. For example, Burt and Knez (1995) in analysing levels of trust between managers in a private company, demonstrated that third parties are often important disseminators of information relating to potential trusteds, and that this information (gossip) influences the calculations of trusters. However, the authors note an important caveat – third parties tend to make only partial disclosures about others. This is because third parties themselves often have incomplete information regarding a relevant other and are also prone to offer biased opinions of others usually because people prefer to communicate information consistent with what they believe the other party wants to hear. An obvious analogy here are national newspapers that are sometimes selective in their use of information to work with a certain editorial position, more commonly referred to as 'framing effects' (see Iyengar 1991; Scheufele 1999).

Information from third parties therefore is not always reliable. Above all else, individuals will rely on their own experiences first, gossip second. Depending on the individual, some may even wish to remain agnostic before committing to trust or distrust (as outlined in the previous chapter). Despite problems in acquiring reliable information, there are social mechanisms in place that create trustworthy individuals.

2.2.1 Social norms and trustworthiness

When cooperating individuals, social groups and organisations interact, they expect a certain standard of behaviour from each other. Individuals expect others to keep promises; social groups expect individuals not to undermine a particular way of life; and organisations, like government, expect citizens to pay taxes and not break the law. But why do we keep promises, conform to a certain lifestyle and pay our taxes on time?

Many scholars believe the coordinating force behind such behaviour is social norms (e.g., see Chong 2000; Coleman 1990; Elster 1989; Putnam 1993). Social norms have two important functions. First, they dictate who or what can be respected by defining the boundaries of our moral horizon (Taylor 1989: 232). Respect is granted when another is not x, y or z. For example, Labour party members do not agree with Liberal Democrats, but they respect them, that is, recognise they have legitimate causes/ends. But if Liberal Democrats adopted racist policies (for example) then a basic standard of politics and the political process will have been broken, that is, the norm that all individuals should be treated with equal moral worth regardless of race. Breaking this norm would see the Liberal Democrats isolated from the political process as without complying with it respect from others cannot follow, as it is an implicit rule for any political party in a liberal democracy. Second, social norms provide implicit or explicit rules for conduct which makes people's behaviour more predictable. It is this predictability that allows individuals to have confidence in the future action of others. But as the following section will argue, people's behaviour might only appear trustworthy, that is, their actions satisfy your expectations and interests *but only incidentally so.* This means that the person trusting will in the long term find that their trust is misplaced. This is because relationships of trust only endure if the individuals involved internalise the relevant social norms which provide them with a maxim for action. This line of argument will demonstrate the benefits of trust over the 'carrot and the stick approach' of incentives and enforcement.

2.2.2 Instrumental adherence and internalisation

According to Coleman, a norm is 'the state in which a socially defined right to control an actor's action is held not by the actor but by others' (Coleman 1990: 266). An important condition under which this occurs is when an actor's action has externalities, that is, consequences for the lives of others. The social group will then assume the right to control these actions by punishing the individual for acting otherwise via the imposition of social sanctions (see Axelrod 1997: 46–7 and Putnam 1993: 171–2). In this sense, social norms are mechanisms by which the common good of the group is protected. Because they influence the rational calculations of individuals, 'social norms establish ideal forms of behaviour, assign priority to different points of view and ways of life, and affect individual choice by coordinating expectations' (Chong 2000: 5). Such coordination creates stable and repeated behaviour within groups, and this ensures a certain level of predictability about others' actions. As Putnam (1993: 177) claims: 'Individuals are able to be trusting because of the social norms and networks within which their actions are embedded.'

When concerned with the processes by which social norms coordinate individuals, two differing interpretations can be given. The difference depends on whether individuals are viewed as instrumental, strategic actors with fixed preferences, or actors that are also motivated by a set of dispositions and values.[1] The former, and most common view, is that norms affect individuals as external factors. The norm itself does not figure within an individual's psychology, but the various incentives for acting in accordance with the norm do; hence, norms are only of interest with the benefits they bring by upholding them, or the costs incurred for violating them. Hume (1751) originally put forth the necessary connection of social conventions and rational calculation governed by utility (justice as artificial virtue), a position implicit in the work of March and Olsen (1989) and Axelrod (1997). This is also the position Coleman takes:

> I have little to say about the compliance with norms, because compliance or noncompliance is merely the result of the application of the principle of maximising utility under different conditions. (Coleman 1990: 286)

And likewise, Putnam:

> History determines the stable outcome of any given society…but once in this setting [a society governed by the norm of reciprocity and trust] rational actors have an incentive to act consistently with its rules. (Putnam 1993: 178–9)

According to these positions, social norms are nothing more than a collection of individually rational behavioural regularities. If we take this interpretation to be true, then, as a corollary, we have to assume social sanctioning to be an effective process to coordinate rational individuals. However, the validity of this assumption is questionable on two accounts: (1) the problem of monitoring; and (2) the need for mechanisms to ensure violators of a social norm will be punished.

In attempting to overcome collective action problems and to ensure the provision of public goods, there is a consensus that third party enforcement, along the lines of Hobbes' Leviathan, is not an option. The problem is that it is difficult to detect those free-riding on a public good when general and not universal cooperation for their supply is required (Weale 2001: 5). It is thought that the strength of implicit rules of conduct within society – as a means to coordinate individuals – is that society, as opposed to the state, can enforce standards more effectively. No doubt this is true. But we should ask: is more effective, effective enough? that is, can social sanctioning alone guarantee a minimum compliance with a norm? Putnam thinks so:

> Novembers here are windy, and my leaves are likely to end up on other people's yards. However, it is not feasible for my neighbors to get together to bribe me to rake. The norm of keeping lawns leaf-free is powerful in my neighborhood, however, and it constrains my decision as to whether to spend Saturday afternoon watching TV... [But] non-rakers risk being shunned at neighborhood events, and non-raking is rare. Even though I prefer watching the Buckeyes to raking up leaves, I usually comply with the norm. (Putnam 1993: 171)

But Sidgwick, amongst others, was suspicious of social sanctions and their ability to make duty and self-interest coincide as 'Social no less than legal penalties are evaded by secret crimes... for what one requires for social success is that one should appear, rather than be, useful to others' (Sidgwick 1890: 166–8).

In concurring with Sidgwick's suspicions, two invalid assumptions seem to be made in Putnam's anecdote. First, that the neighbourhood – even granting strong social networks – is able to isolate and detect Putnam's tree as the one causing the mess; and second, the neighbourhood can monitor Putnam's efforts. With this latter point, it seems quite easy for a rational actor to appear to be doing his bit, without ever actually doing it. Although in the absence of big brother society can keep a closer eye on individuals than the state, the detection of a crime and the monitoring of the suspect are still problematic in the social world as they are in the legal.[2]

But, even if we are generous and grant social sanctions effectiveness if they are used, one problem remains – how can we be sure they will be used? Can we trust that violators will be punished? Axelrod (1997) notes that norms, such as reciprocity, will not sustain in the absence of a mechanism that maintains 'vengefulness' above a sufficient level, where 'vengefulness' represents the motivation to punish those who have failed, to punish violators of norms. To maintain sufficient levels of vengefulness, there must exist a metanorm – a norm that says one must punish those who do not punish violators (Axelrod 1997: 52). We find that such a norm is not without exemplars: the boy who is grounded for allowing his younger sister to paint the cat; the citizen who knowingly fails to report a crime and is consequently charged with negligence of civil duty; perhaps even those who harbour terrorists are punished for failing to uphold an international norm. But this just replaces the mystery of how norms are maintained with the equally perplexing question of how metanorms are maintained. Answering this latter conundrum is now the task in hand.

2.2.3 The internalisation of norms

Implicit within accounts of metanorms (especially Axelrod 1997: 55–63) is that they exist independent of the norm they seek to defend. Indeed, by granting them a 'meta' status, we seem to be casting them out into a realm where they have a life of their own. Coleman (1990: 282–6), on the contrary, felt no need to ascribe to a separate mechanism to maintain the sanctioning against violators of a norm, as individually it is in the interest of each to uphold the norm, which logically entails the sanctioning of others who break it.

While I agree that we do not need to appeal to a mechanism existing independent of the norm itself, to assume that individual rational actors will burden the costs of punishing defectors is, I think, simply another way to restate the problem of free-riding. For Coleman's argument to work, we have to assume that society can detect and monitor those who fail to punish violators (no more difficult than detecting and monitoring the violator in the first place). So, even if we relax this questionable assumption, we are left with a rational actor who should behave for the good of all by punishing the defector. But as we know, in a rational world, what is in the interest of each does not equate with the interest of all. As punishing a single defector entails certain costs (time, effort and perhaps even retaliation from the violator herself) but little, if any, immediate benefits, we should expect the violation to go unpunished. Indeed, it takes a brave perhaps reckless individual to single-handedly tackle a gang of youths vandalising a public space.

So what could promote such heroism? The process of internalisation seems to me to be the most influential factor in determining (1) whether or not a norm is acted in accordance with, and (2) the extent to which individuals are willing to punish violators. The internalisation of norms refers to the process by which 'an individual acquires a preference for conformity to a behavioural standard and suffers some psychological cost – guilt is an appropriate term – when she fails to conform, whether or not others are aware of her violation' (McAdams 1997: 338). It is a process then that is an extension of, as opposed to apart from, the norms themselves.

Ultimately, the difference between complying with a norm because of environmental considerations versus intrinsic ones is related to the difference between shame, which is externally generated, and guilt, which is internally generated.[3] Most individuals motivated by the former will simply ignore the norm, as coordinating individuals through shaming is not sufficiently widespread given that social sanctions are not widely effective. In contrast, if people accept the expected behaviour as in line with their pre-dispositions, they will be likely to blame themselves if they fail to live up to expectations and seek to change their behaviour. 'The crucial point is that the reason rules are acknowledged is that they are seen to have authority; it is not that they are seen to have authority because they are in practice acknowledged' (Weale 2001: 5). Thus, if norms are to be acted in accordance with, they must hold an authoritative grip on individuals, where an agent's 'inner point of view' cannot be ignored. 'As a result, compliance based on intrinsic forces such as guilt is more stable than compliance based on extrinsic forces such as shame' (Etzioni 2000: 160). Not only does internalisation lead to more stable compliance for individuals, it also means those same individuals are more likely to punish defectors. If social norms are internalised to such an extent that they become a trait of an individual – as opposed to merely a state – then an observed violation of the norm will arouse greater anxiety in the observer. This anxiety provides greater motivation to punish the violator than would normally be if the norm didn't constitute a trait (Marcus et al. 2000: 60–4 and ch. 5).

We have then two different processes of internalisation, one being 'ethical internalisation' (or 'rational internalisation') and the other 'non-rational internalisation'. The former is shaped throughout our civil life, and is characterised by our acceptance or rejection of reasons to conform to a social norm.[4] However, to believe something to be right cannot be equated with doing what is right; one can be rather conversant with Kant for example, and still act immorally. The presence of our traits and habits – the 'non-rational' process of the internalisation of norms – primarily explains this discrepancy. The socialisation influences that pre-date civil life, namely school, family and the community, are all part of the non-rational process of the internalisation of norms, factors that even determine the extent to which an individual will trust (Newton 1999b: 172). These form our dispositions, and are prior to any conscious decision-making (Marcus et al. 2000: 39–41). Indeed, what we get anxious about and therefore are more likely to act upon, is essentially determined by such dispositions. So for example, a concern for the decay in moral values will be more apparent to Christian fundamentalists than to those for whom Christian values are of lesser importance. And, of course, whether one is a practising Christian is determined more often than not by the family, school and community that shape dispositions.

The reason why social norms are maintained then is only made explicable when we assign a central role to the process of internalisation. It is only under conditions where norms are internalised do we find stable and regular behaviour, which makes individuals within a community predictable, and ultimately, trustworthy. By internalising norms, individuals adopt expectations of themselves and others from a 'moral perspective' which guides the kind of actions they wish to follow and wish others to follow (Ostrom 2003: 41).

The preceding arguments have stated that it is reasons internal to an agent, as opposed to external, that provide the significant motivational postulates for individuals. As a corollary, some of the more prominent rational choice accounts of social norms fail to account for their maintenance as they presuppose an invalid view of agency – namely, outcome orientated individuals, governed by environmental constraints and their effects. As Green and Shapiro note,

> once the move is made to abandon the 'internal' reading, it is difficult to see how we can illuminate structural relations and causes ... as an external reading is compatible with so many divergent empirical outcomes. (Green and Shapiro 1994: 23)

Green and Shapiro also note, however, that 'internal' rational choice theories do exist, which treat intentions as causes. But if we accept this assumption, then we need to remove the 'as-if' assumption of behaviour found within external rational choice accounts and replace it with an account of the psychological microfoundations of judgement and action (Elster and Hylland 1986: intro; Green and Shapiro 1994: 20–3). This means that accounting for norms such as reciprocity and the resulting trustworthiness requires an understanding of the process of internalisation.

2.2.4 Confidence and convergence on a maxim

A judgement that something is 'good' is commonly cited as a primary motivational factor within the formation of intentions. According to Kant, the concept of 'good' in practical deliberation has two roles: one to refer to some value the object has itself, and another to motivate, that is, play some effective causal role in action determination (Kant 1964: 4). Insofar as they are genuine, these judgements of a good imply the presence of some desire. 'Desire', in rational choice terms, is generally understood as that psychological state of the agent which aims at satisfaction. There is, however, a notion of 'desire' which refers to the affective mental entities that are less, or not at all amenable, to deliberative constraints of any kind. For now, our concern is with the former notion.

Intentions then are formed with an object in mind that is judged to be good, and – leaving aside our affective desires – an agent consequently 'wills' the appropriate action to accord with what is deemed good. This can often lead to the formation of a maxim.[5] So, for example, consider the scenario where an old lady has to cross a busy main road that is absent of safe points of crossing. An individual decides to help the old lady across to the other side. This intention is formed on the basis of some maxim, which might be 'I will always help the needy if I am able to'. So, in the presence of this maxim, it seems that we could trust this person to help the old lady.

What we can deduce from this example is that a true relationship of trust only attains insofar as individuals act on similar maxims. This is to make a Kantian point; we wouldn't necessarily trust a person because they merely act in accordance with a certain principle, but we would if we believe they act *from* a certain principle.[6] To take another example, I wouldn't trust Fred to attempt to return a lost bag of money to its rightful owner – perhaps by handing it over to the police – simply because he has never stolen before. And to give a political example, I doubt the underprivileged in Britain trust the Conservative Party to alleviate their undesirable position simply because the party leadership has now said that is party policy. If I knew Fred disapproved with theft on principle then I would expect that principle to over-ride the economic incentive to keep the bag of money, and hence I would trust him to attempt to return it. Likewise, if certain sections of the public believed that the Conservative Party cared about the underprivileged as a matter of principle as opposed to adopting the policy position as an electoral strategy, then they would probably be trusted on the matter. In both cases, to outwardly act in accordance with a principle is not the same as acting from the principle, and only with the latter are we given any sort of guarantee about the behaviour of others.

Figure 2.2 below outlines the movement from social norms to trust. As stated, mere instrumental adherence to a social norm will create a behavioural regularity in an individual, but such an individual will be liable to defection if they see an opportunity to gain short-term benefits without jeopardising long-term pay-offs. For example, a purely rational actor will accord with tax laws less when the system of punishment is perceived to be ineffective (Smith and Kinsey 1987: 646). Hence, trust decisions based on confidence can lead to that trust being misplaced.

But pure adherence with a social norm based solely on an underlying principle/maxim is likewise not sufficient for the attainment of trust. The reservation is that the recognition of one's duty does not necessarily stand in a one-to-one relationship with the fulfilment of one's duty, as 'a commitment to self-sacrificing motivation as a routine feature of social life is simply implausible' Weale (2001: 8) So self-sacrificing commitment aside, relationships of trust maintain when both actors involved recognise the benefits to each other's self-interest (Hardin 1998). But this must come with a guarantee that the relevant other will not defect; the guarantee comes in the form of a maxim that provides the motive to act in a reciprocal manner where self-interest is sufficiently 'long sighted' (Lane 1972).

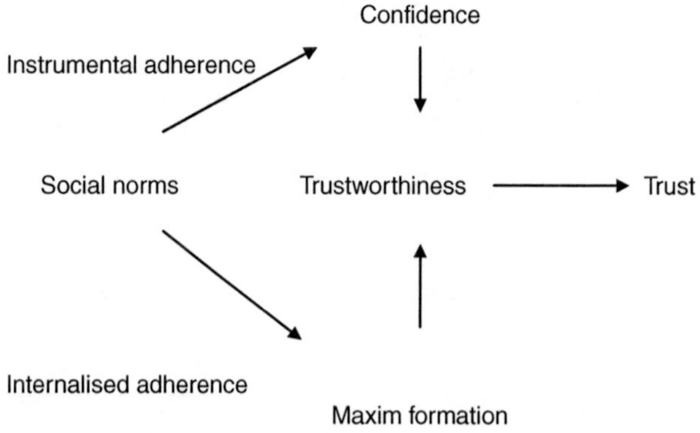

Figure 2.2 Social norms and trust

2.3 Trust in people and government: misnomers?

The implication for relationships of trust, as stated, is that they can only be maintained within close and ongoing interactions. This ostensibly poses a problem for the validity of the notions of 'trust in society' (people in general) and 'trust in government'. The validity of 'thin' types of trust, like trust in government, have been questioned. Some argue that trust, by its very nature, can only be found in 'thick' personal relationships that are close and ongoing (Coleman 1990; Hardin 1999). If we recall that trust requires another to promote our interests qua our interests, it is difficult to envisage a situation in which this condition can be fulfilled unless the truster personally knows and cares for our individual interests. For example, Coleman argues that trust is the concept through which risk is evaluated, and it is a function of: (1) the probability that the trusted is trustworthy, and (2) the potential net gain (utility) of cooperating, given the trusted is trustworthy (Coleman 1990: 99). He argues that cooperation is produced consciously by explicit communication about joint interests and joint sanctioning, in which sanctions are seen as a 'public good' (1990: 116). Due to the formal nature of such bargaining, Coleman believes trust can only be fostered in informal, small, closed and homogenous communities, which are able to reinforce normative sanctions. It is for this reason that Hardin (1998) also believes that trust in government does not exist, as institutions like government cannot operate with the specific interests of individuals in mind and form intentions based on those interests. Ullmann-Margalit (2002: 6) likewise argues that it is 'the impersonality... in the institutional case [which means] it is a misnomer to talk of trust'. As such, we should only speak of confidence in government (Hardin 1998: 13–14).

The problem with this line of thinking is that it conflates idealisation with abstraction, introducing normative concerns when discussing trust as an empirical phenomenon. The public is informed, to a certain extent, of the role, conduct and performance of political actors and institutions, and this influences expectations with regards to whether the beliefs and actions of government harm or promote our interests (Levi 1999: 4–5). From this basis, a judgement of the trustworthiness of political actors and institutions is made. While ideally we shouldn't ask questions of trust until we have sufficient information and knowledge that the relevant other considers and acts on our specific interests (i.e., we ought to remain agnostic), individuals nonetheless hold beliefs about the trustworthiness of government officials based on limited knowledge. Inferences are made about what motivates political actors from very little, and perhaps even unreliable information.

The problem implicit in Hardin's account is a presumption of psychological egoism on the behalf of political actors.[7] The position seems to conflate two distinct conditions: government takes an individual's interests into account, and government takes individuals into account. Of course, it is true that government cannot fulfil the latter condition, which Hardin and Ullman-Margalit point out, as the relationship between citizen and government is impersonal. But in this instance, it is the *interests* of an individual that are important for relationships of trust, not necessarily the actual person. Citizens have a relationship with government not because they meet politicians on a regular basis but because government and politicians are supposed to represent the interests of their citizens. The fact that citizens possess 'other regarding' interests, such as the protection of human rights for example, means that citizens can make judgements as to how trustworthy they believe government is in satisfying this interest. Our link to government – psychologically speaking – is through such interests and also through our reference group ('people like me'). If government produces outcomes unfavourable to people like me (e.g., cutting student grants), or violates principles that are for the benefit of all (the protection of Human Rights), then I am perfectly entitled to judge government as untrustworthy. To deny that we can, assumes that government has to satisfy each citizen personally. This is implausible given that no citizen is narcissistic enough to wake up in the morning and ask: 'right, what is government going to do for me personally today?' And as people don't, there seems little reason to believe that trust in government is actually a misnomer.

The second objection to talk of trust in government is that government is an institution, and institutions do not form intentions and possess motives (Hardin 1998). This objection is undoubtedly true – to think otherwise would be to reify the institution of government. The problem again is that this is to remove trust in government out of the context of empirical exploration. The crux is whether or not survey respondents when asked about trust in government only think of 'government' as the institution, or whether the notion of 'government' also includes politicians. The high correlation between trust in politicians and trust in parliament (0.370***, ESS round 3, 2006 working sample) suggests that both are shaped with the other in mind – politicians can only ever be as good as the set of institutional practices, but then sound institutional practices require the competent conduct of political officials. So while as an analytical truth trust in government is a misnomer, as an object of empirical study it is not, for the concept of 'government' necessarily implies 'politicians', a group of intention forming actors sometimes motivated for their common good, that is, the success of their governing president/party, and sometimes motivated otherwise.

Similar reservations can be held regarding trust in society (see Milner 2002). The difference is there is some merit to the claim that social trust is a misnomer as an idealised concept (i.e., something desirable for communities to have) and as an object of empirical study. Whilst we are usually able to make decisions of how trustworthy our family and friends are, perhaps even our neighbours, it becomes less clear how we can even begin to evaluate the motives and intentions of 'people in general'. A notable difference between the general object of 'government' and the general object of 'people' or 'society' is that the individuals and actions of government are constantly in the public spotlight whilst people's lives, except for a handful of criminals and celebrities, are exclusively private. It is no surprise then that generalised social trust questions are predominantly interpreted by survey respondents with close family and friend relationships in mind (Sturgis and Smith 2008). Indeed, given the requirements of what constitutes a relationship of trust, it seems difficult to think of any other way one could respond to such questions. Social trust then, as prompted by current survey questions, is not in fact generalised. Overcoming this problem is a concern for Chapter 5.

2.4 What trust does

A form of life based on trust and engagement brings individuals immense benefits, particularly true for social trust. Berkman and Glass (2000) argue that ongoing connections with other people provide individuals with subjective well-being (see also Diener 2000). One important mechanism at work is how engagement affects the serotonergic system in our brains (Tse and Bond 2002). This mechanism demonstrates bi-lateral causality and so increased levels of serotonin will provide motive to engage further.

If this relationship is true, then it should be the case that countries with higher levels of social trust are also the happiest countries. As can be seen from Figure 2.3 below, for Western Europe, a very strong positive association does exist, with low social trust countries like Italy also scoring the least happy, all the way up to high trusting and happy countries such as Finland and Denmark.

The nexus between trust and happiness can also be triangulated by using a different measure of well-being. Socially trusting societies might be happier, but are they more satisfied with life in general? Not surprisingly, the virtuous circle of living in a trusting society does indeed lead to greater satisfaction with life, as Figure 2.4 below demonstrates.

Apart from happiness and satisfaction with life, trust has other benign by-products. As a non-enforcement and non-incentive based mechanism,

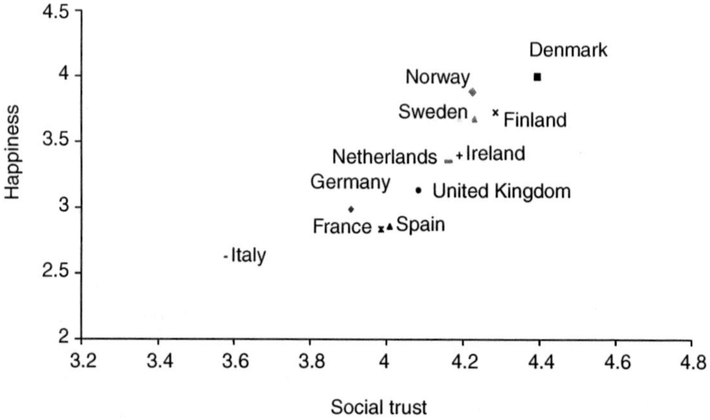

Figure 2.3 Social trust and happiness
Note: Figures are mean values from five point scales.
Source: ESS round 3, 2006.

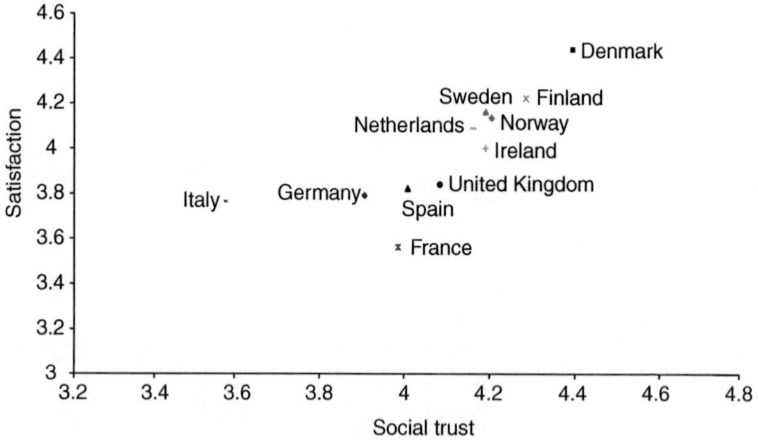

Figure 2.4 Social trust and satisfaction with life
Note: Figures are mean values from five point scales.
Source: ESS round 3, 2006.

trust is posited as an (if not the most) efficient and stable way of overcoming the problems of creating cooperative relationships (Hollis 1998: 8). The argument is that trust binds and invigorates cooperative behaviour. It facilitates the formation of a sense of common identity and purpose, and limits the need to monitor the behaviour of others thus reducing transaction costs. Groups in society can then bond and pursue mutual interests effectively and with ease. Quite simply, trust 'lubricates social life' (Putnam 2000: 21).

Trust also lubricates political life. As Figure 2.5 demonstrates, countries with higher levels of trust in government also have the highest levels of turnout in general elections for legislative assemblies.[8] Despite the anomalies of Germany and Finland, the positive correlation between the two appears to be strong.

By mediating between citizenry and government, different levels of political trust change the nature of citizen–government relationships by altering the capacity for government to govern and for organised interest groups to pursue their interests more effectively. Gamson has argued that when the level of political trust is high,

> the authorities are able to make new commitments on the basis of it and, if successful, increase support even more... [But] when it is low and declining, authorities may find it difficult to meet existing commitments and to govern effectively. (Gamson 1968: 45–6)

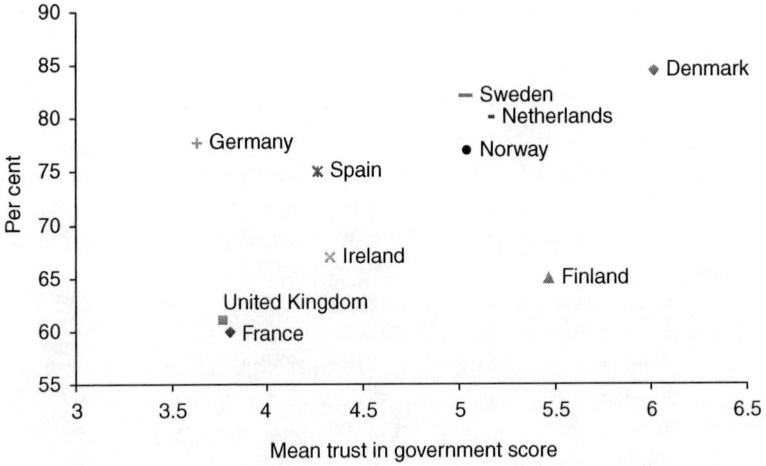

Figure 2.5 Political trust and general election turnout

Source: ESS round 3, 2006.

Not only does trust ease the formation of relationships but it also improves the relationship by making individuals feel secure enough to grant freedom to others. Granting freedom to others allows them to develop skills and knowledge that could improve the efficiency of cooperating with such an individual or organisation in the future (Levin 2003: 6). At a political level, the benefits of extending trust and cooperation across different interests has important implication for the quality of policy output. For example, trust, or a lack of it, is a decisive factor in the formation of political constitutions. Weale (2002: 8) asks why political constitutions exist with a large number of veto points built into them given problems such as 'log-jam':

> The obvious answer is the lack of trust on the part of political actors in the good intentions of those with whom they will have to interact. This lack of trust potentially has a number of sources, but one obvious basis is that the political actors who have to operate within the political constitution represent heterogeneous interests or ideologies. For example, veto points may be built into federal political systems because when the constituent units come together their representatives fear that in pooling their sovereignty with others they may be handing over control over their vital interests to others who may not respect their wishes.

Constitutions built on such Madisonian principles have a tendency to produce ineffective government. Obvious examples are the European Union's inability to make alterations to the Common Agricultural Policy and the failure of a number of US administrations to make substantial health care reforms, most notably Bill Clinton's.

Constitutional design and social life minus trust decreases spontaneous sociability and cooperation between individuals and organisations. Spontaneous sociability refers to the 'capability to form new associations and to cooperate within the terms of reference they establish' (Fukuyama 1995: 29). An implication of spontaneous sociability is that adherence to the boundaries of group membership, such as family or company, is less relevant than is the development of cooperation between groups. Combining a high degree of generalised trust and spontaneous sociability allows for the growth of trust-based cooperative networks. This is what Putnam (2000: 16) refers to as 'bridging social capital' – trust and cooperation that extends across disparate social groupings.

2.4.1 Reducing transaction costs

Specifically, it is the reduction in transaction costs between individuals that enhances cooperation. As the previous chapter demonstrated, in the absence of personalised knowledge about others, trust must be individually negotiated or substituted for other beliefs (see also Barber 1983; Sitkin 1995). Indeed, some argue that all there is to some forms of cooperation is individual negotiation:

> What transaction cost economics says... is that because opportunistic agents will not self-enforce open-ended promises to behave responsibly, efficient exchange will be realized only if dependencies are supported by credible commitments. Wherein is trust implicated if parties to an exchange are farsighted and reflect the relevant hazards in terms of the exchange? I maintain that trust is irrelevant to commercial exchange and that reference to trust in this connection promotes confusion. (Williamson 1993: 469 quoted in Levi 1999: 3)

This echoes the early view of Axelrod (1984) in The Possibility of Cooperation. If two actors realise that it is in their long-term self-interest to keep promises and maintain the relationship, why is trust needed at all?

There seems to be much truth to this claim. An example will clarify the point. One rule of thumb for drivers is that they should pay very close attention to other drivers, bearing in mind that at any moment they could make an error. In reality, our level of attention does not consistently accord with this standard. The reason is that the advice asks us to presume a certain level of distrust towards other drivers. But in our practical deliberations as drivers, trust and distrust are not issues. We know nothing of the intentions and past behaviour of other drivers, and because we lack such knowledge, we have no basis upon which to presume trust or distrust. We are confident, however, that if we are personally driving safely, no harm will come to ourselves or any other. We are also confident that as it is in every driver's interest to also drive safely, they will probably do so. We negotiate this interaction with others without recourse to beliefs of trust or distrust, and by and large, we negotiate it successfully and without harm.

The argument I wish to defend here is not that only trust is adequate for cooperation, but rather all things being equal, cooperation based on trust is more beneficial than cooperation based on enforcement or incentives. Where the environments of commercial exchanges and negotiating traffic differ is that in the former trust, at the very least, is possible. Commercial exchanges operate in an environment where individuals and organisations deal with others who have a reputation or status that signals how trustworthy they have been in the past. When confronted with other motorists, no such information is available. And in environments where trust is possible, it can (and perhaps should) be harnessed and used to greater effect than a carrot (incentives) or stick (enforcement) approach.

Recognition of this has led a number of theorists to focus on the role of trust in reducing the costs of interpersonal and intra- and inter-organisational transactions (Arrow 1972: 23; McAllister 1995: 25; Bromiley and Cummings 1996: 302–10; Uzzi 1997; Putnam 2000). Trust is seen as an efficient lubricant to economic exchange. It is the most efficient mechanism for governing transactions, functioning as 'implicit contracting' (Arrow 1974: 23). In most transactions, particularly economic, individuals have incentives to lie and defect. This is why

> virtually every commercial transaction has within itself an element of trust, certainly any transaction conducted over a period of time... [and] it can be plausibly argued that much of the economic backwardness in the world can be explained by the lack of mutual [trust]. (Arrow 1972: 357)

Of course, the main beneficiary of trust is time. Without trust, the only way mutual confidence between two business organisations can develop is for both to research the past activities of the other. Absent such bureaucratic tasks, attention can be directed towards fulfilling current contractual obligations or arranging new ones. So rendering the need for monitoring others redundant grants freedom to all parties involved to pursue more fruitful projects. Furthermore, the good will present in trusting relationships will also facilitate the actors' willingness to share ideas and information and to clarify goals and problems (Moorman, Zaltman and Deshpande 1992: 316–20).

2.4.2 Promoting economic growth

The impulse of introducing social and institutional phenomena into economics was given by the new institutional approach of economics (see North 1990 and Williamson 1981 for example). Transaction costs, uncertainty, imperfect information, social and cultural restraints were all increasingly cited as determinants of economic development and as such integrated into neoclassical frameworks. This was complimented with advances in game theory and micro-economic analysis that likewise started to focus on the concept of trust. In the trust game proposed by Berg et al. (1995), individuals are able to achieve a higher but uncertain payoff by trusting that the anonymous counterpart is willing to cooperate and reciprocate the trust placed. Berg et al. (1995: 128) state that social norms govern the decisions of the individuals to trust and to reciprocate the placed trust.

However, it was Putnam (1993) who first highlighted the role of social norms, in particular trust and reciprocity, for economic development and thus initiated various empirical studies on the topic. Putnam compares the governmental performance in the northern and southern regions of Italy by looking at differences in the civic community in these regions. His argument is that regions with a stronger sense of community have higher levels of trust which, in turn, contribute to the effectiveness and stability of democratic government and a superior economic performance. In this sense, cooperation and trust emerging from civic responsibility resolve collective action problems and lead to mutual benefits. According to Putnam, societies evolve towards one of two broad equilibria: first, a desirable equilibrium ('virtuous circle') with high levels of civic engagement, cooperation, trust and performance; or second, an undesirable equilibrium ('vicious circle') with isolation, exploitation, distrust and stagnation, for trust tends to be self-enforcing and cumulative. The former possesses a community of fidelitists the latter a community of opportunists.

Fukuyama (1995) also argues for the link between trust and economic performance with a cross-country evaluation of differences in economic performance to variations in trust.

> economic activity represents a crucial part of life and is knit together by a wide variety of norms, rules, moral obligations, and other habits that together shape the society. As this book will show, one of the most important lessons we can learn from an examination of economic life is that a nation's well-being, as well as its ability to compete, is conditioned by a single, pervasive characteristic: the level of trust inherent in the society. (Fukuyama 1995: 7)

He states that generalised trust accounts for the superior performance of institutions, especially firms. The need for cooperation and the dependence of cooperation on trust determines the success of a firm in implementing an efficient organisation, adopting changes in technology, acquiring qualified personnel and achieving economic objectives. Fukuyama explicitly distinguishes between family ties and generalised trust wherein the first is harmful for firms and the latter leads to economic superiority.

There are three paths to sociability: the first is based on family and kinship; the second on voluntary associations outside kinship such as schools clubs, and professional organisations, and the third is the state. There are three forms of economic organisation corresponding to each path: the family business, the professionally managed corporation, and the state-owned or -sponsored enterprise. The first and third paths, it turns out, are closely related to one another: cultures in which the primary avenue towards sociability is family and kinship have a great deal of trouble creating large, durable economic organisations and therefore look to the state to initiate and support them (Fukuyama 1995: 62).

In the field of Economics, a wealth of literature particularly throughout the 1990s began to accumulate on the positive effects that trust has on societies supporting Fukuyama's claims. Helliwell (1996a, b) for example demonstrates the positive effects of trust on productivity growth and investment activity for a selection of OECD countries. La Porta et al. (1997) likewise conducted a comparative study on the economic effects of trust. The empirical tests suggested that a one-standard-deviation increase of trust increases growth by 0.3 per cent (La Porta et al. 1997: 315), where as Zak and Knack (2001) and Whiteley (2000) suggest that the effects of a one-standard-deviation increase in social trust is actually over 0.3 per cent growth.

As a way of adding further evidence to this purported link between social trust and economic growth, the following chart (Figure 2.6) plots the 2003 GDP growth rate for West European countries against a measure of social trust from round 1 of the ESS (2002).

2.5 The causal order of trust and behaviour

Despite numerous examples of aggregate associations between trust and benign outcomes such as higher turnout in elections, the research programme in trust extends itself to a more 'scientific' concern: does trust cause certain types of outcomes or is trust the result of these outcomes? The only way to demonstrate this empirically is to utilise longitudinal (panel) data usually favoured with a lagged regression method approach (e.g., Whiteley 2000). For some, this is the only way to explore trust empirically.

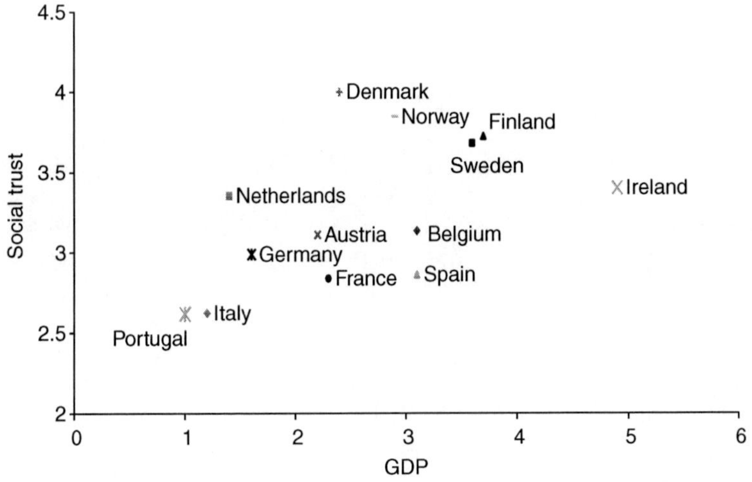

Figure 2.6 Social trust and GDP

> Such a concern with causal ordering is not merely the pedantry of 'the quibbling econometrician'... For despite the correlational evidence, where we find education, income and occupational status to be significant predictors of [social] trust in a cross-sectional regression, there is the very real possibility that some unmeasured characteristic is the true cause of the observed associations. (Sturgis et al. 2007: 3–4)

This is certainly true and such methodological developments have advanced the research programme on trust to a new level. However, there are still two important issues that need to be raised when evaluating such advanced methodological approaches in contrast to standard cross-sectional analyses. First, there is always a trade-off between method-driven research and theory driven research. If the aim is to test the causal relationship between a limited set of variables (e.g., educational attainment on social trust) then longitudinal data from panel surveys often suffice. However, if the research is more theory-driven and a wider range of hypotheses are to be tested, then only cross-sectional datasets contain the long list of variables required to do so.

The second issue refers to the limited inferences that can be made regarding causal ordering in cross-sectional analyses. In the long run it could be argued that the concern of whether trust comes before or after certain behaviours might not be so important to render cross-sectional analyses futile or unimportant. The reason is that there are plenty of good arguments and evidence to suggest that a bi-lateral relationship exists between social trust and institutional outcomes (e.g., Szreter 2002; Letki and Evans 2005), as well as political trust and political behaviour (Hetherington 2004; Keele 2004). Put another way, trust can create new forms of behaviour as well as provide a mechanism that maintains behaviours. Either way, it is the belief that relevant others will fulfil their promises and satisfy your interests that establishes/ maintains the cooperative behaviours so important for civil society. This acceptance of trust as a cause *and* effect leads us back to a line of thinking highlighted at the beginning of this current wave of trust research which argues that 'linear causal questions must not crowd out equilibrium analysis' (Putnam 1993: 181).

This is not to argue against attempts to unravel the causal relationships within trust relationships. They undoubtedly help us to better understand the nature of trust relationships. It is, however, to acknowledge that cross-sectional analyses can still illuminate where and to what degree trust – social and political – plays a role.

2.6 Conclusion

The three general benefits of trust – spontaneous sociability, the reduction in transaction costs and greater economic growth – while distinct in essence, are highly correlated empirically (Fukuyama 1995: 17). But for trust to work its benign effects, certain conditions must be met if individuals and organisations are to reap such benefits.

I have argued that trust requires both stable, repeated behaviour and a belief that the trusted is acting for a common good. Insofar as social norms provide a mechanism to create behavioural regularities, I initially argued that rational choice theories presuppose a view of agency that cannot be applied to explain their maintenance. Social sanctioning alone is neither widespread nor effective enough to guarantee a minimum compliance with social norms and only through the process of internalisation will individuals be less inclined to violate a norm for reasons of guilt. Furthermore, only when internalisation occurs will individuals possess enough 'vengefulness' to punish defectors. A view of agency that emphasises the (external) environmental constraints and their associated costs and benefits is, therefore, inadequate for analysing social norms.

It was suggested that trust is not merely the ascribing of probabilities to others' behaviour, but the assigning of a quality to the person herself, more specifically, to the nature of their intentions. So, assuming perfect information, trust is the recognition of a 'good character', with the essence of this character being that an agent acts from a self-prescribed maxim. If individuals have the same objects of intention, that is, they share the same conception of a good, then a relationship of trust is made possible. If those same individuals also share a maxim that motivates action in relation to this good, then a trust relationship will attain. However, if we believe an individual to be governed by a particular maxim (e.g., 'I will never steal') then we still require knowledge of their behaviour as proof of this intention (i.e., they actually demonstrate they don't steal). On the other hand, if we view some behavioural regularity that is in accordance with a norm – where the norm is an expression of a common good – then we still need assurances that individuals are acting from a belief in the norm, and not merely in accordance with it.

Thus, the argument can be simplified as follows: Social norms coordinate a multitude of individuals, and the self-prescribing of maxims bind those same individuals to appropriate conduct. Hence, convergence on a maxim in the presence of a social norm is necessary and sufficient for trust. The incidence of 'good character' then is central to levels of trust between people. This incidence of good character sets the upper level of trust possible within a society. However, actual trust within a society always falls short of this upper level. The reason for this is that the formation of trust relationships requires reliable information regarding the motives, intentions and competence of relevant others.

Part II
Explaining Trust

Trust as we have seen is a crucial belief for individuals when negotiating the social and political world in a way that best satisfies their interests. But for scholars and policymakers alike, trust is viewed as a resource for society given the range of benign outcomes high levels of trust can produce. This section updates the vast amount of comparative research into explaining trust by utilising data from the European Social Survey 2005.

Chapter 3 begins by reviewing the theoretical approaches used to explain trust in society and government. It will be demonstrated that differences in these approaches differ first and foremost on assumptions about human agency, in particular the degree to which socialisation processes manage thoughts and behaviour. **Chapter 4** goes on to test the different explanations of trust with data from a range of West European nations. Not only are levels of trust the outcomes of enquiry, but also how trust is associated with behavioural outcomes important for civic culture concerns. Despite illuminating some aspects of how trust works empirically, **Chapter 5** offers a critique of such comparative analyses. The nature of these approaches dictates that research is conducted at a high level of abstraction. A corollary of this is that important contextual information is lost in terms of measuring and explaining trust. An implication is that trust is best studied at a lower level of analysis.

3
Frameworks of Trust

3.1 Introduction

The current wave of cynicism towards the individuals and institutions of government comes on the back of a tide of mass economic, political and social change across Western Europe, America and Japan. As Jan W. van Deth (van Deth and Scarbrough 1995: 1) notes: 'Within just a few decades, political institutions, party systems and political cultures ... lost their traditional roots.' Not only was there a rise in 'unconventional political acts' with greater 'elite challenging behaviour' (Inglehart 1999), but also the actual content and structure of society changed. Immigration levels from the 1950s increased decade by decade;[1] rising capitalism led to greater wealth inequalities and the demise of traditional industries (Sennett 1999); religious orientations faded (Jagodzinski and Dobbelaere 1995); and the mass media became the main source of information, given it power to frame and alter perceptions of government and society (Curran and Seaton 1985).

Contemporary research on trust reflects these concerns. For some, low trust and scepticism is the product of increasing individualistic and atomised societies indicating that the cultural basis of Western societies is problematic (Uslaner 2002; Knack 2003). For others, the problem is a question of reinvigorating social and political institutions (Levi 1998; Whiteley 1999; Rothstein and Stolle 2003). To what degree either position is true has important implications for addressing the democratic issues of participation and effective institutional performance. If trust in institutions like government has social origins, then policy makers attempting to improve participatory democracy need to extend their concerns to the social order of society. Likewise, if social trust (deemed as important for a happy and healthy citizenry) has political origins, then policy makers need to be sensitive to the trade-off between institutional performance and institutional intervention in society.

The culture versus institutional divide in terms of accounting for the origins of trust is a useful starting point often adopted by scholars (such as Mishler and Rose 2005 and Nannestad and Svendsen 2005). After reviewing the basic tenets behind either position, this chapter goes on to develop a more nuanced typology of explanations for trust. Implicit in various approaches are assumptions made regarding the status of agency, specifically to what degree individuals are shaped by social processes. Furthermore, approaches can also be separated according to the nature of their origins, that is, whether the approach originates outside of the social or political relations in question.

3.2 Trust – general approaches

To what degree individuals are an expression of themselves or the people and society around them has pervaded the social sciences, amongst other disciplines such as psychology and philosophy, for decades. Two traditions within political science that find expression on this matter are cultural approaches and institutional approaches. The divide represents different assumptions regarding human nature which relate to the structure/agency debate. Cultural theories leave little room for individuality to determine levels of trust, whereas institutional theories emphasise individual rationality over and above social structures and context.

Cultural theories begin with an assumption that trust is an emergent property of social relations (see Eckstein et al. 1998). Across a lifetime, individuals learn to trust or distrust by experience. Initially, the relevant others are parents and immediate family, but over time, the set of interactions widens to incorporate school friends, colleagues and neighbours (Fukuyama 1995). The outcome is a generalised sense of trust or distrust in other people, that is, 'social trust' (see Newton 1999b: 168).

The causal mechanisms at work with this approach are early socialisation processes. Such an interpretation posits trust in political actors and institutions as originating outside the political system in cultural norms, where social trust and political trust interact across time. From a cultural perspective, institutional trust is an extension of interpersonal trust, learned early in life and, much later, projected onto political institutions, thereby conditioning institutional performance capabilities (cf. Almond and Verba 1963; Putnam 1993; Inglehart 1999; for criticisms, see Jackman and Miller 1996; Levi 1996; Foley and Edwards 1999).

Institutional theories, by contrast, hypothesise that trust in government and society is strictly 'endogenous'. By this it is meant that they are directly determined by closer correlates within the political world. On this reading, trust in government is determined simply by the actions of government, and trust in people is simply determined by the perceived actions of people. Indeed, many theorists adopt such positions, where institutional trust is the expected utility of institutions performing satisfactorily (see for example Dasgupta 1988; Coleman 1990; Hetherington 2004). As such, trust in government is a consequence, not a cause, of institutional performance. The implication is that trust in institutions, be they social or political, are rationally based; it hinges on citizen evaluations of behaviour and outcomes.

3.2.1 Degrees not absolutes

The underlying concerns behind the culture/institutions dichotomy are thus two-fold. First, the level of individuality behind thought and action, and second, the origins of explanations. Despite these differences it is not necessarily the case that the effects of cultural influences are denied in institutional approaches, and institutional effects are denied in cultural approaches.

> On the contrary, insofar as political institutions persist and perform relatively consistently over successive generations, political socialization and institutional performance should exert very similar and reinforcing effects on trust in institutions. (Mishler and Rose 2001: 31)

Any single explanation of trust will therefore – either explicitly or implicitly – make assumptions about the degree to which individualism is present, not whether it is present at all. So between the black and white world of culture and institutions are various shades of grey where human agency is more or less individualistic. Thus we can imagine social action as rational but within social enablements and constraints, with individuals interpreting rules both individually and collectively. (see Hay 1995: 189. Also Weaver and Rockman 1993: 1–41). To understand this better scholars have invoked the notion of 'roles'. According to Hollis (1994) roles have three intertwined factors – the role players' judgement, the conflict between role players, and the conflict between roles. All roles have certain goals that the actor must at the least strive to achieve, but the means to fulfil a given end is up to the discretion of the role player. This is where individuals have to work out priorities. As such 'self, roles, and reasons cannot be disentangled' (Hollis 1994: 195). Two individuals in the same institution, in the same role (i.e., in the same context), will invariably bring with them their different ideas and priorities; their different 'self' formulating different means to fulfil an end. 'When thinking about roles we [are] inclined to invoke a self, distanced from the role it plays and perhaps even, in principle, from rules it follows' (Hollis 1994: 197).

The broad spectrum of explanations on trust can therefore be separated by degrees of individuality, where broad and general analyses that focus on culture and context are opposed by increasingly institutional and individually based approaches. This is neatly demonstrated by Figure 3.1. The next level of analysis down from cultural approaches are 'embedded' institutional explanations. This type of explanation embraces the social capital thesis, and encompasses both cultural and institutional factors. Such approaches posit individual socialisation experiences as sources of significant variation in trust that can explain differences within as well as between societies. Finally, at the lowest level of analysis, 'unencumbered actor' theories argue that individual preferences and experiences condition individual evaluations of social and political institutions.

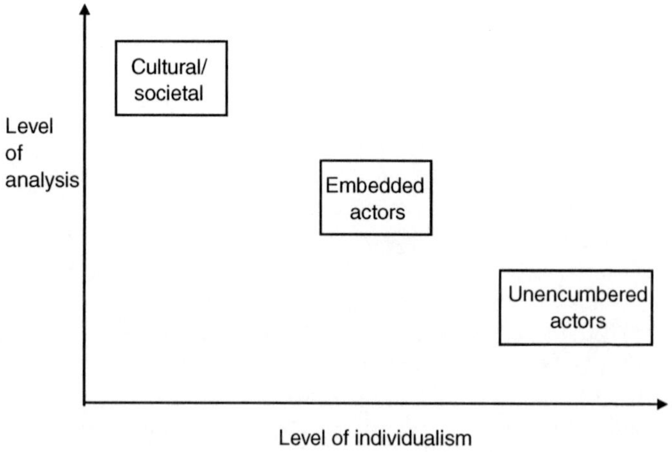

Figure 3.1 Approaches to trust

3.3 Explaining social trust – specific approaches

To manage the vast array of explanations on offer for social trust, it is useful and ultimately illustrative to separate 'endogenous' explanations from 'exogenous' ones. The former relates to factors that are automatically highly correlated with social trust where an equilibrium outcome is formed. The obvious and often cited example here is that of social networks and their hypothesised interaction with levels of trust. Exogenous factors represent random causal variables that *might* influence levels of trust given that certain prior conditions are met. Applying this way of thinking to Putnam's (1993) *Making Democracy Work*, the invasion of the Norman's provided an exogenous 'shock' to the levels of social capital in Italy, whilst the default path dependent strategies of trusting (for those in the North) and distrusting (for those in the South) provide the endogenous explanation for levels of civic engagement and government performance.

Using this final distinction allows for an analytical framework for explaining social trust to be developed. Table 3.1 below outlines the different explanations to be reviewed in this section.

The first types of explanations to consider are the ones that view individuals as being primarily shaped by surrounding social influences.

3.3.1 Societal factors endogenous to social relations

As mentioned, according to cultural theories (for example Fukuyama 1995), the potential for societies to promote social trust between citizens is primarily determined by longstanding cultural experiences Specific societal level theories build on this position by expanding on the roles and experiences that would determine levels of trust. Scholars have emphasised family background, local organisations such as schools and voluntary groups, as well as peer group influences (Stolle and Hooghe 2004: 425). This view suggests that core values of social trust

Table 3.1 Analytical framework for explaining the trustworthiness of society

	Endogenous to social relations	**Exogenous to social relations**
Societal factors	Family background	Education, income, wealth
Embedded actors	Social networks; voluntary orgs; neighbourhood	Group RD
Unencumbered actors	Crime	Media effects; egoistic RD; values

are acquired early in life and that this creates stable and entrenched features of an individual's character observable throughout their life (Sapiro 2004. See also Kohlberg 1981). Implicit in this approach are also the effects of certain life 'events', such as being made unemployed. However, the strength of prior socialisation processes keeps an individual's patterns of thought and behaviour in tact (Stolle and Hooghe 2004: 423).

3.3.2 Societal factors exogenous to social relations

Building on the endogenous factors to social trust are scholars that believe early life experiences to hold less of a lasting effect on an individual's life. Flanagan and Sherrod (1998) for example provide evidence to suggest that between the ages of 14 and 25 divergent life paths and events can have a dramatic effect on political socialisation. Character development and life opportunities, it is deemed, are primarily shaped by early adult experiences such as exposure to divorce, poverty or discrimination (Delhey and Newton 2003: 5).

Underlying this type of explanation then is where individuals are located in society's ladder. Seligman, for example, argues that trust cannot develop in hierarchal cultures. Such rigid social orders are akin to Putnam's notion of 'social cleavages' (Putnam 2000) where economic resources are stratified. This can create feelings of injustice towards the privileged from those of a low social status while those of a high social status might adopt the belief that those less privileged than themselves represent an underclass. Such discrete groups represent heterogeneity within a community, and as recent research into social capital points out, people trust more easily people who are similar to themselves, that is, 'people like me' (Alesina and La Ferrara 2002; Putnam 2007). Heterogeneity itself is often measured along different lines, primarily wealth (i.e., inequality), ethnicity, religion, occupation and education achievements (see for example Rothstein and Uslaner 2005).

3.3.3 Endogenous explanations for embedded actor approaches

The third type of explanation for social trust focuses on levels and types of interactions within a society which embodies the social capital thesis. Analytical developments in this field identified two broad types of social capital: bonding and bridging (Putnam 2000; Stone 2003). This advance in social capital theory differentiates the types of relationships with those close to them who share a similar social identity, with those unlike them but with equal social status. Where as the previous approach focused on the structure of society, which in theory determines 'generalised trust', this approach is centred on localised interactions. The hypothesis is that social trust is primarily an expression of belonging to neighbourhood and getting involved in community affairs. It is through these actions that a collective 'we' spirit is adopted signalled by higher trust in others.

3.3.4 Exogenous explanations for embedded actors

According to social psychologists, trust is closely linked with the status of an individual's reference group (Cook 2004). While exogenous societal factors assume that disparities in social indicators such as education and wealth create social cleavages (that is, in and out group statuses), exogenous explanations for embedded actors assumes that before such heterogeneity arises individuals must (1) see the conditions of their reference group relative to other groups in society, and (2) feel that any perceived differences are unjust. Intuitively it seems plausible that if people are satisfied when social conditions are good, then satisfaction should rise as conditions get better. Despite this scholars have suggested that political unrest can occur as a result of improving conditions (Gurr 1970). For example, why did Blacks in America during the 1960s resort to political violence when their socio-economic position seemed to be improving? (Useem 1975). RD theory states that discontent towards the structure of society is not related solely to a person's or group's objective socio-economic condition, rather when an individual's situation is seen relative to their past or other individuals and groups in society. The theory of relative deprivation (RD) states that feelings of frustration that lead to aggression are a product of individuals becoming aware of an unjust condition they are subject too through a process of comparison. It occurs when either Adams' (1963) or Homans' (1961)[2] rules of equity are violated (Zimmermann 1983: 31). While RD has been used primarily to account for political violence (see for example, Grindstaff 1968; Gurr 1970) I propose that it could also be used to explain other forms of political unrest, namely low levels of social trust as well as political trust.

3.3.5 Endogenous explanations for unencumbered actors

Studies have demonstrated that exposure to crime can affect social trust (Lederman, Loayza and Menendez 2002). However, the relationship of cause and effect between crime and social trust is not clear (Akcomak 2008). Studies have suggested that social trust and indeed social capital in general reduces crime. What seems intuitively true, however, is that crime is generally regarded as a threat to the interests of individuals and a violation of a societal norm. Given the conceptual status of trust as outlined in chapter 1, it is entirely plausible that exposure to crime would reduce the perception of how trustworthy people are.

3.3.6 Exogenous explanations for unencumbered actors

The final explanations for social trust occur outside of direct social relations and are factors that are highly individualised. The first hypothesis is that individual values and characteristics determine levels trust. Eric Uslaner (2002: 572) argues that social trust is not dependent upon the experience of reciprocity but mostly upon the two characteristics of optimism and capacity to control one's own life. Scheufele and Shah (2000) likewise also found that individual values have an impact on levels of social trust, in particular self-confidence. Related are the findings of Delhey and Newton (2005) that suggest catholic countries are less trusting of each in comparison to predominantly protestant nations. The second hypothesis is an extension of the theory of relative deprivation. Whilst people can fell deprived because of the social status of their reference as outlined earlier, they can also feel deprived because of their own personal conditions. This is referred to as egoistic RD (Runciman 1966). The third and final hypothesis is the type and level of information people receive about people in society. The main channel for this is through the mass media. Indeed, research has indicated that some forms of media usage actually promotes trust (Norris 2000; Newton 1999a), possibly highlighting the instrumental role that information plays in decisions of trust.

3.4 Trust in government – specific approaches

Trust in government was originally discussed in the early 1960s by Robert Lane, William A. Gamson, Almond and Verba, and David Easton (Lane 1962; Almond and Verba 1963; Gamson 1968; Easton 1965). Easton proposed that political systems are an input and output oriented process, where support for the system (the input) stood in relation to the nature and policy outputs of government. In 1975 Easton re-conceptualised the idea of political trust as more diffused in relation to support of the political system, and more precise in relation to political objects such as politicians. The consensus then was to use the term political trust synonymously with the terms political support or confidence. As such,

Table 3.2 Analytical framework for explaining government trustworthiness

	Endogenous to political system	Exogenous to political system
Societal		Wealth, education
Individual socialisation	Group RD	Social capital
Individual evaluations	Government represents; Government fair	Media effects, egoistic RD, values

trust in government survey questions were deemed to simply measure the level of satisfaction with the policy outputs of government.

Many explanations for the declining trustworthiness of government now focus on widespread social changes. The obvious example here is the social capital thesis (Coleman 1990; Putnam 1993, 2000, 2007). One obvious feature about this explanation is that it focuses on factors exogenous to the political system. This is contrasted with endogenous explanations emphasising 'civic' concerns such as the quality of policies produced by government and how representative political parties are. Table 3.2 outlines the types of explanations on offer to account for variations in the trustworthiness of government.

3.4.1 Societal

A group of influential scholars in the US believe that civic engagement (including trust) is determined by an individuals access to certain resources (Bartels 2003; Verba, Schlozman and Brady 1995). Indeed, if we think about the types of individuals that have the time, interest, and just as importantly, incentive to think and act politically, then such individuals usually have a higher than average socioeconomic status (Parry et al. 1992). As such, trust in government itself could also be directly affected by factors such as levels of wealth and education.

3.4.2 Exogenous individual socialisation processes

According to Putnam, in America at least, social trust is on the decline (Putnam 2000). Concomitant with this decline is a sharp and widespread fall in the number of voluntary local community activities. It is this increasing absence of face-to-face activities that accounts for falling levels of social trust, electoral turnout, and even economic growth (Putnam 2000: 291 and 319). More crucial for the concerns here, Putnam argues that declining social capital is probably the reason for declining trust in government (Putnam 2000: 347. See also Putnam

1995). Putnam's (2000) overarching concern is with the decline in 'bridging' social capital which undermines the principle of generalised reciprocity and ultimately civic engagement.

The argument is that social capital reinforces government legitimacy through a two-part process: from the premise that social capital strengthens the norms of society, high levels of social capital are associated with high levels of tax compliance (Putnam 2000: 348). If individuals see such compliance, they feel that the tax system is working and therefore see government as an efficient institution. As such, without high levels of tax compliance, individuals will perceive an inefficient and perhaps unjust tax system imposed by government (Putnam 2000: 347).

However, not all agree that civic engagement builds trust. Stolle (2001) for example demonstrated that trust and reciprocity are not associated with membership of voluntary organisations. This is supported by individual level research which finds marginal or no correlation between social trust and measures of trust in government (Orren 1997; Hall 1999; Kaase 1999; Newton and Norris 2000). Nonetheless, a more recent individual level analysis found a strong and statistically significant correlation between social trust and confidence in parliament (Zmerli, Newton and Montero 2007).

3.4.3 Endogenous individual socialisation processes

Another explanation already mentioned that emphasises socialisation processes is the theory of Relative Deprivation (RD). Due to increasing heterogeneity within societies, the number of possible inter-group comparisons has increased over the past thirty years. Furthermore, due to improvements in the media, the amount of information to make social comparisons has increased. Juxtaposed with economic inequalities and regional deprivation, possible states of RD are entirely plausible.

The fact that the number of possible inter-group comparisons has increased means very little if individuals do not actually think of themselves in group terms. But individuals have found that the most efficient way to pursue their interests is through a collective:

> Most individuals ... want to protect what they regard as their legitimate interests from others ... [and] it is sufficiently strong to create the basis for organized and opposed interest groups, based on class, ethnic, linguistic, religious or regional identities. Limited generosity therefore involves an unwillingness to carry disproportionate burdens or disadvantages relative to one's reference group, but it does not involve a desire to disrupt a satisfactory balance of interests among potentially antagonistic groups if it can be established. (Weale 1999: 11)

Weale suggests that the conflicts of interest within societies are between groups (see also Crozier et al. 1975: 161), and that this is a result of them persisting under undesirable and unjust conditions. If individuals have become increasingly more aware of the differences within their society, due to improved information networks through the mass media, this allows them to make judgements about their own personal position or their own reference group's position relative to others. Furthermore, when having made that judgement, if they perceive their own group's position to be unjust, it's possible they will hold their government responsible for it (Tyler, Rasinski and McGraw 1985; Miller and Listhaug 1998: 216).

Group RD (see Runciman 1966) then captures a situation where individuals suffer a sense of injustice on behalf of their reference group (for example Black minorities in America during the 1960s). Group RD presupposes that an individual is (1) in a state of deprivation and (2) feels this deprivation in relation to other groups in society. A final condition for states of RD to affect factors such as trust in government, is that government must be held culpable for unjust conditions (Sanders and Tanenbaum 1983).

3.4.4 Exogenous individual evaluation explanations

A different variant of RD is Egoistic or Individual RD (Runciman 1966: 154). This is purely an individualistic judgement. No socialisation process takes place. It is the outcome of an individual not fulfilling life expectations which they believe they deserve. This could be in terms of social status, finances, access to public services, and other goods and resources regarded as important to helping them lead a life that befits the type of person they are.

One could argue that egoistic RD is an expression of an individual's underlying value system. Such expectations can extend to many areas of life, and indeed according to Inglehart (1997), the number of postmaterialistic values in many Western democracies has increased. Postmateralists are seldom concerned with material and security issues, but rather with values such as individual freedom, human rights and the protection of the environment. With more postmaterlialists demanding more from government, the consequence is that trust in government has declined (Inglehart 1997: 225). These individuals are also more inclined to participate in elite-challenging activities such as third-party voting and public protesting than non-postmaterialists (Inglehart 1997: 220. See also Hetherington 2004). A slightly different take on this value change is that individuals have become more individualistic (Sennett 1999).

Also shaping individual judgements is the role played by the media. It has been suggested that political cynicism is a product of the role of private interests creating a bias portrayal of the news. The argument is that the media will primarily design a news story so it will 'sell', as opposed to making it above all else informative and educational (see Davis and Owen 1999: 192; Keane 1991: 39). While journalists tend to cover bad news, their profession is also mechanical rather than ideological, with personal career and corporate profit motives the goal and not a commitment to uncovering truth (Schudson 1995: 14). Ultimately, according to Postman (1987), the actual content of television is one of fragmented news (on average 45 second news slots), that is without context, consequences, values, and therefore without essential seriousness; 'that is to say news as pure entertainment' (Postman 1987: 102).

Contrary to these claims are the arguments of Dalton (1996), who suggests that the modern mass media has allowed for a process of 'cognitive mobilisation', by which political skills and knowledge of the public are improved. His analysis argues that two prerequisites are essential for this process to happen – easy access of political information, and the ability for the public to absorb and understand this information. The expansion of the mass media, especially television he argues, has increased the accessibility of political information.[3] But, regardless of whether the media has a positive or negative effect on its users, the fact that the media has become so dominant as a political informer suggests that, at the very least, it must have had some direct impact on the way individuals think about society and politics. Furthermore, Bacharach and Gambetta (2001) remind us that for trustworthy making characteristics to be shown, effective communication is required. With the media being the single biggest political communicator, it has a privileged opportunity to shape political views and opinions and influence government trustworthiness.

Norris (2000) and Newton (1991) argue that it is not necessarily the media in its entirety that matters but the specific content. The former concludes that watching television is not consistently associated with lower levels of confidence in political institutions (Norris 2000: 239). The latter likewise presents evidence to suggest that television as the culprit of political malaise is a spurious correlation, while there is much greater support for mobilisation. Viewing the television news regularly is associated with relatively high levels of political knowledge, interest and understanding, and has no impact on factors such as trust in officials and system efficacy. Newton concludes that watching television news appears to have a positive effect on levels of knowledge, interest, and understanding, and has no independent negative effect on levels of political malaise (Newton 1997). Other scholars, however, have also produced evidence to suggest negative framing effects, particularly from the tabloid press that undermines faith in government and society (Putnam 1995; Iyengar 1996).

3.4.5 Endogenous individual evaluation explanations

Literature on Deliberative Democracy posits the link between government and citizens as being mediated by concerns of representation and due process (Warren 2002). Citizens are not unreasonable in their demands by having expectations that exceed the capabilities of government (see Tyler 1990. Contrast with Bok 1997). Rather, citizens make reasonable demands for a political system that is representative of diverse interests (Held 1996), and is transparent in that policy makers and the policy making process are open and honest, something of a pressing issue in an e-Government era (Kim 2007). If individuals perceive the political system to deviate from these standards of representativeness and openness, then the trustworthiness of government will be questioned.

Public institutions, like government, should make decisions as if they operated behind a 'veil of ignorance' (see Rawls 1972: 5). They are only trustworthy when seen to be treating each group in society fairly, that is, with equal moral worth. Levi argues that for modern institutions to be trustworthy 'there also needs to be rules and institutions that [are] transparent and procedurally fair and that have mechanisms for ensuring the credibility of government actors' policy promises' (Levi 1996: 51). Levi cites the research of Tyler and Caine (1981) who provided evidence of procedural fairness as an important reason why people accept their fines. Individuals that are convicted of speeding, traffic accidents, drug possession, drunk driving and other crimes, would accept their fines as long as they perceived the procedures as fair. This included not only their own personal experiences with public authorities, but also their perception of how others in similar positions are treated in the eyes of the law. He concludes that this:

> supports the suggestion by political scientists that maintaining the 'appearance of justice' in government is important. Based on these findings ... it would be expected that a decreased belief that government functions through 'fair' procedures would be particularly destructive to citizen support for political leaders and institutions. (Tyler and Caine 1981: 653)

As an extension of this line of thinking, scholars have argued that trust in government is influenced by political scandals and corruption (Orren 1997), where the Watergate and Iran-Contra affairs have all be demonstrated to effect trust in government (Citrin and Green 1986: 431–6).

3.4.6 Endogenous government performance explanations

In contrast to process explanations of government trustworthiness, others emphasise the outcomes of government policy. Studies in political economy for example suggest that voter perceptions of government depend on governments stimulating a prosperous national economy,[4] as government performance is primarily judged in terms of objective economic indicators. Given such concerns, there seems plausible evidence to suggest that if governments fail, and fail repeatedly, to improve such vital policy areas, then citizens will trust government less to deliver. Recent studies offer some evidence which supports such a claim (Bok 1997; Keele 2004; McAllister 1999; Miller and Listhaug 1999). Indeed, a deep recession in the early 1990s and the ERM crisis are seen as the primary reasons why the Conservative Party lost the British public's trust. Government policy 'successes' not only satisfy certain interests – for example, the minimum wage introduced in 1998 improved the lowest earners incomes without damaging the macro economy – but also show that what politicians say and what they do can actually match. Acting in accordance with manifesto commitments demonstrates that politicians can keep promises; implementing a successful policy demonstrates they are also competent. Promise keeping and competence are the crux of trust relationships, as they are indicative of a 'good character' (see Chapter 2).

3.5 Conclusion

The research programme into explaining trust in society and government has moved away from testing specific hypotheses to more general theoretical positions. As we have seen, such tests theorising the origins of trust in government are distinguished along two dimensions. *Cultural theories* differ principally from *institutional theories* with regard to the extent that individualism plays its role in human agency. Explanations can also be couched in endogenous or exogenous terms, where by political trust originates from within the political system (endogenous) or from wider social relations (exogenous). Similarly, social trust either originates from within immediate social relations (endogenous) or from the effects of institutional performances and the structure of society (exogenous).

To what degree social life and political life overlap then are key concerns behind research into trust. By applying the theoretical frameworks established in this chapter to comparative data from Europe, the following chapter offers some preliminary analyses to determine the extent to which this is true.

4
Comparative Overview
Trust and Civic Cultures

4.1 Introduction

The pressures of the average day mean that citizens find it difficult to devote much time to politics and civic life. Not only this, regular involvement in such activities on a regular basis is very much restricted to a minority of people (Pattie et al. 2004). A recent concern for political elites and scholars is that even the few popular forms of participation, such as voting in national elections, are in decline (Dalton 2002). Indeed, political scientists have explored the 'crisis of democracy hypothesis' for decades. It is an issue that has been re-visited a number of times, such as the debate between Arthur H. Miller and Jack Citrin on declining trust in government (Citrin 1974; Miller 1974), or the Crisis of Democracy report to the trilateral commission (Crozier, Huntington and Watanuki 1975). Later, the Beliefs in Government project (BiG) investigated whether different aspects of support in government was declining in Western Europe (see Kaase and Newton 1995), while in Disaffected Democracies (2000) Susan Pharr and Robert Putnam ask 'What's troubling the trilateral countries?' (America, Europe and Japan).

While not new concerns, one might say – upon reflection – that they are somewhat surprising. Almond and Verba reported over 40 years ago that Britain possessed a 'balanced civic culture' (1963: 455). Specifically, they reported that Britons 'were trusting of each other and of the political system' (Seyd and Whiteley 2002: 2). Almond and Verba concluded that the same is true for Americans who also had a vibrant civic culture, one based on high participation. But despite the ongoing concern of the health of Western democracies, the only sober conclusion to be made now is that 'there's no immediate crisis in the citizen support in these states' (Kaase and Newton 1995: 141). This is echoed by Pharr and Putnam's contention that there exists 'no evidence of declining commitment to the principles of democratic government...on the contrary, if anything, public commitment to democracy per se has risen in the last half century' (Pharr and Putnam 2000: 5).

The aim of this chapter is to update these civic culture concerns. Using the European Social Survey 2005, information from a host of West European nations is utilised to establish the factors that account for different levels of trust and the civic behaviours associated with more or less trust in people and government. Despite illuminating cross-cultural differences and similarities, the results in this chapter suffer from the standard limitations of cross-sectional, comparative research. First, cross-sectional data are inadequate in terms of teasing out cause and effect. However, and as noted in Chapter 2, Putnam (1993: 181) reminds us that the social scientific pursuit of unravelling linear causation shouldn't distract us from analysing equilibrium outcomes. Second, and more importantly, is the lack of contextual data which is often the case with comparative datasets. Given this caveat, the empirical results in this chapter should be treated as a general exploration of the associational outcomes of trust across West European countries.

4.2 The parameters of trust

The previous chapter reviewed the literature on both social and political trust and derived a theoretical framework based on the different types of explanations on offer. The implications of this framework are a series of general hypotheses to test. Trust is shaped by:

GH1: Societal norms
GH2: Individual socialisation processes endogenous to social relations/the political system
GH3: Individual socialisation processes exogenous to social relations/the political system
GH4: Individual evaluations endogenous to social relations/the political system
GH5: Individual evaluations exogenous to social relations/the political system

The first consideration is whether trust in people and trust in government varies beyond country differences. If GH1 is correct and that variation in trust between individuals in primarily accounted for by differences in societal norms, then we can conclude that trust is very much an emergent property of social relations. Beyond societal norms, are the more localised (GH2 and GH3) and individual specific (GH4 and GH5) hypotheses.

4.3 Behavioural correlates of trust

Working from the premise of a participatory model of democracy, the irreducible concern of the civic culture thesis is an understanding of the conditions that facilitate citizen participation in the political process (Muller and Seligson 1994). Recently scholars have analysed the issues of participation through the concept of citizenship. If citizens are to adopt the Rousseauian idea of 'civic religion' where by the needs of society are placed prior to the needs of individuals (i.e., the general will before the will of all), then increasingly diverse and cosmopolitan polities need to engender a sense of common identity and purpose.

According to T. H. Marshall, citizenship is 'a status bestowed on those who are full members of a community. All who possess the status are equal with respect to the rights and duties with which the status is endowed' (Marshall 1992: 18). It is the nature of these rights and duties that is the source of conflict over the exact meaning of citizenship. Political theorists often invoke – either implicitly or explicitly – one of three types of models of citizenship (see Marshall 1992: 18–20; Carens 2000):

1. Legal citizenship
2. Political citizenship
3. Moral citizenship

These are useful separations as they unpack the different conceptions of rights and responsibilities that a Western democratic civic culture contains. Model number one predicates citizenship simply on legal status. The implication is that a 'good' citizen need only comply with their respective country's laws and occasionally legitimate governments through a national election (Schumpeter 1942).[1] Model number two presumes that the role of citizenship goes one step further than mere acquiescence by including a wider behavioural component. This usually comes in the form of acquiring greater awareness of basic political facts (also referred to as 'civic literacy'). However, it has been argued that fleeting political participation and interest is simply not enough for democratic societies to flourish (Habermas 1981; Barber 1983). Instead, model number three argues that citizens not only need to be active citizens, they also need to be virtuous citizens. This is to recognise that being a good citizen does not always equate with being a good person. By combining law and virtue, this model 'obliges citizens to use their political resources and skills to participate well, that is, to maintain not just effective laws but a decent state' (Ricci 2004: 8).

Models of citizenship and concomitant duties

	Type of model		
Type of duty	**Legal**	**Political**	**Moral**
Voting	X	X	X
Party orientated		X	X
Civic literacy		X	X
Secondary associations			X
Protesting/demonstrating			X

Scholars have remarked, often with some force, that model number one leads to government by elites (Talisse 2005). As such, this model does not seem conducive to democratic governance at all. The deficiencies of this model, however, are extremely useful in terms of uncovering a minimal set of responsibilities that a majority of citizens must fulfil in order for democracy to, at the very least, survive. The two obvious ones already mentioned are:

Law-abiding behaviour
Voting in free, fair and regular elections

Civil Society, as we know it, would cease to exist without mass compliance of national laws. Furthermore, civil unrest would be the end result without some mechanism by which citizens can express consent towards laws.

4.3.1 Political deference and participation

The two previously mentioned behaviours are also subsumed in citizenship models two and three. Where scholarly opinion is most divided, is whether citizens ought to be closer to model number two or three (for example, compare Parkinson 2003 with Dryzek 2000). The crux is the extent to which citizens should defer to the decisions made by political elites and the extent to which they should actively participate.

The literature on trust in government is the most useful way of understanding the level of deference citizens have towards their respective political authorities. Scholars in this field note that we should only expect (and should only want) citizens to trust when the relevant other is trustworthy (Hardin 2002). This is what standard survey questions on trust capture; how trustworthy government, politicians or people in general are perceived to be. As such, high trust scores towards government reflect deference; low trust scores towards government reflect disrespect. However, it is not always clear how deference and disrespect should be evaluated. Do high levels of deference capture widespread normative agreement on the actions of government or do they capture blind adherence? (Held 1996: 195). Likewise, do high levels of disrespect capture a critical citizenry (Norris (ed.) 1999) or a cynical one?

In terms of political participation, a wider set of activities are deemed as essential to the workings of democracy beyond that of law abiding behaviour, voting and the acquisition of basic political knowledge. Subsumed in model three are the following less obvious activities, but nonetheless activities that are still deemed of significant value to the workings of democracy. They are political party orientated acts (Seyd and Whiteley 2002) and participation in local organisations and social networks (Putnam 1993, 2000).

In the majority of Western democracies, parties are the most prominent way by which interests are aggregated. The importance of their role cannot be underestimated (see McDonald and Budge 2005). Particularly, they provide electorates with a set of alternative policy proposals upon which a government is chosen. Similarly, the role of Non-Governmental Organisations, such as Oxfam or Amnesty, should not be underestimated. Not only do they try to alleviate the suffering caused by social and economic problems through direct action, but they also lobby on behalf of deprived groups and raise awareness of issues. The Criminal Justice System (CJS) also requires citizen input on a regular basis. In particular, jury and lay magistrate positions are occupied by citizens, the former requiring acquiescence when called upon, the latter relying purely on independent volunteering. Finally, and as argued by Putnam (1993), a strong civic tradition reinforces government legitimacy through a two-part process: high levels of trust and social interactions strengthen the norms of society, which in turn reduces the element of free-riding in society (for example tax evasion; see Putnam 2000: 347–8). Second, a population with widespread social trust and participation is proficient in articulating its interests clearly, which in turn makes for efficient and effective government (Newton 1999b: 178).

4.3.2 Civic literacy

Henry Milner (2002) argues that research into trust in society is something of a misnomer. The real driving force behind social and political participation, he contends, is 'civic literacy' – the stock of political interest and knowledge that individuals possess. Public policies that encourage media consumption and adult education improve the quality and availability of information for political thought and debate. A consequence is that individuals are mobilised, cognitively speaking, where civic interest and awareness is stimulated.

This position is closest to citizenship model number three. The role of a citizen should be constructed in terms of activities that go beyond the formal types of participation, activities that place children and adults into situations where they are required to cooperate and share ideas and information to achieve a common goal. The idea is that this will promote the character traits essential for citizenship. At the very least then, model three of citizenship argues that the 'ethic of compromise' is prominent amongst citizens (see Dobel 1990 for a discussion on its centrality to building a strong, liberal democratic political community).

4.4 Data and country selection

In order to (1) test which of the five general hypotheses shape decisions of trust and (2) whether trust is associated with the three main areas of civic activities, it is necessary to initially specify the country selection and dependent variables that will form the forthcoming regression analyses.[2]

Throughout this chapter, the empirical analyses will be focused on a selection of West European countries using the European Social Survey, 2006–07. Despite holding data on twenty-one nations throughout Europe, the analyses will be restricted along two dimensions. First, East European countries will be excluded from the analysis. The reason for this is that, in comparison to West European countries, these countries are undergoing a process of democratisation where old social and political institutions are being replaced by newer ones. The unique dynamics taking place in this region means that any comparative analyses need to treat Eastern Europe as a separate region for study. Indeed, the fact that this region is democratising makes it a fruitful area to analyse and understand how trust in institutions is built and maintained (see for example Raiser et al. 2001). The second dimension along which the country selection is restricted is in terms of voting in elections. As one of the behavioural outcomes to be predicted by levels of trust is voting, it makes sense to exclude those countries where voting is compulsory. Given such a legal requirement for citizens of some countries, levels of trust can have no observable effect on turnout.

Given the above restrictions, the map (Figure 4.1) highlights the countries to be included in the analyses: the UK, France, Spain, Germany, Netherlands, Italy, Denmark, Sweden, Finland and Norway.

Figure 4.1 Countries in the working sample

Source: Map adapted from: http://upload.wikimedia.org/wikipedia/commons/thumb/1/1d/Western-Europe-map.png/200px-Western-Europe-map.png

The focal point will be the two prominent types of trust – trust in people and trust in government. To measure these items, the following questions from the ESS will be used:

Social trust

'Most people can be trusted or you can't be too careful'
'Most people try to take advantage of you, or try to be fair'
'Most of the time people are helpful or mostly looking out for themselves'

Trust in government

'How much trust do you have in [your own country's] parliament?'
'How much trust do you have in politicians?'

For each of these trust questions, respondents are asked on an 11-point scales to signal how much trust they have in other people in general, where 0 is the least trusting answer and 10 is the most trusting. A consensus has emerged amongst scholars using comparative data st that single item measures of social trust are inadequate (e.g., Veenstra 2002), while some do likewise for trust in government as well (e.g., Hibbing and Morse 2001). Following on from such research, the three items on social trust and the two items on political trust will be merged to form a social trust and political trust index respectively. As such, throughout the forthcoming analyses, social trust will refer to an average score of the above three measures, where as trust in government will refer to an average score of trust in parliament and politicians.

In terms of using trust variables to explain political behaviour, the ESS offers three items of importance in relation to the citizenship models outlined earlier. They are:

'Did you vote in the last general election?'
'Have you worked for a voluntary organisation in the last 12 months?'
'Have you worked for a political party in the last 12 months?'

The first item can obviously be used to gauge voter turnout and by combining the second and third items it is possible to generate a three-point scale variable for wider civic acts (where zero = no participation; one = worked for either a voluntary organisation or party; and two = worked or both).

4.5 Models of social trust

This list of general hypotheses can be broken down further into specific hypotheses for both types of trust. Social trust is shaped by:

SH1: Country differences
SH2: Nature of family relations
SH3: Wealth inequalities
SH4: Extent of social networks and civic participation

SH5: Neighbourhood satisfaction
SH6: Group relative deprivation
SH7: Perceived levels of crime
SH8: Media effects
SH9: Egoistic relative deprivation
SH10: Individual values

To gain an understanding of which of the five general hypotheses best predicts levels of trust, each of the specific hypotheses above will be 'nested' into regression models.

4.5.1 Social trust models

The first model to consider is the cultural model which simply assumes trust to be a pure expression of prevailing social norms in society. This model includes a set of country dummies from the working country selection sample and is specified as follows:

1. Cultural model:

$$\text{Trust} = a + \text{France} + \text{Spain} + \text{Germany} + \text{Netherlands} + \text{Italy} + \text{Denmark} + \text{Sweden} + \text{Finland} + \text{Norway} + e$$

where,
a = constant
e = error term.
Note: UK is reference group country.

The second model to consider is the endogenous societal norm model which assumes trust to be an expression of family background including the closeness of ties of kinship:

2. Societal model:

$$\text{Trust} = a + \text{Family background} + \text{See family/friends} + e$$

where,
Family Background = highest educational qualification attained by mother and father
See Family/Friends = 'how often see close family and friends'.

The third model to test is an extension of individual socialisation processes endogenous to social relations.

3. Individual socialisation model:

$$\text{Trust} = \text{a} + \text{Neighbourhood} + \text{Voluntary associations} + \text{Discrimination} + \text{Group RD} + \text{Religion} + \text{e}$$

where,
Neighbourhood = Satisfied with neighbourhood
Voluntary associations = Active in voluntary associations
Discrimination = Member of a discriminated group
Group RD = Student/Retired/Unemployed
Religion = Protestant/Catholic.

4. Endogenous individual evaluations model:

$$\text{Trust} = \text{a} + \text{Crime1} + \text{Crime2} + \text{Individualism} + \text{Ideology} + \text{e}$$

where,
Crime1 = General perception of crime
Crime2 = Asked for assistance with a crime
Individualism = People should take responsibility for their own life
Ideology = Self Left-Right ideological position.

5. Exogenous individual evaluations model:

$$\text{Trust} = \text{a} + \text{Media} + \text{Egoistic relative deprivation}$$

where,
Media = Read papers/Listen to radio/Watch television
Egoistic relative deprivation = Satisfied with life.

4.6 Results – social trust

Presenting the results separately for each model means it is possible to evaluate the explanatory strength of each in its own right. The cultural model outlines the societies that have a strong prevailing social norm of trusting others relative to the UK. As can be seen in Table 4.1, the coefficients for the three Scandinavian countries – Denmark, Norway and Sweden – confirm the results of other studies that demonstrate widespread trust in this region (Delhey and Newton 2005). Only Portugal appears to be less trusting socially than the UK, whilst Italy proves to be indifferent statistically. The adjusted R square figure

Table 4.1 Explaining social trust

	Cultural Model		Societal		Individual socialisation		Endogenous individual evaluations		Exogenous individual evaluations	
Variables	**Beta**	**Sig.**	**Beta**	**Sig.**	**Beta**	**Sig.**	**Beta**	**Sig.**	**Beta**	**Sig.**
Age	**–.081*** **	.000	–.010	.262	.005	.694	**–.070*** **	.000	**–.091*** **	.000
Gender	–.018	.022	–.016	.055	**–.107*** **	.000	–.004	.626	**–.033*** **	.000
Education	**.262*** **	.000	**.248*** **	.000	**.234*** **	.000	**.272*** **	.000	**.246*** **	.000
Income levels	**.050*** **	.000	**.097*** **	.000	**.075*** **	.000	**.118*** **	.000	**.061*** **	.000
Ethnicity	–.001	.896	.008	.350	.004	.659	–.013	.121	.014	.083
Denmark	**.146*** **	.000								
Finland	**.083*** **	.000								
France	**.023* **	.013								
Ireland	**.065*** **	.000								
Italy	–.008	.351								
Netherlands	**.101*** **	.000								
Norway	**.128*** **	.000								
Portugal	**–.063*** **	.000								
Spain	**.035*** **	.000								
Sweden	**.202*** **	.000								
Father ed.			.006	.604						

Mother ed.			**.093*** **	.000						
See friends			**.096*** **	.000						
Intimate			**.066*** **	.000						
Neighbourhood					**.281*** **	.000				
Voluntary orgs					**.080*** **	.000				
Discriminated					–.016	.055				
Student					**.074*** **	.000				
Unemployed					**–.026** **	.002				
Retired					**–.038*** **	.000				
Catholic					**–.120*** **	.000				
Protestant					–.014	.130				
Crime							–.005	.564		
Help people							**.125*** **	.000		
Left-right (self)							**–.121*** **	.000		
TV									**–.066*** **	.000
Radio									.008	.321
Newspapers									**.070*** **	.000
Ego RD									**.115*** **	.000
R Square	.182		.151		.239		.150		.147	
N	13967		12926		11046		13103		12640	

suggests that just over 18 per cent of variation in the dependent variable is captured by country variation, leaving a lot to be accounted for.

The next model, societal, tests the claim that deeply rooted family factors shape social trust. In terms of family background, having an educated mother is positively associated with trust (.093***), and in terms of ongoing relationships regular interaction with close friends and family (.096***) with the added benefit of social support (.066***) likewise boost levels of trust. Overall, however, this model fares no better than the cultural model in terms of explanatory power.

Individual socialisation processes, however, prove to be more significant. This is particularly true for attachment to one's neighbourhood. The strong positive coefficient for this variable (.281***) suggests that generalised trust measures are indeed driven by localised factors. This is supported by the weak but significant positive effect of activities in voluntary associations (.080***). It also seems to be the case that belonging to specific groups in society, namely the unemployed and retired, reduces levels of social trust (–.026** and –.038*** respectively), whilst being a student is associated with higher levels (.074***). Finally, and in line with previous research (Rothstein and Uslaner 2005), the presence of Catholicism is negatively associated with social trust.

Surprisingly, perceptions of crime are not associated with less trust in people. More important it seems are people's individual values as demonstrated by the endogenous individual evaluations model. Altruistic values, signalled by a willingness to help people, is positively associated with social trust (.125***), which is complemented by the fact that being right-wing ideologically speaking is associated with less trust in people (–.121***). This makes intuitive sense given that individuals of the Right place a strong emphasis on individualism and personal responsibility, the implication being that any perceived inappropriate behaviour, however defined, is necessarily the fault of individuals. This effect is compounded by people's tendency to remember the negative aspects of life which makes distrust a prominent default position.

The final model confirms that receiving information about society from different sources has different impacts on levels of trust. Watching television is associated with less trust, while reading newspapers is associated with greater trust. This provides evidence for both media malaise and media mobilisation theories, with the latter criticising TV for sensationalising and magnifying the negative aspects of human affairs (Postman 1987; Putnam 1995), with the latter suggesting the mass media can act as a cognitive mobiliser (Dalton 1996; Newton 1999a).

In order to evaluate the relative importance of each variable that proved to be a significant predictor of social trust, a composite model was derived. Table 4.2 below presents the results.

The first obvious point about the results is the fact that all of the variables, with the exception of being retired, remain statistically significant. This demonstrates the multi-faceted nature of trust, and indeed points to numerous origins both directly related and indirectly related to social relations. Nonetheless, outside of the country variables,

Table 4.2 Composite model of social trust

Variable	Beta	Sig.
Age	–.001	.953
Gender	**–.075*** **	.000
Education	**.202*** **	.000
Income levels	.020	.062
Ethnicity	.005	.547
Denmark	**.119*** **	.000
Ireland	**.087*** **	.000
Italy	**.023* **	.041
Netherlands	**.115*** **	.000
Norway	**.079*** **	.000
Portugal	**–.034** **	.003
Spain	**.039*** **	.000
Sweden	**.206*** **	.000
Mother ed.	**.058*** **	.000
See friends	**.057*** **	.000
Intimate	**.041*** **	.000
Neighbourhood	**.252*** **	.000
Voluntary orgs	**.047*** **	.000
Student	**–.025** **	.004
Unemployed	**.048*** **	.000
Retired	–.010	.279
Catholic	**–.022* **	.047
Help people	**.130*** **	.000
Left-right (self)	**–.142*** **	.000
TV	**–.037*** **	.000
Newspapers	**.032*** **	.001
Income	**.056*** **	.000
Adj R Square	.310	
N	9892	

Note: France was dropped from the regression equation due to being a constant.

the strong neighbourhood (.252***) and individual value effects (help people: .130***; left/right: –.142***) should be highlighted. It should also be highlighted that higher education, as we would expect, is also strongly and positively associated with higher levels of social trust (.202***).

4.7 Models of Political Trust

To recall, Political trust is shaped by:

SH1: Country differences
SH2: Social capital
SH3: Group relative deprivation
SH4: Evaluations of the party system
SH5: Media effects
SH6: Egoistic relative deprivation
SH7: Individual values/ideology
SH8: Policy satisfaction
SH9: Perceptions of the macro economy

Again, following a 'nested' approach, the following general models are tested:

1. Cultural model:

Trust = a + France + Spain + Germany + Netherlands + Italy + Denmark + Sweden + Finland + Norway + e

where,
a = constant
e = error term.
Note: UK is reference group country.

2. Societal model:

Trust = a + Social trust + Social networks + e

where,
Social trust = generalised perception of the trustworthiness of others
Social networks = how often see close family and friends.

3. Individual socialisation:

Trust = a + Discrimination + Group RD + Ideology + e

where,
Discrimination = Member of a discriminated group
Group RD = Student/Retired/Unemployed
Ideology = Self Left-Right ideological position.

4. Exogenous individual socialisation:

Trust = a + Media + Egoistic RD + Individualism + e

where,
Media = Read papers/Listen to radio/Watch television
Egoistic RD = Satisfied with life
Individualism = People should take responsibility for their own life.

5. Endogenous individual evaluations:

Trust = a + Policies + Parties + Interest + e

where,
Policies = Satisfaction with policy outcomes on salient issues
Parties = Close to a party
Interest = How much interest in politics.

4.8 Results – political trust

The cultural model of trust in government in Table 4.3 suggests significant variation across individuals from different countries. The theme of Scandinavian exceptionalism is continued with Denmark and Finland in particular both having strong positive coefficients (.308*** and .321*** respectively). Similar to social trust, only Portuguese individuals appear to be less trusting of government relative to citizens from the UK.

The results from the societal model suggest that social trust is positively associated with trust in government and strongly so (.374***). In fact, this societal model explains the same amount of variation in trust in government than all of the variables in the cultural model put together (R square = .191). Further to this are the impacts of the individual socialisation variables. First and foremost are the surprisingly positive effects of holding rightwing tendencies on trust in government. One possible reason for this result is the recent electoral success of

Table 4.3 Explaining trust of government

Variables	Cultural Model		Societal		Individual socialisation		Endogenous individual evaluations		Exogenous individual evaluations	
	Beta	Sig.	Beta	Sig.	Beta	Sig.	Beta	Sig.	Beta	Sig.
Age	**.043*** **	.000	.004	.618	**.026***	.023	**–.044*** **	.000	**–.018** **	.010
Gender	**.044*** **	.000	**.022** **	.003	**.037*** **	.000	**.027** **	.001	–.005	.441
Education	**.102*** **	.000	**.093*** **	.000	**.153*** **	.000	**.127*** **	.000	**.079*** **	.000
Income	**.077*** **	.000	**.060*** **	.000	**.101*** **	.000	**.054*** **	.000	.011	.142
Ethnicity	.004	.606	.001	.890	.000	.968	.003	.697	**–.017***	.016
Denmark	**.308*** **	.000								
Finland	**.321*** **	.000								
France	**.039*** **	.000								
Ireland	**.129*** **	.000								
Italy	**.051*** **	.000								
Netherlands	**.133*** **	.000								
Norway	**.142*** **	.000								
Portugal	**–.074*** **	.000								
Spain	**.136*** **	.000								
Sweden	**.164*** **	.000								

Social Trust			**.374*** **	.000						
Voluntary			**.096*** **	.000						
See Friends			.001	.360						
Discriminate					**–.075*** **	.000				
Student					**.089*** **	.000				
Unemployed					**–.037*** **	.000				
Retired					**.044*** **	.000				
Left-right					**.143*** **	.000				
TV							**.026** **	.007		
Radio							.014	.135		
Newspaper							**.087*** **	.000		
Ego RD							**–.182*** **	.000		
Help people							–.010	.254		
Education									**.150*** **	.000
NHS									**.213*** **	.000
Economy									**.411*** **	.000
Interest									**.173*** **	.000
R Square	.191		.191		.079		.092		.452	
N	14702		14594		13860		12048		14170	

rightwing parties in Western Europe (see Mudde 2007). Being retired is positively associated with trust in government (.044***) and likewise being a student (.089***) which is contrasted with the effects of discrimination (–.075***) and being unemployed (–.037***).

While the media variables in the social trust model demonstrated the utility of malaise and mobilisation theory, the results for the exogenous individual evaluations model for trust in government provide support for the mobilisation model only. Both watching television and reading newspapers promote greater trust in government (.026*** and .087*** respectively). The final variable in this model suggests that the presence of ego RD – the gap between individual expectations and reality – has a relatively strong negative impact on trust in government (–.182***).

The final model which centres upon perceived performance of government and political interest overwhelming demonstrates the strongest explanatory utility accounting for nearly 50 per cent of variation in the dependent variable (R square = .452). Specifically, satisfaction with the way government has handled the economy has the largest say in promoting trust (.411***), followed by perceived performance on national health systems (.213***), political interest (.173***), and finally performance on national education systems (.150***).

Again, taking all of the significant variables together and placing them into another regression equation produces a composite model to test the relative importance of each. Table 4.4 below presents the results.

Taking all of the variables into account, government performance related variables plus social trust prove to be the most important. This suggests a neutral conclusion between cultures and institutions, where trust in government does appear to be shaped by wider social relations, but the strong 'endogenous' effects of institutional performance appear to have primacy. It should also be noted that levels of cognitive engagement as measured by political interest is also an important predictor of trust in government.

4.9 Models of political behaviour

Building on the analysis of citizenship and duties earlier on, we now turn our attention to trust's association with important behavioural outcomes for democratic societies. To recall, these include voting and voluntary activities in organisations. This will be tested against the previously derived models. The explanatory utility of trust in government will be explored by building the term into the exogenous individual evaluations model.

Table 4.4 Composite model of trust in government

Variable	Beta	Sig.
Age	.001	.928
Gender	**–.019***	.012
Highest education	**.069*****	.000
Income levels	.017	.062
Ethnicity	.004	.754
Denmark	**.027*****	.009
Finland	**.024***	.036
Ireland	**–.054*****	.000
Italy	**.073*****	.000
Netherlands	**–.048*****	.000
Norway	**–.032****	.003
Portugal	**.037*****	.000
Spain	**.055*****	.000
Sweden	**.050*****	.000
Social Trust	**.149*****	.000
Voluntary	**.037*****	.000
Discriminate	**–.023****	.003
Student	**.037*****	.000
Unemployed	**–.021****	.006
Retired	–.011	.251
Left-right (self)	.010	.208
TV	–.013	.117
Newspaper	**.031*****	.000
Ego RD	.008	.336
Education	**.107*****	.000
NHS	**.148*****	.000
Economy	**.248*****	.000
Interest	**.134*****	.000
R Square	.302	
N	11635	

4.10 Results – trust and behavioural outcomes

Table 4.5 below presents the results for predicting voter turnout. Unlike the trust variables, voter turnout demonstrates less variation at the individual level across countries, with a handful of countries (such as Denmark, Sweden and Italy) demonstrating a slightly higher propensity to vote relative to the UK. Little explanatory utility is also found with the societal model where being unemployed and suffering from ego RD are marginally associated with a decreased likelihood of voting (–.051*** and –.058*** respectively).

Table 4.5 Explaining vote turnout

	Cultural Model		Societal		Individual socialisation		Endogenous individual evaluations		Exogenous individual evaluations	
Variables	**Beta**	**Sig.**	**Beta**	**Sig.**	**Beta**	**Sig.**	**Beta**	**Sig.**	**Beta**	**Sig.**
Age	**.213*** **	.000	**.205*** **	.000	**.200*** **	.000	**.206*** **	.000	**.153*** **	.000
Gender	.003	.695	.008	.325	.001	.860	.000	.975	**–.029*** **	.000
Education	**.127*** **	.000	**.118*** **	.000	**.080*** **	.000	**.107*** **	.000	**.040*** **	.000
Income levels	**.096*** **	.000	**.085*** **	.000	**.086*** **	.000	**.089*** **	.000	**.071*** **	.000
Ethnicity	**–.048*** **	.000	**–.048*** **	.000	**–.058*** **	.000	**–.050*** **	.000	**–.047*** **	.000
Denmark	**.077*** **	.000								
Finland	–.003	.745								
France	–.014	.154								
Ireland	**.030** **	.002								
Italy	**.085*** **	.000								
Netherlands	.010	.297								
Norway	.016	.105								
Portugal	.009	.327								
Spain	**.050*** **	.000								
Sweden	**.084*** **	.000								

Discriminated			–.010	.239						
Student			–.017	.052						
Unemployed			**–.051*** **	.000						
Retired			–.027	.063						
Ego RD			**–.058*** **	.000						
Social trust					**.085*** **	.000				
Meet People					**.022* **	.011				
Voluntary Orgs					**.079*** **	.000				
Education							–.003	.728		
NHS							–.006	.545		
Economy							**.070*** **	.000		
Interest							**.186*** **	.000		
Trust Govt.							**.121*** **	.000		
TV									.008	.363
Radio									**.017* **	.044
Newspapers									.011	.225
R Square	.079		.070		.077		.162		.047	
N	15207		13866		13119		13805		14491	

Table 4.6 Composite vote turnout model

Variable	Beta	Sig.
Age	**.140*** **	.000
Gender	**–.027** **	.003
Education	**.055*** **	.000
Income levels	**.047*** **	.000
Ethnicity	**–.046*** **	.000
Denmark	**.037** **	.002
Finland	**–.035** **	.004
Ireland	**.023* **	.033
Italy	**.101*** **	.000
Netherlands	–.019	.098
Norway	.004	.752
Portugal	.009	.409
Spain	**.039*** **	.000
Sweden	**.066*** **	.000
Student	**–.044*** **	.000
Unemployed	**–.048*** **	.000
Retired	–.014	.222
Ego RD	–.010	.352
Social trust	**.027** **	.009
Meet People	**.021* **	.028
Voluntary Orgs	**.043*** **	.000
Economy	.010	.412
Interest	**.179*** **	.000
Trust Govt.	**.114*** **	.000
Radio	**.026** **	.006
Adj R Square	.138	
N	10,992	

Further evidence is provided to support the claim that social life is related to civic engagement. The individual socialisation model suggests that social trust (.085***), social networks (.022***), and being active in voluntary associations (.079***) are all positively associated with voting.

Greater explanatory power is found with individual evaluations endogenous to the political system. Marginal positive effects are found with satisfaction with the economy (.070***), while political interest (.186***) and trust in government (.121***) prove to be stronger predictors of turnout. Finally, marginal positive effects are found for listening to the radio (.017*).

Turning to the composite model (Table 4.6 above), it can be seen that the most important predictors of vote turnout in the model are political interest (.179***) and trust in government (.114***). The effects of the societal variables – trust (.027**), see friends (.021*), and voluntary organisations (.043***) – are small but still significant. However, it should be noted that this model is relatively weak with only around 14 per cent of the variation accounted for in the dependent variable (R square = .138).

As Table 4.7 demonstrates, predicting wider civic acts is just as difficult as predicting vote turnout, where all models demonstrating low R square values. Yet again, wider social variables prove to have some say in participation rates, with those discriminated against (.056***) more inclined to engage in voluntary activities. Negative motivations for participating are further supported with the marginal positive effect ego RD has on civic acts (.022*). The most important social effects, however, are found with the social trust and see friends/family variables (.101*** and .082*** respectively).

Turning to the individual evaluation models, the political interest and trust in government variables prove to be the strongest predictors again (.196*** and .091***). Alongside satisfaction with the NHS (.036***) and the economy (.033***), this endogenous individual evaluations mode proves to be the strongest predictor of civic acts. Finally, dual media effects are demonstrated again, with TV watching promoting civic malaise (–.042***) and reading newspapers promoting civic engagement (.061***).

Table 4.8 presents the composite model for civic acts.

The results suggests that, principally, levels of civic acts are determined by political interest (.192***), interactions in social networks (.081***), and trust in government (.083***). The table also confirms that discrimination and social trust still prove to be significant although relatively weak predictors of civic engagement.

4.11 Conclusion

The results from the social trust models offer evidence to suggest the importance of environmental conditions, in particular satisfaction and attachment to surrounding neighbour, and internalised values, notably individualism. In a wider sense, this establishes the primacy of endogenous socialisation process and exogenous individual evaluations in terms of explaining levels of social trust. The results from the trust in government models highlight the explanatory utility of three types of approaches. First, further evidence is provided for the claim that trust in government has social origins, demonstrated by the association

Table 4.7 Explaining civic acts

	Cultural Model		Endogenous societal		Endogenous individual socialisation		Endogenous individual evaluations		Exogenous individual evaluations	
Variables	**Beta**	**Sig.**	**Beta**	**Sig.**	**Beta**	**Sig.**	**Beta**	**Sig.**	**Beta**	**Sig.**
Age	**.091*** **	.000	**.205*** **	.000	**.200*** **	.000	**.206*** **	.000	**.153*** **	.000
Gender	**.083*** **	.000	.008	.325	.001	.860	.000	.975	**–.029*** **	.000
Education	**.136*** **	.000	**.118*** **	.000	**.080*** **	.000	**.107*** **	.000	**.040*** **	.000
Income levels	**.045*** **	.000	**.085*** **	.000	**.086*** **	.000	**.089*** **	.000	**.071*** **	.000
Ethnicity	–.003	.740	**–.048*** **	.000	**–.058*** **	.000	**–.050*** **	.000	**–.047*** **	.000
Denmark	**.028** **	.002								
Finland	**.092*** **	.000								
France	–.012	.199								
Ireland	–.014	.155								
Italy	**–.021* **	.023								
Netherlands	–.003	.787								
Norway	**.053*** **	.000								
Portugal	**–.044*** **	.000								
Spain	**.050*** **	.000								
Sweden	**.042*** **	.000								

Discriminated			**.056***	.000						
Student			**.072***	.000						
Unemployed			.003	.730						
Retired			–.006	.563						
Ego RD			**.022***	.017						
Social trust					**.101***	.000				
Meet People					**.082***	.000				
Education							.007	.463		
NHS							**.036***	.000		
Economy							**.033***	.000		
Interest							**.196***	.000		
Trust Govt.							**.091***	.000		
TV									**–.042***	.000
Radio									.013	.122
Newspapers									**.061***	.000
R Square	.060		.052		.059		.101		.047	
N	16092		14600		13936		14592		15325	

Table 4.8 Composite civic acts model

Variable	Beta	Sig.
Age	**.095*** **	.000
Gender	**.062*** **	.000
Education	**.050*** **	.000
Income levels	**.037*** **	.001
Ethnicity	.002	.790
Denmark	.007	.572
Finland	**.085*** **	.000
Ireland	.008	.434
Italy	.000	.968
Netherlands	**–.023***	.040
Norway	**.049*** **	.000
Portugal	**–.035*** **	.001
Spain	**.057*** **	.000
Sweden	.016	.162
Discriminated	**.042*** **	.000
Student	**.023***	.024
Income	–.003	.792
Social trust	**.033*** **	.001
Meet People	**.081*** **	.000
NHS	–.002	.832
Economy	**.043*** **	.001
Interest	**.192*** **	.000
Trust Govt.	**.083*** **	.000
TV	**–.051*** **	.000
Newspapers	**.054*** **	.000
Adj R Square	.118	
N	11,494	

between social and political trust even when a host of other factors are controlled for. Second, trust in government above all else, seems to be driven by satisfaction with the outputs of government, especially the economy and public services such as health care systems. Finally, factors that tap into cognitive engagement, in this instance, political interest, provide additional insight into the factors that foster perceptions of governmental trustworthiness.

Both types of trust also seem to have significant associations with different levels of political behaviour. Trust in government, along with levels of political interest, prove to be the best predictors of vote turnout, while the same is also true for wider civic activities in voluntary associations. It should also be noted that *some* explanatory utility is found with social trust and other social capital related variables (such as meeting friends). Nonetheless, as the composite models demonstrate, when controlling for other relevant factors, these positive effects become marginal.

Variation in trust can also only be marginally accounted in terms of the society an individual belongs to. The 'cultural' models never explained more than 8 per cent variation in either trust in society or government. However, with the exception of the endogenous individual evaluation models, the same is true for all other types of explanations. The first reason for this, and it is a problem often found in contemporary analyses of political trust, is the sole focus on specific beliefs in government – primarily perceived trustworthiness of politicians or confidence in parliament – as the variables to be explained and the variables that could explain political behaviour (see also Kaase and Newton 1995; Nye et al. 1997; Norris 1999; Pharr and Putnam 2000; Hetherington 2004). The second problem was the inability to fully implement the conceptual framework in Chapter 3; comparative dataset always offer more countries to work with, but often they offer fewer variables too. Thus despite illuminating some of the features surrounding trust and social and political life, comparative analyses often leave a lot of variation in trust and behavioural outcomes unaccounted for.

5
Exploring Trust
A Critique

5.1 Introduction

Despite theoretical developments, research in the field of trust is viewed as underdeveloped. Hibbing and Theiss-Morse argue that 'research on public attitudes toward government lags far behind research on participation and vote choice in terms of the scholarly resources (grant money, journal space, etc.) devoted to it' (Hibbing and Theiss-Morse 2001: 2). The primary reason for this, I will argue, is that definitions of trust in government are too close to purported explanations of trust in government.

It is argued that social scientists should treat the concept of trust as an 'explanation based generalisation', that is, as an abstraction that captures as many of the important phenomenal relationships in question, what Messick and Kramer (2001: 90) call an adequate 'working definition'.[1] The problem with this approach is that the type of explanation that will be employed determines the definition of trust. Without sufficient distance between the thing to be explained and the explanation, it is not clear that trust in people or government are discrete objects of enquiry. What is required is formal theorising, setting out a cognitive map of the components of trust in order to distinguish between the explanans and the explanadum.

Nonetheless, operationalising a concept and then seeking to measure it is often highly problematic, and this is especially true for concepts that are not directly observable such as beliefs and psychological traits. By not being directly observable, they are best thought of as latent constructs, and psychologists make use of multiple measures when attempting to gauge such constructs. A further argument put forward in this chapter is that research into trust has over-relied on single item direct measures of trust. Instead, by (1) formalising trust relationships and (2) by making the conceptual move of viewing trust as a latent construct, empirical investigations into trust can significantly reduce the problem of attenuation when trying to measure it.

The implication of treating trust as a latent construct means that object such as trust in government or trust in society are in fact *attitudes*. While particular instances of trust decisions are 'beliefs' based on current information as outlined in Part I, the diffused nature of the two objects of 'society' and 'government' means that social researchers are asking individuals to call upon generalised orientations when thinking about people in general and the individuals and institutions of government.

5.2 Conflating explanations and definitions

Conflating what trust is with what explains trust makes the divisions between description and explanation even harder to see. Fukuyama's (1995) conception of trust, for example, is a cultural interpretation. Trust in public authorities, he argues, is part of a 'shared moral community' (Fukuyama 1995: 89). On this definition, trust in government is an emergent property of basic social relations. Virtually from birth, individuals learn to trust or distrust other people or institutions by experiencing how others in the culture treat them and how, in return, others react to their behaviour. This represents both a cultural definition and explanation of trust in government.

Institutional theories emphasise that trust in government and distrust are rational responses by individuals to the performance of institutions (North 1990). Whereas cultural theories view institutional design as deeply conditioned by culture and substantially path dependent, institutional theories hold not only that institutional structure is a function of rational choice or intentional design (see Orren and Skowronek 1995) but also that the choice of institutional designs has real consequences for government performance and thus for public trust in institutions (e.g., Stark 1995). Hetherington (2004: 15) offers the most clearly institutional based definition of trust in government: 'political trust [is] the degree to which people expect that government will work to produce outcomes consistent with their expectations'. Again, like Fukuyama, this definitional statement also contains an explanation – trust is an expectation, and so trust in government is explained by government fulfilling expectations. Hardin (1999) even admits that his 'encapsulated interest' account of trust is both 'a definition and explanation' (Hardin 1999: 11).

The closeness of definitions and explanations of trust in government has caused severe theoretical and methodological problems. Instead of looking for factors independent of the thing to be explained, definitions of trust in government presuppose explanations. In doing so, some accounts of trust in government are tautological. Without sufficient distance between the phenomenon in question and the logical explanation behind it, it becomes impossible to identify causal mechanisms that determine any explanations (Elster 1999: 5–7).

5.3 Beliefs and attitudes

There is no actual consensus about the definition of an attitude, but in general, attitudes tend to be evaluative in their nature, for example, good versus bad; liberal versus conservative; positive versus negative. Baron and Byrne (1984: 126) define attitudes as 'relatively lasting clusters of feelings, beliefs, and behaviour tendencies directed towards specific persons, ideas, objects or groups'. Such a characterisation of attitudes is common throughout literature of social psychology, and it identifies how attitudes are made up of more than one entity. One problem with this definition is that it conflates psychological and cognitive variables (feelings and beliefs) with behavioural outcomes. This is similar to the conceptual problems found within the social capital thesis where 'norms' and 'networks' are referred to under the same heading (Newton 1999b).

A further qualification to the previous definition is that due to the multidimensional nature of attitudes, they often provide a general and as mentioned earlier evaluative orientation to persons or objects. For example, if your only experience of 'young offenders' is when a 16-year old stole your car, you might develop a negative attitude towards that particular group of young people. And once formed, such attitudes are relatively stable and notoriously difficult to alter.

This is an example of a type of heuristic at work. When evaluating and trying to predict behaviour, individuals employ a device known as a 'heuristic' that provides simple rules or principles for making complex inferences quickly (Gilovich et al. 2002: 204). In a world where time and information are limited, and one is under constant pressure to make decisions, heuristics are a useful cognitive shortcut. The implication is that people are more cognitive 'satisficers' than 'optimisers' (Simon 1982: 240–2). For example, some people believe that if a particular food is high in fibre, then it must be good for you – a simple rule that avoids the arduous task of analysing each food item's ingredients and their health consequences.

Individuals employ one of three types of heuristics: (1) representative; (2) attitude; or (3) availability (Kahneman and Tversky 1973). Representative heuristics are a strategy for making judgements based on the extent to which current events or stimuli are associated with other events or stimuli. The process at work is whether obvious features of an object are representative of, or similar to, the presumed characteristic of a category (Aronson 1999: 134–7). I am sure all of us at some point have had to sit a job interview, and the interviewer goes through the same process. Although the interviewer has some knowledge of our past behaviour – presented before her in a 'Curriculum Vitae' – a decision on our future behaviour is made at least in part on the character assessment made throughout the interview. This is presumably the first time the two people have met, and as the interviewer knows nothing of the interviewee's general behaviour the interviewer looks for particular cues: the tone of the interviewee's voice; the level of eye contact; the posture of the applicant; the time it takes the candidate to respond to a question; the attire worn by the applicant. Some, albeit unethically, might even consider the sex, race, class or nationality of the applicant as a cue for their future behaviour. All of these factors are likely to contribute to the interviewer's overall assessment of how trustworthy the candidate is by mapping cues about the person's character with what the interviewer believes to represent a good worker.

An attitude heuristic is the tendency to judge things or events based on recalling the emotional response associated with it (Pratkanis 1989: 72). As a dog bit me when I was a child, my immediate reaction to most dogs now is fear and contempt. The process at work is one of inferring facts from an attitude, by recalling a past negative or positive response to a person or object, and using that as the basis for current judgement.

Finally, availability heuristics are strategies that judge the *likelihood* of an event on the basis of how quickly instances or associations come to mind (Slovic 1987: 281–2). Such information will be recalled because (1) it is from an extreme emotional response, (2) because it is a recent event or (3) because it is a repeated event. It is thought that specific phobias develop because of an intense emotional experience in childhood (McNally 1987: 285). I frequently have safe experiences with dogs, but the one extremely painful experience when I was younger means that I overestimate the likelihood of it happening again and adopt a general strategy of avoiding dogs.

In contrast to attitudinal heuristics, beliefs are much easier to define. According to the Oxford English Dictionary, a belief is a 'mental acceptance of and conviction in the truth, actuality, or validity of something; something believed or accepted as true, especially a particular tenet or a body of tenets accepted by a group of persons'. In its simplest form then, a 'belief' indicates what someone thinks is true. So for example, the statement 'that cat is black and white' is a belief statement as it asserts a claim about the world. Whether the cat actually is black and white is not important. Beliefs do not have to be objectively true – only that the person thinks it to be true is of concern.

In between beliefs and attitudes are values. Much like attitudes, it is difficult to offer an accurate and consistent definition, especially given their intimate relationship with attitudes. But social psychology again offers minimal conditions that make values distinct from attitudes:

- Values are described as what a person wants to be true
- Values are conscious judgements, and can be viewed as an 'expected standard'

So not only do values guide the behaviour of the individual, but they also act as a 'benchmark' to evaluate the behaviour of others. In this sense social norms form part of our system of values and are formed, maintained or abolished depending on the nature of the ongoing interaction between beliefs and attitudes.

In terms of empirical research, although we cannot see, touch or feel attitudes, beliefs, and values we can infer them from an individual's behaviour (what they do), speech (what they say), or non-verbal behaviour (how they look). Figure 5.1 below outlines the process by which attitudes are formed.

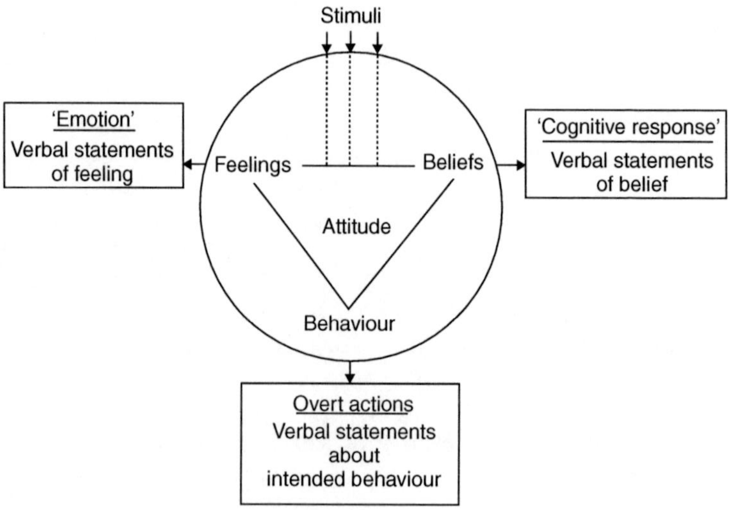

Figure 5.1 The formation of attitudes

Source: Spooncer, F. (1992) *Behavioural Studies for Marketing and Business*, Leckhampton, UK: Stanley Thornes Ltd.

Individuals receive information about the environment around them (stimuli). Given the information is relevant in some way to an individual's deliberative process,[2] two responses follow: an emotional reaction and the possible formation of a belief. For example, residents in Florida when told that a hurricane is expected within the next 48 hours (information) initially feel anxious about the imminent threat to their property and lives (emotional reaction). They then begin to realise that in order to minimise structural damage to their property they need to secure loose fittings and windows and they need to temporarily relocate away from the danger area so the risk to their lives is also minimised (the formation of beliefs).

5.3.1 Trust as an attitudinal heuristic

Because the object of social trust and political trust questions are often diffused ('people in general'), and because the object is seldom indexed to particular actions (e.g., trust people to pay their taxes), trust questions are best thought of as directly tapping into an underlying attitude. The one problem with this assertion is in relation to political trust items and more specifically the notion of 'government'.

It has been remarked that when an interviewer asks an American interviewee what they think about the 'government in Washington', the respondent is probably thinking about the 'federal' government and all its apparatus (the executive, both legislative houses and the judiciary). However, ask the same question to a Briton about the 'government in Westminster', the respondent will most likely be thinking of the government of the day, that is, the Labour or Conservative Government (King 2000: 121). This has important implications for comparative research into trust in government, where like is possibly not being compared with like due to different understandings on what the object of government refers to. The implication might also go deeper than that. While it is possible for different political cultures to have different usages for the term government, so too could different types of citizens. If this is true, then questions on 'government' might contain a high degree of individual level heterogeneity effecting the robustness of the measures.

In the light of this, the belief of 'government' trustworthiness (i.e., the incumbent government) could also be treated as part of a wider attitude where 'government' takes on a more general status, that is, an orientation towards all of the prevalent political actors and institutions.

5.4 Building a conceptual model

Beyond the direct questions of trust in government/politicians or confidence in parliament are more specific questions relating to leaders, parties, influence on politics and overall satisfaction with the political system. But in order to capture trust between governed and government it is necessary to first understand what it is that democratic citizens would demand from government to make the institution seem trustworthy. The same can also be done for social trust by pinpointing different forms of social cleavages along attitudinal lines. Figure 5.2 below recalls the three types of information required to form beliefs in trust.

5.4.1 Dimensions of trust in government

When considering the perceived intentions of the actors of government, citizens will use certain cues to determine what such intentions are. The first and most obvious channel of information is what prominent political actors are saying, or at least reported to be saying, about their respective policy programmes. This is where political leaders take centre stage, with increasing interest in European Political Science on the electoral effects of political leaders (Schmitt and Ohr 2000; King 2002). As Schmitt and Ohr (2000) notes,

> voters are not [necessarily] expected to choose the party whose policy positions come closest to their preferences, but the one who emphasises the 'right' problems (i.e. those they themselves are most concerned about) and who seems to be capable to do something about them. If this process works well, a government will be finally installed which attributes high priority to the concerns of a majority of voters and 'does something about them'. The latter aspect – doing something – brings political leaders [into] a model of contemporary political representation. (Schmitt and Ohr 2000: 4)

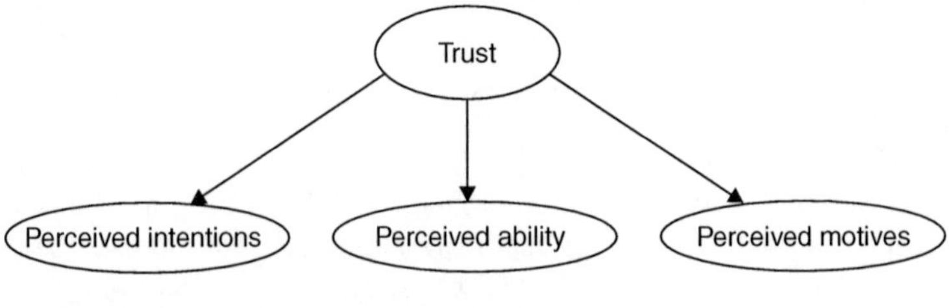

Figure 5.2 Trust relevant information

Further to this, individuals will also employ a representative heuristic and infer policy intent from the main political parties. The degree to which the ideological positions and policy platforms of parties accord with our own political views would have a say in how trustworthy we perceive government as a whole to be.

Also available to citizens are availability heuristics that inform us of how likely party X is on fulfilling its promise on policy Y. I know many voters who will never forgive the Conservative Party for Black Wednesday and likewise the Labour Party for the Winter of Discontent. The Essex Model (1997) used to predict current voting behaviour at the time even included the 1982 Falklands War as an explanatory factor. Personal harm, economic depressions and war all incite extreme levels of anxiety in people, which is why they remain relevant for current judgement long after they happened (Marcus et al. 2000). Recent events are also likely to be prominent in our minds. And it is not just the recent that is important, but also the ongoing. Trains that repeatedly fail to run on time and more alarmingly fail to run on the tracks, suggest a continuing trend of government's inability to improve public transport. If an individual associates such negative events and outcomes with a certain political party, or even worse holds them directly culpable for them, then that party will be deemed as untrustworthy.

Nonetheless, when we evaluate the behaviour of another, it is not always good enough that they simply behave as we hope they would. An important criterion is that the act was motivated for the right reasons. To recall an old term, we want people to possess a 'good will' (Kant 1964: 15). Whether George W. Bush and Tony Blair decided to invade Iraq for reasons of Weapons of Mass Destruction or for wider strategic reasons is a fundamental question. As their 'true' intentions have been called into question, it is undoubtedly one of the biggest questions of trust any elected leader could be asked to answer. Not only does it have immediate implications for International Law and diplomacy, but also for why the United States and Britain are countries with a history of waging military campaigns abroad and why they continue to do so. And with this example in mind, it is easy to see why questions of trust always bring a strong moral flavour to proceedings. Of course, the removal of the Baath Party regime in Iraq and the promise of free and fair national elections is a desirable outcome. But our common intuitions about integrity demand that such acts are committed for the right reasons, that the act was indeed committed with the interests of the ordinary people of Iraq in mind (promotes their interests qua their interests). How we judge what the true motives of others are is highly

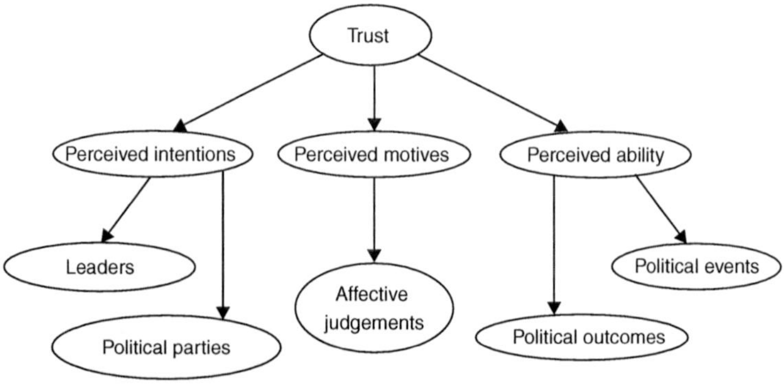

Figure 5.3 Trust in government components

susceptible to our affective intelligence and to a certain degree the type of political or social creed others represent.

Figure 5.3 above summarises the three dimensions of trust in government and their respective components.

5.4.2 Components of trust in government

Turning to the literature that attempts to explain political thought and behaviour, researchers tend to make use of a standard set of public opinion indicators.

Leaders

Knowledge of leaders and of their perceived characteristic and qualities is posited as an important explanatory variable for their impact on vote choice (Clarke et al. 2004: ch. 8; Vetter and Gabriel 1998: 75). Scholars have made use of various items relating to the leaders of main political parties such as direct trust questions and whether respondents 'like' the leader in question (Clarke et al. 2004) as well as the degree to which they are perceived as competent (Bartle and King (ed.) 2006). Indeed, all of these items on perceptions of leaders are implicit judgements of how trustworthy they appear by prompting survey respondents to evaluate the character and past behaviour of the individual in question.

Political parties

The notion of 'party identification' is a pervasive, and problematic, concept in the field of political behaviour. It is commonly measured using one or both of two questions: which party voters 'feel closer' to and which party voters 'think' of themselves as identifying with. The problem is that this

> cues respondents to accept a party label and, thus, it inflates estimates of the proportion of party identifiers in the electorates and the proportion who switch their identifications over time. More specifically, some respondents are not true identifiers, but when prompted to select a party, they oblige the interviewer and do so. (Clarke et al. 2004: 196)

Similar problems have been noted elsewhere with both measures of party identification, with evidence to demonstrate that the concept is highly sensitive to question wording (Bartle 2001; Margetts et al. 2005). Aside from identification measures, social surveys have introduced more stable measure of evaluations of political parties. Similar to the items now found in relation to leaders, data is now generated on the extent to which parties are trusted, liked and perceived to be competent (found in recent British Election Studies).

Affective judgements

Jon Elster in a fascinating book entitled *Alchemies of the Mind*, notes that 'emotions have cognitive antecedents and cognitive consequences' in which it is possible to analyse 'emotional patterns that are related to general features of social life' (Elster 1999: 106 and 139). It is precisely such a view that is supported by the theory of *Affective Intelligence*.

According to George Marcus et al. (2000), emotions play an independent role in human agency, as opposed to emotions being only managed through reason. This reverses the role of affect and cognition, in which individuals are not forward looking and outcome orientated, but rather retrospective and dispositional in their behaviour. Only when an external event arouses an emotional response do individuals engage with the social and political world:

> We posit that individuals monitor political affairs by responding habitually, and for the most part unthinkingly... by relying on past thought and evaluation. [T]he central claim of our theory is that when citizens encounter a novel or threatening actor, event, or issue... a process of fresh evaluation and political judgment is triggered. (Marcus et al. 2000: 1)

This central claim accords with a psychological mechanism that Herbert Simon noted over thirty-five years ago. Generally, individual behaviour is goal-orientated in which attention is directed towards outcomes that satisfy certain preferences. However, humans have an *interrupt mechanism*. This redirects attention towards higher priorities regardless of the pursuit of prior antecedent goals (Simon 1967: 143). This emotional response is the pivotal factor that accounts for changes in behaviour; it raises mental awareness and provides physiological motives to act. This reflects the instrumental role that emotions play in the formation of beliefs and attitudes as outlined in the previous section.

In response to these developments in the way we think about human agency, social surveys now include items that ask respondents how they 'feel' about object X. For example, British Election studies now ask respondents how they feel about leaders, parties and economic outcomes (macro economic and personal finances). Combined with standard questions on what the respondent 'thinks' about such objects, researchers can now triangulate measurements to gain a clearer understanding of general respondent orientations and underlying attitudes towards political figures and outcomes.

Political outcomes

According to Almond and Verba (1963), a democracy requires a balance of efficacy and trust amongst its citizens in order to perform effectively. The public needs to feel that public officials represent their views, but they should also be equally willing to trust public officials to make the right decisions for them on their behalf. This is the crux of Locke's notion of the government holding 'a trust' with the people (Locke 1988: 426–7). As such, good citizenship is a balance between constructive criticism of government and reasonable deference to its decisions. The best political systems foster such efficacy and trust between governed and government.

Where citizens are generally asked to defer to the decisions of government is in terms of policy decisions on position issues that engender 'alternative and highly conflictual responses' (Nelson 1984: 27). This can be contrasted with valence issues that are characterised by 'a single, strong, fairly uniform emotional response and do not have an adversarial quality' (Nelson 1984: 27; see also Campbell et al. 1960; Stokes and DiIulio 1993). So beyond the basic democratic issue of representation, citizens also demand benign outcomes in terms of the salient issues of the day, be they positional or valence issues.

Political events

Key political events as mentioned earlier can hold sway over an individual's judgement long after the event has happened. Indeed, the sentiment behind this is that trust is difficult to make and easily broken.

Sometimes it is just too difficult to forgive and forget. The Brent East (2003) by-election result in the UK, for example, was primarily determined by protest voting against the government's decision to invade Iraq, and numerous political commentators have remarked that the Invasion of Iraq will mar Tony Blair's legacy as Prime Minister.[3]

5.4.3 Dimensions of trust in society

A crucial dimension for social trust is the extent to which others in society are perceived to be a motivated by the same principles/values. Social psychologists would refer to this as perceptions of 'in-group/out-group status'; Political Scientists would probably make recourse to the prevalence of particular social norms. In either case, the important empirical referent is the same – the perception that most people have internalised rules that coordinate their actions and make them predictable and cooperative.

The factors behind social cleavages which often determine in and out group status are numerous. Individuals can object to the way people think and behaviour because their basis for doing so is perhaps discriminatory, harmful to others, or to use a stronger term, irreducibly immoral. Alternative or different lifestyles therefore can invoke anxiety and even provoke social clashes between individuals and groupings. Areas of ethnic or racial tensions, for example, are symptomatic cases of inherent distrust between social groups. The degree to which we find others trustworthy is primarily informed by the level of appropriate behaviour (however defined) we witness in our daily interactions with others, as well as the occasional and random event that touches our lives, usually some form of personal attack. This is summarised in Figure 5.4.

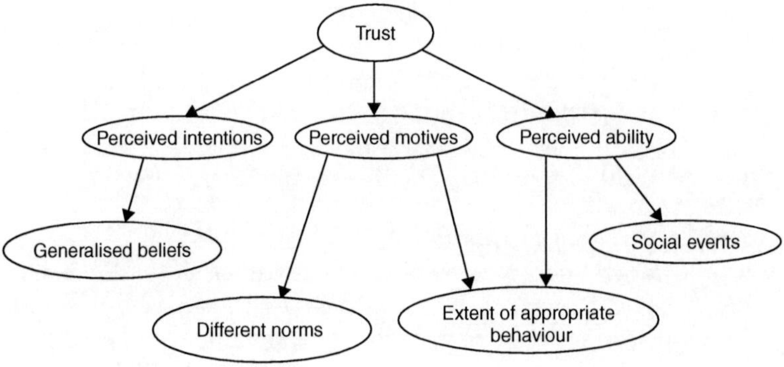

Figure 5.4 Trust in society components

5.4.4 Components of trust in society

Generalised beliefs

Treating trust as a general attitude in Western liberal democracies means that the concern is not the 'thick' and particularised trust in people we are familiar with, that is, people like ourselves. This is a crucial aspect of social relations relatively homogenous and smaller societies, not true for regions such as Europe and the USA.

> Generalised social trust in people we do not know personally, but with whom we interact constantly, is comparatively more important in modern large-scale, urban industrial society ('a society of strangers'), and likely to have implications for their democratic politics. (Zmerli and Newton 2006: 4)

Generalised measures of trust then reflect a bond that people share across a society, which extends beyond potentially divisive social characteristics such as levels of wealth and differences in colour, creed or religion. It is the foundation of a cooperative spirit that brings people together for common and mutually advantageous purposes.

Different norms and lifestyles

A challenge to the development of generalised is particularised trust which often leads to 'bonding' forms of social capital. Putnam (2000) notes that a by-product of this is sometimes the 'dark side of social capital', which gives rise to organisations such as the Ku Klux Klan. The reason for this is that

> particularised trust reflects social strains, where each group in a society looks out for their own interests and places little faith in the good intentions of others. Particularised trusters may be as involved in civic life as generalised trusters, but they will restrict their activities and good deeds to their own kinds. Evangelical Christians in the United States, a group with high in-group trust and low trust in others, are very active volunteers and donors to charity—but only with and for their own faith communities. (Rothstein and Uslaner 2005: 8)

Sometimes the problem is not so much the lifestyle that people lead, rather the values and opinions that they hold. Racist sentiments, for example, are held by people whose actual lifestyles are very much like any other person's. By the same token, an individual's social attitudes and political views can accord with the majority of society's, but isolated

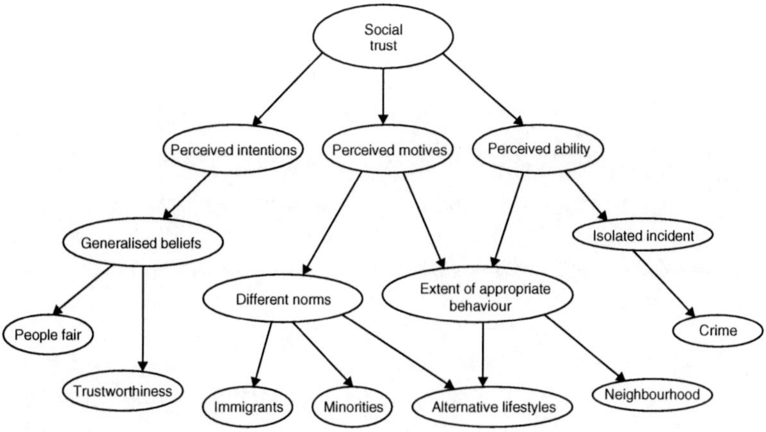

Figure 5.5 Qualitative structure of social trust

acts, for example the use of recreational drugs, can provoke moral outrage from others.

Extent of appropriate behaviour

The perceived extent of certain immoral or anti-social behaviours is perhaps best thought of as a measure of social 'confidence' rather than trust, although Chapter 1 highlighted the importance of confidence in the logic of trust. We can think of social confidence as being driven by the close interactions we have with people in our own neighbourhood. If people reside in areas where there is a high degree of conformity regarding basic societal rules (respect for private property, for example), then trust will flourish. Occasionally, some of us have the misfortune of being the victim of a random crime which could quite easily undermine any trust present.

Taking all of the above factors into account, Figure 5.5 summarises the qualitative structure of social trust.

5.5 Conclusion

Noting that standard, single and direct measures of trust are inadequate to fully capture peoples orientations towards government and society, scholars have decided to merge at least two single measures of trust to produce a more robust measure (e.g., Zmerli, Newton and Montero (2007) for social trust, and Miller and Listhaug (1999) for political trust).

This goes some way to acknowledging that trust in society and government are latent constructs that take on a status that is closer to attitudes than single beliefs. Nonetheless, without formalising the antecedent conditions of trust, the concept is never properly operationalised for social scientific enquiry.

The implication of this is that scholars are left to rely on the assumption that survey respondents interpret the meaning of direct trust questions in similar ways. Indeed, one of the great advantages for deriving the components of trust – intentions, motives and capability – is that researchers don't actually have to rely on direct measures of trust in order to analyse trust in society or government. By formalising what trust is, a whole array of other social survey items become useful, if not desirable, when measuring perceptions of how trustworthy others are.

Part III

Trust in Britain

Whilst the previous section illuminated some of the general features that determine levels of trust across a host of nations, a deeper explanatory understanding can only be offered using more detailed data that can better capture the context within which decision of trust towards people and government are made. As such, this section departs from analysing trust from a comparative perspective and focuses on data from one country, namely Great Britain.

The aim of **Chapter 6** is to explore how best to make use of such data. Building on the qualitative framework derived in Chapter 5, the various attitudinal components of trust in society and government are measured using data from the most recent British Election Study (BES). By providing improved measures of trust, **Chapter 7** goes on to establishing a more contextualised explanatory framework. Not only will the results provide a better understanding of the links between social trust and trust in government, but also a vastly improved understanding, relative to the comparative analyses, of how trust in government works. **Chapter 8** is the final chapter in this section and seeks to untangle one of the overarching problems when analysing trust – to what degree is it a cause or an effect of social and political behaviour? By using repeated measures data from the BES, some light can be shed on this empirical puzzle.

6
Exploring Trust
A Quantitative Review and Trends

6.1 Introduction

As we have seen, empirical investigations of trust invariably restrict analyses to account for variation in single, direct measures. Conceptually speaking, this need not be the case; the empirical net for trust is much wider than it is often assumed to be. This chapter uses country specific data from Britain and explores the added value of more detailed datasets. Principally, this means a reduction in attenuation when trying to measure trust and more contextualised social and political data to help understand how it works. In particular, attention can be given to (1) how social trust can be better measured using beliefs that evaluate the different norms and lifestyles in society, and (2) how trust of government can be better measured with reference to perceptions of leaders and parties.

As such, this chapter builds upon the qualitative models in Chapter 5 and by taking advantage of a more detailed country specific dataset, develops a set of quantitative models that uncover the structure of attitudes of trust towards society and government. As will be argued, a crucial caveat when widening the empirical net is to introduce statistically robust measures that specifically tap into the perceived intentions, motives and behaviour of potential trusteds. As trust in society and government are diffused and perhaps vague constructs, these research programmes require developments in measurements that resolve the problems of attenuation, not increase them. Put another way, elaborate conceptual models as outlined in Chapter 5 are only as useful as the measurements available.

Using British Election Study (2005) data, the next section outlines the survey questions to be used in the forthcoming chapters. It is also illustrative to analyse the structure of beliefs in society and government with the aid of factor analysis. Once this has been established the next task is to provide an overview of these trust items by tracking their trends across time. As we shall see, one trend in particular is illuminating – government is the only major public institution in Britain in which trust is falling.

6.2 Building on the qualitative model – measuring political trust

Taking advantage of the more comprehensive list of variables in British Election Study data, the following survey questions are used.

6.2.1 Direct trust questions

For direct trust in government measures, the following questions are used:

- 'How much do you trust the present government?'
- 'Now, thinking about political institutions like Parliament, please use the 0 to 10 scale to indicate how much trust you have for each of the following, where 0 means no trust and 10 means a great deal of trust.'
- 'How much do you trust the Parliament (at Westminster)?'
- 'How much do you trust politicians generally?'
- 'How much do you trust... Labour Party... Conservative Party.... Liberal Democrats?'
- 'Now, please use the 0 to 10 scale to indicate how much trust you have for each of the party leaders, where 0 means no trust and 10 means a great deal of trust. How much do you trust Tony Blair?'

6.2.2 Efficacy and system questions

- 'On a scale from 0 to 10 where 10 means a great deal of influence and 0 means no influence, how much influence do you have on politics and public affairs?'
- 'On the whole, how satisfied are you with the way democracy works in Britain?' (BES 1997)
- 'On the whole, are you satisfied or dissatisfied with the way that democracy works in this country?' (BES 2001)

These system questions utilise a four-point scale, where answers range from (1) satisfied, (2) fairly satisfied, (3) not very satisfied, to (4) not at all satisfied.

The core trust in government items of direct measures, efficacy and system satisfaction can be complemented by related implicit trust variables. To recall, the related objects are political leaders, parties, perceptions of the incumbent government and perceptions of 'government' generally.

Leaders

- 'Now, some questions about the party leaders. Using a scale that runs from 0 to 10, where 0 means a very incompetent leader and 10 means a very competent leader, how would you describe Tony Blair?'
- 'Now, let's think more generally about the party leaders. Using a scale that runs from 0 to 10, where 0 means strongly dislike and 10 means strongly like, how do you feel about Tony Blair?'

Parties

It was noted in Chapter 5 that standard party identification questions are highly problematic. As such, other measures of party evaluations will be used. These are generated using the following questions:

- 'Using a scale that runs from 0 to 10, where 0 means extremely untrustworthy and 10 means extremely trustworthy, how much do you trust the ... Labour ... Conservative ... Liberal Democrat Party?'
- 'On a scale that runs from 0 to 10, where 0 means strongly dislike and 10 means strongly like, how do you feel about the Labour ... Conservative ... Liberal Democrat Party?'

Incumbent government/government

- 'Please tell me if you agree or disagree with the following statement: Government treats people like me fairly.'

As the list above demonstrates, the British Election Study 2005 includes direct and indirect trust questions on the three objects of government: politicians, parliament and 'the' government. These are complemented by the standard measure of efficacy and system satisfaction. Figure 6.1 outlines these objects of beliefs in government and their corresponding survey questions.

Previously, scholars have combined trust in politicians and trust in institutions items together to form a political trust index in an attempt to provide a more accurate measure of trust in government (for example, Miller and Listhaug 1999: 211–12). Other research has demonstrated that such a dimension of beliefs in government is found alongside two other dimensions. According to Pattie and Johnston (2001), citizens make clear distinctions between the trust, efficacy and satisfaction

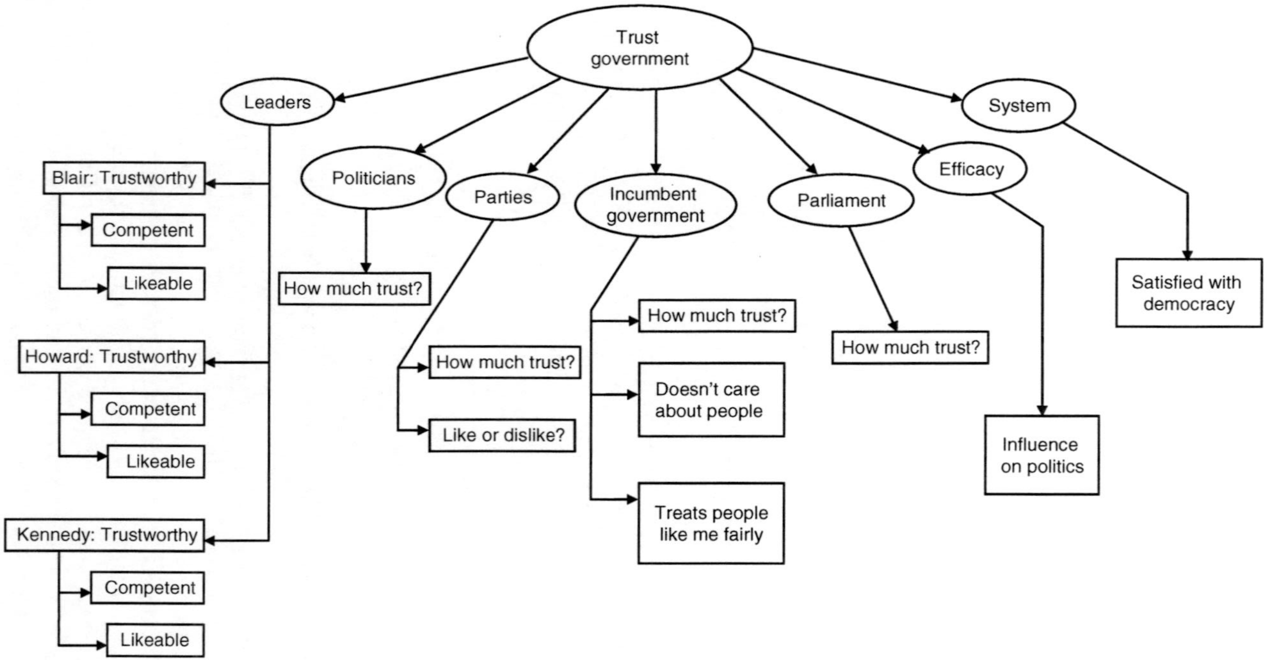

Figure 6.1 Quantitative structure of trust in government

with the overall system. To uncover which items can be merged and what the various underlying dimensions of beliefs in government are, it is necessary to employ a sophisticated statistical technique. By employing factor analysis, we can judge whether these beliefs are indeed reducible to three separate underlying components or whether they are so highly inter-related that they form a single component.

6.3 The structure of political trust

Factor analysis is a statistical technique used to gauge latent constructs within a group of variables (see Child 1990: 2–7. Also Child 2006; Lewis-Beck (ed.) 1994). As such, it is an appropriate technique to employ when determining underlying psychological dimensions (factors) amongst a set of cognitive beliefs. By running a factor analysis on the conceptual model in Figure 6.1, the various dimensions of beliefs in government can be uncovered. Due to the extremely high correlation between the three types of leader evaluation variables (trustworthiness, competence and likeability) these items are merged into a single leader index. The same is also true for the two measures of trust in political parties. Table 6.1 presents the results.

Table 6.1 Factor analysis of beliefs in government, Britain 2005

	Rotated component			
	1. Trust 'Government'	**2. Trust Conservatives**	**3. Trust Lib. Dems**	**4. Influence**
Trust Tony Blair	.850			
Trust current government	.845			
Trust Labour Party	.802			
Trust parliament	.732			
Trust politicians	.720			
Trust Michael Howard		.873		
Trust Conservative Party		.821		
Trust Charles Kennedy			.815	
Trust Liberal Democrats			.873	
Democracy satisfaction	.595			
Government is fair	.634			
Influence on politics				.966
Eigenvalue	4.426	1.856	1.269	1.009
% variance explained	36.9	15.5	9.7	7.4

Notes: Extraction method: Principal Component Analysis.
Rotation method: Varimax with Kaiser normalization.

As would be expected, the variables on party leaders and parties separate out into intuitive components – trust in the Labour Party leader is statically associated with trust in the Labour Party itself. The first three components represent implicit trust judgements about the Labour Party, the Conservative Party and the Liberal Democrats respectively. The results also reveal that satisfaction with the overall system loads onto the trust in incumbent government dimension while feelings of influence on politics represents a dimension in its own right.

A further feature should be noted. It is interesting to find that the two generalised trust items – parliament and politicians – load onto the trust Labour Party component. Previous analyses into trust in government have followed the normal practice of distinguishing between trust in people and confidence in institutions and subsequently using confidence in political institutions as an indicator of political support. The reason is that

> this taps into a more stable and bedrock set of attitudes than trust in particular political leaders or governments. Confidence in political institutions, therefore, is a better measure of support for the underlying institutions and system of democracy, as against support for particular political leaders or particular parties in government. (Zmerli and Newton 2006: 6)

The results from the previous factor analysis suggest that this is not the case, and for the UK at least, trust/confidence items on institutions are heavily associated with evaluations of the incumbent government.

We have then four dimensions of beliefs in government: trust in the incumbent government, trust in the main opposition party, trust in the third party, and finally feelings of influence on politics and the political process. By running a second order factor analysis (i.e., attempting to reduce these four dimensions of beliefs in government further), it is possible to see whether a latent construct of simply trust in government (both incumbent and the overall institution) exists. The results suggest one underlying dimension (eigenvalue = 1.562, 40 per cent of variance explained). It is this measure of trust in government that will be used as the dependent variable in the forthcoming regression analyses in Chapter 7.

6.4 Building on the qualitative model – measuring social trust

The following questions are used to measure social trust.

6.4.1 Direct trust questions

- 'Using this card, generally speaking, would you say that most people can be trusted, or that you can't be too careful in dealing with people?'
- 'Do you think that most people would try to take advantage of you if they got a chance or would they try to be fair?'

For both questions, respondents are given a card with an 11-point rating scale on which to place themselves, where 0 = no trust at all (or similar negative response), and 10 = complete trust. Recent research demonstrates that with the aid of metric equivalence tests these items can be considered as a reliable and cross-culturally valid measure of social trust (Reeskens and Hooghe 2008).

6.4.2 Different norms and lifestyles

In terms of gauging the extent to which others share similar norms and values, it is important to measure a sense of belonging to local communities, which should have a significant impact on how trustworthy people in general seem, as well as the degree to which people from different backgrounds and people with different lifestyles should be tolerated, that is, not viewed with disdain. The following questions have been targeted as useful:

- 'Please tick one box on each line to show how much you agree or disagree with each of these statements. I feel like I belong to this neighbourhood.'
- 'How strong are your feelings of attachment to your neighbourhood?'
- 'Please tick one box on each line to show how much you agree or disagree with each of these statements: People in Britain should be more tolerant of those who lead unconventional lifestyles.'
- 'There is a lot of talk about democracy these days and people have different opinions about what a democracy should be. Please tick one box on each line to show how much you agree or disagree with each of these statements. In a true democracy, the majority has a responsibility to protect the rights of all minorities.'
- 'Please tick one box on each line to show how much you agree or disagree with each of these statements. Immigrants increase crime rates.'

- 'Please tick one box on each line to show how much you agree or disagree with each of these statements. Immigrants generally are good for Britain's economy.'
- 'Please tick one box on each line to show how much you agree or disagree with each of these statements. Young people today don't have enough respect for traditional British values.'

6.4.3 Extent of appropriate behaviour

Finally, to gauge general perceptions of appropriate behaviour in society, the following question has been targeted as useful:

- 'Let's talk for a few minutes about how things have been developing in Britain in the last few years. How would you describe the crime situation in Britain these days?'

6.5 The structure of social trust

Table 6.2 presents the results of the factor analysis for the social trust items. A clear component that concerns itself with people different from the norm is derived from the ten items, which could be potentially useful in terms of gauging the extent to which individuals are inclined to bridge their social capital to others not like themselves. The second component is a strong neighbourhood orientation, where as the third component derived from the data represents the two generalised measures. The final point to note is how respondents interpreted the 'young people do not have enough respect' item. Found in the same component as general perceptions of crime, it seems that this item is an evaluative response as to how young people are perceived to behave, and whether such behaviour is in accordance with prevalent social norms and values. In short, whether the behaviour is 'appropriate'. Figure 6.2 summarises the results of Table 6.2.

Following on from reducing the four beliefs in government components to one underlying trust in government dimension, the same procedure will be conducted on the four social trust components. Verifying the idea of trust as a latent attitudinal construct, the four social beliefs are reduced to a single dimension (Eigenvalue = 1.493, 39 per cent variance explained). Again, it is this measure that will be used as the dependent variable for analysing social trust in the forthcoming chapters.

Table 6.2 Factor analysis of beliefs in society, Britain 2005

	Rotated component			
	1. People Different	**2. Neighbourhood**	**3. Generalised**	**4. Appropriate behaviour**
Majority's responsibility to protect rights of minorities	.708			
Immigrants good for the economy	.688			
Should be tolerant towards alternative lifestyles	.630			
Immigrants raise crime	.600			
Attachment to neighbourhood		.927		
Feel belong to current neighbourhood		.921		
People fair			.882	
Generalised trust			.877	
Young people not enough respect				.747
General perception of crime				.685
Eigenvalue	2.381	1.953	1.196	1.082
% variance explained	23.8	19.5	12	10.8

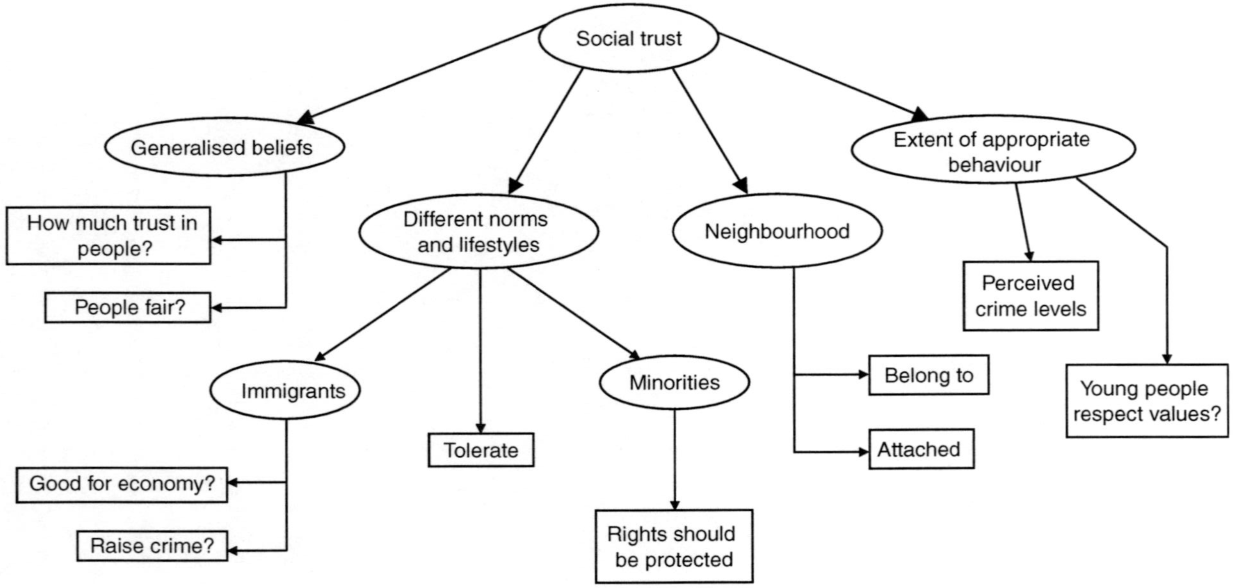

Figure 6.2 The four components of social trust

6.6 Trends in beliefs of government, Britain, 1987–2005

6.6.1 Efficacy, trust and system evaluation

According to Almond and Verba (1963), a democracy requires a balance of efficacy and trust amongst its citizens in order to perform effectively. The public needs to feel that public officials represent their views, but they should also be equally willing to trust public officials to make the right decisions for them on their behalf. As such, good citizenship is a balance between constructive criticism of government and reasonable deference to its decisions. The best political systems foster such efficacy and trust between governed and government.

Between 1987 and 2005 in Britain, the number of respondents perceiving government as untrustworthy consistently outweighed the number perceiving government as trustworthy. Figure 6.3 demonstrates that the number of cynical respondents (government is untrustworthy) is roughly 50 per cent in 1987 sustaining at a level between 70 and 75 per cent between 1997 and 2005. The number of respondents

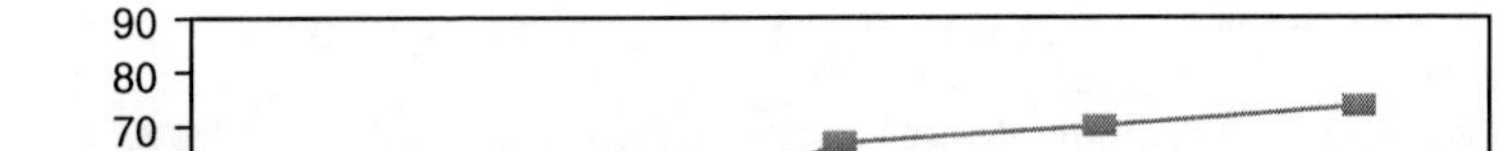

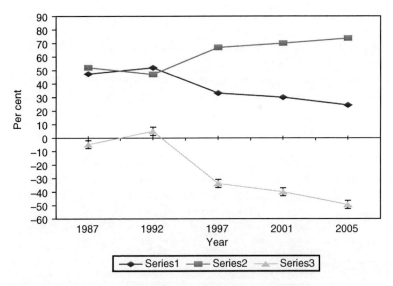

Figure 6.3 Government trustworthiness in Britain, 1987–2005

Sources: BES panel data, waves 1987–1992 and 1997–2001; BES 2005. Figure presents respondents answering most of the time (1) and some of the time (2) as viewing government as trustworthy and those answering some of the time (3) and almost never (4) as viewing government as untrustworthy. N = 3394, 1559, 3504, 2333, 3245 (BES panel data 1987 wave, 1992 wave, 1997 wave and 2001 wave respectively plus BES cross-section data 2005).

believing government to be trustworthy fell consistently from around 52 per cent in 1992 to under 30 per cent in 2005. So both cynicism and a lack of positive faith in government have been on the increase over the past two decades.

The trust index (government is trustworthy minus government is untrustworthy) also in Figure 6.3 demonstrates that from balanced cynicism in 1987, nearly 40 per cent more of the public believe government to be untrustworthy than trustworthy in 2005. Even taking into account the possible margin of error in the figures, the 1987 figure in comparison to 2005 figure is still significantly lower. Without a doubt, the British public are losing faith in government.

Chapter 1 addressed the issue of a presumption of distrust in human psychology and demonstrated that between 1987 and 2001 the British public displayed such a presumption towards government. A closer look at this data indicates that there is an increasingly large section of the public that maintains a distrustful position towards government. Figures 6.4a and 6.4b utilise BES panel data for the periods 1987 to 1992, 1992 to 1997, and 1997 to 2001. Figure 6.4a overviews respondents that say they 'almost always' trust government in the first wave of each data set. The percentages displayed represent whether the same individuals maintained their original position of distrust in the final wave 4/5 years later. Figure 6.4b presents the same data, but for respondents that say they 'almost never' trust government.

The bar chart in Figure 6.4a demonstrates that stability and variance in trusting government is constant across time. Over 80 per cent of respondents over a 4/5-year period will change the nature of their trust belief towards government given that their original evaluation was a positive one. However, this cannot be said for respondents' giving an original evaluation that is negative. Two notable aspects should be inferred from Figure 6.4b: (1) In absolute terms, across all three time-frames, stability in distrust towards government is far greater than stability in trust. For example, for the period 1992–1997, a third of all respondents who distrusted government in 1992 still distrusted government in 1997, compared to only 20 per cent starting from a trusting position. (2) The absolute figure for stable distrust towards government increased by at least 6 percentage points between each time-frame. By the period 1997 to 2001, nearly half of all respondents maintained their negative evaluation of government. So not only is cynicism towards government increasing, it is also become more entrenched in the minds of a significant section of the public.

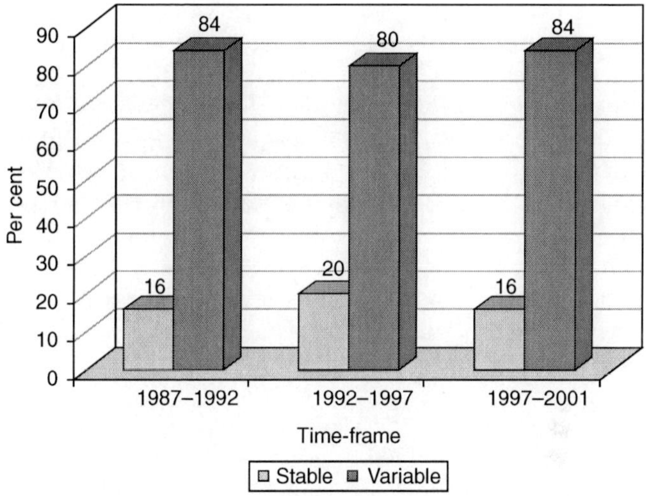

Figure 6.4a Stability of trustworthy beliefs towards government

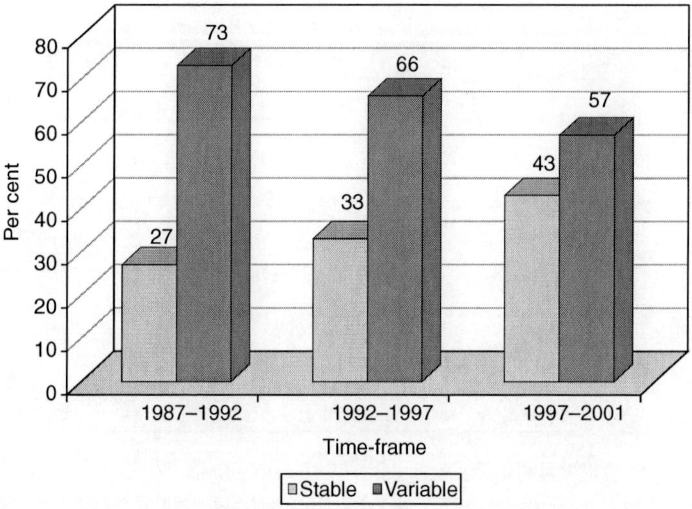

Figure 6.4b Stability of untrustworthy beliefs towards government

Concomitant with the decline in the trustworthiness of government and increasing cynicism is a decline in the level of influence that people feel they can exert on political decisions (see Figure 6.5). From just over a third of the electorate (35.4 per cent) feeling influential in 1987, this figure fell to 27 per cent in 2001. At the same time the number of people expressing little or no influence on the actions of government increased from just under a half in 1987 (48.7 per cent) to 60 per cent in 2005. Note that the percentage decline for those believing government to be trustworthy and the number feeling efficacious towards politics are a near perfect match.

The final important perception of government to highlight is the opinion of the political system as a whole. It could be the case that the two previous trends highlighted are associated with satisfaction with the whole political system. Between 1987 and 2005, satisfaction with the system of government in Britain did fall from 15 per cent of the electorate to just under 9 per cent (see Figure 6.6). However, the notable trend is increasing dissatisfaction with the political system, which rose from 19 per cent in 1987 to over 35 per cent in 2005. So not only is government

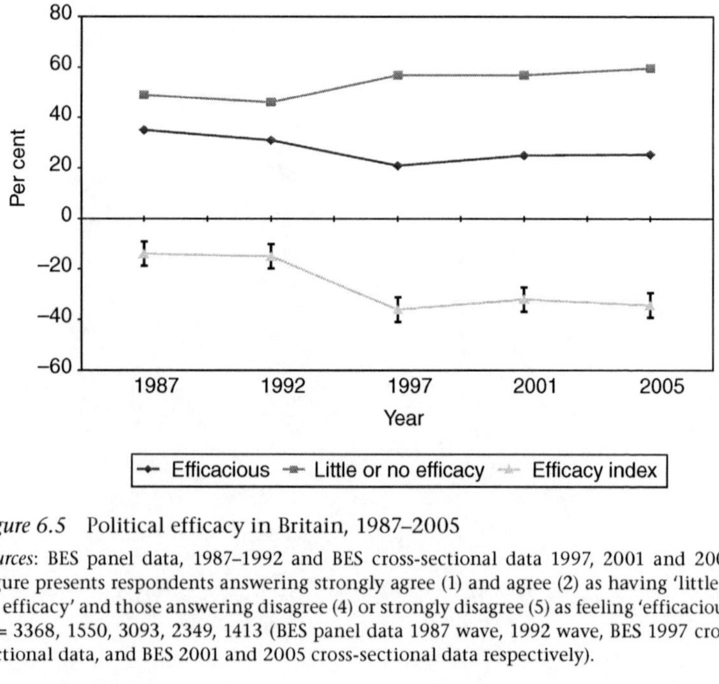

Figure 6.5 Political efficacy in Britain, 1987–2005

Sources: BES panel data, 1987–1992 and BES cross-sectional data 1997, 2001 and 2005. Figure presents respondents answering strongly agree (1) and agree (2) as having 'little or no efficacy' and those answering disagree (4) or strongly disagree (5) as feeling 'efficacious'. N = 3368, 1550, 3093, 2349, 1413 (BES panel data 1987 wave, 1992 wave, BES 1997 cross-sectional data, and BES 2001 and 2005 cross-sectional data respectively).

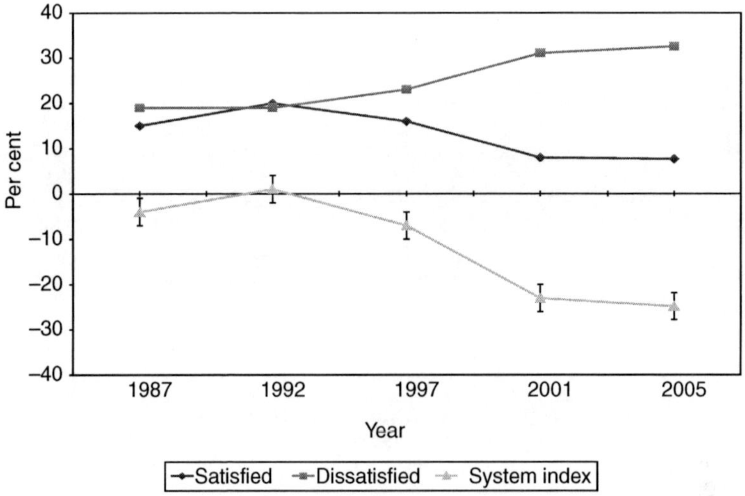

Figure 6.6 Political system evaluation in Britain, 1987–2005

Sources: BES panel data, 1987–1992 and BES cross-sectional data 1997, 2001 and 2005. Figure represents respondents answering 'works well' or 'satisfied' as satisfied and those answering 'doesn't work well' and 'needs complete change'/'not very satisfied' and 'not at all satisfied' as dissatisfied. N = 3370, 1551, 3093, 2347, 3487 (BES panel data waves 1987 and 1992, and BES cross-sectional data 1997, 2001 and 2005 respectively).

considered as less trustworthy, but also the political system as a whole is viewed with increasing scepticism. While Norris (1999) reminds us of Easton's distinction between trust in institutions and trust in the regime – two distinct and separate objects of trust – there is preliminary evidence here to suggest that increasing cynicism of political actors and institutions is 'spilling over' into concerns regarding the workings of the whole political system.

6.6.2 Trust trends in public authorities

Not only are there different objects of trust, there are also different types of trust, that is, trust beliefs and trust attitudes. The trustworthiness of government is a specific belief that informs the general attitude of trust in government. This attitude is a general orientation that determines how and why we defer to public authorities (Miller 1974; Hetherington 2004; Weatherford 1984). Trust is employed as a judgement heuristic to manage situations of risk (Slovic 1987), and 'political' trust is what we call upon to determine whether we can rely on public authorities to satisfy our interests and expectations. It is quite plausible, therefore,

Table 6.3 Confidence in public authorities and trust in society, Britain 1980–2001

Question reads: 'I am going to name a number of organizations. For each one, could you tell me how much confidence you have in them: is it a great deal of confidence, quite a lot of confidence, not very much confidence or none at all?'

Organisation	1980	1990	2001
The Press	28 (70.6)	14.6 (84.7)	18 (75)
The Church	45.7 (53.2)	44.7 (53.2)	38 (43.8)
The Civil Service	45.7 (52.4)	44.6 (54.2)	52.3 (47)
The Armed Forces	80 (18.8)	80.4 (18)	82 (18)
The Police	84.5 (14.5)	76.5 (18.7)	77 (11)

Sources: World Values Surveys, 1980–1981, 1990–1991, and 2000–2001. Figures represent percentage number of respondents answering (1) great deal of confidence and (2) quite a lot of confidence. Negative answers, (3) not very much confidence and (4) none at all, are presented in brackets.

that government's lack of trustworthiness is indicative of an attitude shift towards public authorities. That is, falling government trustworthiness could simply be an artefact of increasing cynicism towards public institutions in general. According to Inglehart (1999), an unwillingness to defer to the decisions taken by public authorities is characteristic of increasing post-materialistic tendencies within modern societies.

However, government lacking trustworthiness cannot be blamed on an increasing tendency amongst the electorate to simply distrust all public authorities. It cannot even be blamed on some. As Table 6.3 shows, there has been no equivalent growing cynicism of the press, the civil service, the armed forces or the police (little or no confidence figures are in brackets). Of the five organisations, only confidence in the church fell consistently between 1980 and 2001, and even then by relatively small margins (7 per cent over 20 years). Over 50 per cent expressed confidence in the civil service at a time when government and politicians are the objects of serious criticism, and even the press were perceived to become more credible during the 1990s.

Subtracting the percentage offering a positive evaluation of public authorities from the percentage offering a negative evaluation will give a net index of the overall confidence of the institution in question. Figure 6.7 charts the changing net confidence. The British public's tendency between 1980 and 2001 was to view the civil service and the armed forces with more confidence, both increasing their net score by over 9 per cent. But while the remaining three public authorities were

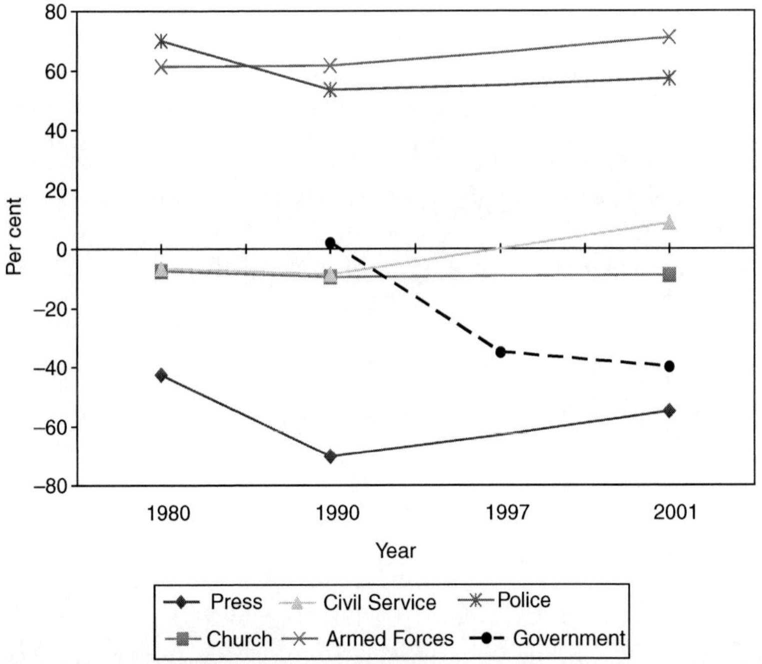

Figure 6.7 Net confidence in public authorities

Sources: World Values Surveys 1980–1981, 1990–1991, and 2000–2001. The 1990 figure for government is from BES panel data, 1992 wave. The following figures are from BES panel data wave 1997 and wave 2001.

viewed with less confidence over the 20 year period, between 1990 and 2001 the public became more confident in them, unlike the institution of government. The implication is clear: growing cynicism is unique to politics and the political process.

6.7 Conclusion

Taking advantage of the qualitative framework established in Chapter 5 and moving beyond simple direct measures of trust, this chapter has used data from Britain to explore the structure of trust dimensions towards society and government. The attitude of trust in government (as opposed to the single belief of trust in the incumbent government) is an expression of four underlying dimensions which include trust in incumbent government as well as trust in the two main opposition parties, and finally feelings of influence on politics. The attitude of social trust is an expression of four underlying dimensions – generalised trust beliefs towards people in society, trust of people in local neighbourhoods, trust in people with different backgrounds and lifestyles, and finally confidence that people in general behaviour appropriately.

Tracking the three trust in government items available across time in social surveys – trust in incumbent government, efficacy, and system – it was demonstrated that long-term declines have occurred in each. Indeed, no public authority apart from government has been the object of increasing cynicism; it is *sui generis* in terms of losing public faith.

7
Explaining Trust in Britain

7.1 Introduction

Upon the formal departure of Tony Blair as Prime Minister of the United Kingdom, his replacement, former chancellor Gordon Brown, signalled that the issue of trust was firmly placed on his agenda:

> To those who feel that the political system doesn't listen and doesn't care, to those who somehow feel powerless and have lost faith ... I will strive to earn your trust. To earn your trust not just in foreign policy but earn your trust in our schools, in our hospitals, in our public services, and to respond to your concerns. (Labour Party leadership acceptance speech 2007)

Such a concern over trust is not without merit. Trust of government in Britain has fallen to record low levels, and the malaise extends to multiple features of the political system. In attempting to better understand the difference between trusters and distrusters, this chapter takes a closer look at party system variables. It will be demonstrated that in order to truly understand trust of government, especially in Britain and probably most of Europe, the starting point must be perceptions of the party system. As the main mechanism by which interests are aggregated (Ware 1996: 5), they often provide the focal point for the political judgement and behaviour of citizens.

This chapter begins by establishing the primacy of parties in government–governed relations, and goes on to track changing trends in the party system in Britain. By including these factors into an explanatory framework, and combining this with improved measures of trust as outlined in Chapter 6, a much improved analysis of trust is offered.

7.2 Trust and political parties

Countries like Britain have a strong party-system in the sense that it is political parties that provide the main link between governed and government. Despite, in theory, the electorate voting for individual candidates to represent their constituency, in effect, it is predominantly the perception of the respective political parties at the national level that shapes partisanship. This is because the party provides individual politicians with a moral resource. Individual candidates contesting a seat will often win or lose depending on the national standing of their respective party. So if the party at the national level becomes unpopular, incumbent MPs in marginal seats have to watch their backs. For example, constituents in Brent East, London, on 18 September 2003, went to the polls in a by-election. Despite historically being a Labour stronghold, the winning candidate – Sarah Teather – was a Liberal Democrat. It is claimed the 29 per cent swing from Labour to Liberal Democrat is best explained by a protest vote over the government's decision to invade Iraq which added to Tony Blair's and New Labour's 'problem of trust'.[1] The outcome was reported less of a triumph for Sarah Teather, but more of a success for the Liberal Democrats and a failure for New Labour.

Furthermore, according to party identification theory (Budge et al. 1976), those who have a strong attachment to a political party are not only more likely to remain loyal to that party in the polling booth, but are also more likely to support the political system. Identifying with a party that accords to the rules of electoral competition in their country should help ensure that they also have respect for and trust in those rules of the political system (Barry 1970; Crewe et al. 1977). If this is the case, then there would be good reason to expect levels of party support to decline as trust in government falls as well.

Parties then provide the critical link between individuals and government by giving individual politicians a moral resource and by legitimising the political system. As such, we should expect to find an ongoing interaction between levels of political trust and the level of support for the party-system.

7.2.1 The falling popularity of political parties

If the British public increasingly believe that the motives of political parties cannot be trusted to serve public interests, then it should be the case that the popularity of political parties has fallen. The evidence is that throughout the late 1970s and much of the 1980s, the popularity of organised political parties did fall, and quite dramatically (Norris 1997; Crewe and Thomson 1999; Dalton et al. 2001). A key indication of this is the rapid decline in individual party membership levels.[2] Figure 7.1 demonstrates the fall from 1960 to 2007. The decline is stark. From nearly 4 million members of all parties in 1960, the same figure on 2007 was closer to 600,000. And not only has overall membership declined. Those who are still members register a weaker degree of identification with their party (Norris 2002: ch. 5). Active engagement and allegiance to all three major parties in Britain has declined considerably, and it is a trend that extends to many developed democracies.

> Not only have national levels of party membership across all of the long-established democracies failed to keep pace with the growth in the size of the national electorates, a trend that was already apparent in the late 1980s, they now are also evidencing substantial declines in absolute numbers. Parties in Western Europe are clearly losing the capacity to engage citizens in the way they once did. Across all of the long-established democracies, these parties are simply haemorrhaging members. (Mair and van Biezen 2001: 13)

Using British Election Study data it is also possible to track the expressed level of party identification as well as the strength of this identification. Despite reservations over the validity of such measures (Green and

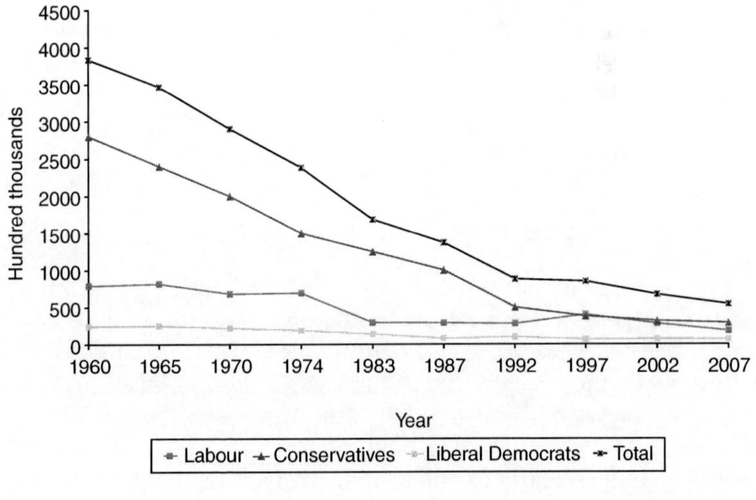

Figure 7.1 Individual membership of the main British parties, 1960–2007

Table 7.1 Party identification, 1987–2005

	1987	1992	1997	2001	2005
Cons	38.6	39.8	26.2	23.5	22.2
Lab	31.4	32.2	42.5	42	33.5
Lib	16.3	11.1	11.7	8.3	11.5
All	86.3	83.1	80.4	73.8	67.2
N	3662	1768	3615	3163	1805

Table 7.2 'Very strong' party identifiers, 1987–2005

	1987	1992	1997	2001	2005
Cons	23.1	19.2	14.4	14.1	11.7
Lab	26.3	22.1	22.3	18.8	16.6
Lib	11.4	9.7	6	6.5	4.8
All	20.3	17	14.2	13.1	11
N	1693	1401	1569	1418	1519

Palmquist 1994), they are the best available items to measure the degree to which the public feels a party represents their interests across time. As Table 7.1 demonstrates, for every election year since 1987, the overall percentage identifying with a party has declined from 86.3 per cent to 67.2 per cent in 2005.

Furthermore, Table 7.2 demonstrates that of those who say they identify with a party, the overall per cent saying this identification is very strong has fallen consistently for each election year from 20.3 per cent in 1987 to just 11 per cent in 2005. What is notable is that this decline has occurred across all parties.

7.3 The changing rationality of parties

A host of literature has been published over the past 10 years on the 'party machine' because politics has become obsessed with style and image over substance (Bartle and Griffiths (eds) 2001; McNair 2003). The British public increasingly think so too. A question repeated in British Election surveys is:

> 'Disagree/Agree: parties are more interested in votes than representing opinions'

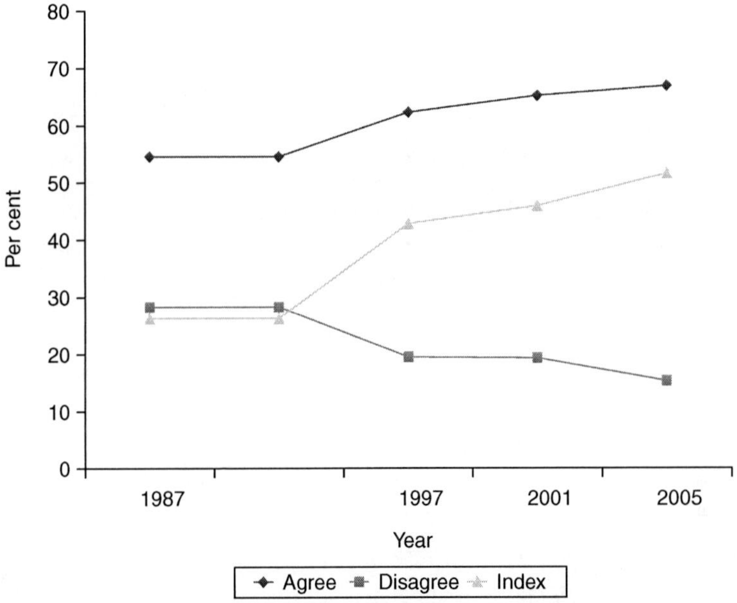

Figure 7.2 Agree or disagree: parties are only interested in votes not opinions
Source: BES cross-sections, 1987, 1997, 2001, 2005. Question was not asked in the BES, 1992. Index is created by subtracting the per cent agreeing with per cent disagreeing.

The opinion that parties alter their policies in order to acquire more votes as opposed to adopting policies because they are believed to be the best for the country is increasing. In the language of trust, parties are not taking our interests into account qua our interests – they are merely considering them as part of their calculations.

As Figure 7.2 demonstrates, this belief has become more widespread between 1987 and 2005. In 1987, 26 per cent more respondents believed that parties are only interested in acquiring votes as opposed to representing opinions, a figure that increased to 51 per cent in 2005. The irony is that as individuals support parties less because they are motivated for instrumental reasons, the response of parties is to become more instrumental in an attempt to win back support. A key characteristic of this 'instrumental' style of politics is that parties have increasingly made recourse to focus groups when developing policy. A primary reason for doing so is to gain a better understanding of the thoughts and opinions of floating voters. Party strategists have recognised that as the level and strength of party identification has fallen, the party that can secure the vote of floating voters will usually win the general election. This has meant that parties 'market' themselves in an attempt to attract voters (Lees-Marshment 2004).

7.4 Expanding the models

Chapter 3 derived explanatory frameworks for trust. With the benefit of more contextualised data, a new set of regression models can be specified with aim of providing a more comprehensive account of trust in society and trust in government. To recall, the main types of explanations identified for trust in government were:

- Wealth and Education
- Group RD and Egoistic RD
- Social capital
- Government represents and Government fair
- Media effects
- Individual values

This creates the following theoretical framework:

Analytical framework for explaining government trustworthiness

	Endogenous to political system	**Exogenous to political system**
Societal		Wealth, Education
Individual socialisation	Group RD; Discuss politics; Ideology	Social capital
Individual evaluations	Policy satisfaction; Parties different; Parties representative	Egoistic RD; Media effects; Values

Specifying regression models for the above yields the following:

1. Societal model:

Trust = a + Wealth+ e

where,
Wealth = (1) Type of occupation (Manual, Semi-skilled, Skilled, Professional)
(2) Type of property (Own/Rent).

2. Individual socialisation:

Trust = a + Discrimination + Group RD + DisPol + e

where,
Discrimination = Member of a discriminated group?
Group RD = Student/Retired/Unemployed; Ordinary people get fair share of wealth
DisPol = Discuss politics.

3. Exogenous individual socialisation:

Trust = a + Social Trust + Social Networks + e

where,
Social trust = generalised perception of the trustworthiness of others
Social Networks = how often see close family and friends.

4. Exogenous individual evaluations:

Trust = a + Egoistic RD + Media + Values

where,
Media = Read papers/Listen to radio/Watch television
Egoistic RD = Satisfied with life
Values = Individualism: People should take responsibility for their own life.

5. Endogenous individual evaluations:

(a) General perception of parties

Trust = a + Motives + Choice + Issues + Party Best + e

where,
Motives = parties interested in votes not government
Choice = perceived difference between main parties
Issues = do parties talk about important issues?
Party Best = is there a party that is best on most important issue?

(b) Evaluation of parties on specific issues

Trust = a + EU + Tax and Spend + Left/Right + e

where,
EU = (Perception of government's policy position – R's policy position on EU)

Tax and Spend = (Perception of government's policy position – R's policy position on taxes)
Left/Right = (Perception of government's policy position – R's policy position on Left/Right scale).

(c) Government performance

Trust = a + EconRet + EconPro + FinRet + FinPro + Crime + Asylum + Health + Terrorism + Economy + Tax

where,
EconRet = Retrospective evaluation of the economy if government is culpable
EconPro = Prospective evaluation of the economy if government is culpable
FinRet = Retrospective evaluation of personal finances if government is culpable
FinPro = Prospective evaluation of personal finances if government is culpable
Crime thru to Tax = Has government handled the issue of... Well?

(d) Civic voluntarism

Trust = a + EfficacyVol + Interest + Knowledge + e

where,
EfficacyVol = Are interest groups more influential than political parties
Interest = How interested is R in politics
Knowledge = Overall score on political knowledge quiz.

(e) Rational choice

Trust = a + EgoBen + CollBen + e

where,
EgoBen = Political activity brings personal benefits
CollBen = Political activity brings collective benefits.

7.5 Results – trust in government

According to the societal model in Table 7.3, wealth items have no impact on levels of trust in government. Of significance but of little explanatory power are the two endogenous socialisation variables that suggest discussing (and hence sharing information about) politics promotes trust in government (.130***), where as perceptions of unfair wealth inequalities reduces trust (–.169***). The next model demonstrates

Table 7.3 Explaining trust in government

	Societal		**Endogenous individual socialisation**		**Exogenous individual socialisation**		**Exogenous individual evaluations**	
Variables	**Beta**	**Sig.**	**Beta**	**Sig.**	**Beta**	**Sig.**	**Beta**	**Sig.**
Age	**.096*** **	.000	.058	.068	**.050***	.041	**.080*** **	.001
Gender	.003	.883	–.006	.800	.027	.226	.006	.790
Education	**.083** **	.005	.049	.054	–.008	.756	**.058***	.029
Income levels	**.058***	.039	–.045	.148	.023	.360	.038	.139
Ethnicity	.000	.986	–.002	.923	–.006	.786	.008	.733
Occupation	–.005	.859						
Own/Rent	.013	.599						
Discuss politics			**.130*** **	.000				
Wealth share			**–.169*** **	.000				
Student			.006	.805				
Unemployed			–.031	.170				
Retired			.057	.075				
Social trust					**.274*** **	.000		
Voluntary					**.082*** **	.000		
Talk local					–.018	.462		
Tabloid							.036	.143
Broadsheet							.008	.741
Individualism							.016	.467
Ego Rd							**–.134*** **	.000
R Square	.013		.048		.087		.028	
N	1931		1941		1894		1942	

Table 7.4 Explaining trust in government – endogenous individual evaluation models

	Parties general		Parties specific		Government performance		Civic voluntarism		Rational choice	
Variables	**Beta**	**Sig.**	**Beta**	**Sig.**	**Beta**	**Sig.**	**Beta**	**Sig.**	**Beta**	**Sig.**
Age	**.099*** **	.000	**.135*** **	.000	**.130*** **	.000	**.076** **	.003	**.080*** **	.001
Gender	.004	.831	–.025	.237	–.030	.108	–.018	.441	–.002	.944
Education	–.001	.981	**.089*** **	.000	.020	.356	**.066* **	.013	**.064** **	.009
Income levels	.019	.394	**.054* **	.021	.006	.769	.040	.129	**.070** **	.005
Ethnicity	.026	.205	.014	.506	.010	.598	.001	.952	–.006	.777
Parties motives	**–.257*** **	.000								
Parties choice	**.115*** **	.000								
Parties Issues	**.129*** **	.000								
Party best?	**.227*** **	.000								
EU distance			**–.153*** **	.000						
Tax & Spend			**–.099*** **	.000						
Left/right Dist.			**–.074*** **	.001						
Iraq			**–.298*** **	.000						
Economy retro					–.017	.615				

Economy pro					**.163*** **	.000				
Finances retro					–.040	.232				
Finances pro					.060	.068				
Govt. Crime					**.107*** **	.000				
Govt. asylum					**.072*** **	.001				
Govt. health					**.148*** **	.000				
Govt. terrorism					**.175*** **	.000				
Govt. economy					**.154*** **	.000				
Govt. tax					**.102*** **	.000				
Efficacy Vol.							**–.084*** **	.000		
Interest politics							**.255*** **	.000		
Knowledge							**–.090*** **	.001		
Selfish benefit									–.003	.903
Group benefit									**.233*** **	.000
R Square	.232		.168		.349		.080		.065	
N	1899		1949		1913		1766		1949	

that higher levels of social trust are in fact associated with higher levels of trust in government (.274***), as to is being active in voluntary organisations (.082***). Finally in Table 7.3, feelings of ego RD demonstrate to be negatively correlated with trust in government (–.134***), although the explanatory strength of the model (R square = .028) proves to be small.

Table 7.4 continues the results from the political trust models and outlines the impact of endogenous individual evaluation explanations. These factors offer a more contextualised approach to understanding trust in government. One of the strongest models (R square .232) is the first model, general perceptions of political parties. All four items are statistically significant and demonstrate that believing parties to be more concerned with votes than government reduces trust (–.257***), while believing parties offer a real choice of alternative policy programmes increases trust (.115***). Similarly, the perception that parties are (1) concerned with the most important issues of the day and (2) capable of doing a good job on that issue also promotes greater trust.

Moving onto specific issues surrounding party politics, using distance measures on policy items helps to account for some of the variation in trust in government. Not being in accordance with government policy on the EU, Tax and Spend, and Left-Right positioning all reduce trust. However, these negative effects are not as strong as the issue of Iraq, where disagreeing with UK intervention has seemed to have a reasonably strong effect (–.298***). The strongest model in terms of explanatory power is the performance model (R square = .349), supporting Easton's (1965) and recently Hetherington's (2004) claim that trust in government is primarily a function of policy outputs. The results here suggest that the economy, the health service and terrorism are all key concerns, where satisfaction on such items leads to greater trust towards government.

The one variable to stand out in the civic voluntarism model is interest in politics, which demonstrates a reasonably strong positive effect on trust (.255***). Interestingly, levels of political knowledge are negatively correlated with trust in government (–.090***) suggesting a presence of 'critical citizens'. However, this effect disappears and becomes positive when political interest is not controlled for. Furthermore, belief that interests group are more influential than parties not surprisingly correlates negatively with trust (–.084**), and finally, holding the view that political activity brings collective benefits is associated with higher trust in government (.233***).

Evaluating all of the significant variables in a composite model allows for nearly half of the variation in trust in government to be accounted for (Table 7.5, R square = .470). The two dominant variables to effect this

Table 7.5 Composite government trust model

Variables	Beta	Sig.
Age	**.115*****	.000
Gender	–.017	.381
Education	–.009	.669
Income levels	–.039	.113
Ethnicity	.032	.077
Discuss politics	.022	.305
Wealth share	**–.047***	.036
Social trust	**.093*****	.000
Voluntary	**.064*****	.001
Ego RD	–.036	.059
Parties motives	**–.085*****	.000
Parties choice	**.069*****	.001
Parties issues	**.056****	.003
Party best?	**.083*****	.000
EU distance	–.026	.194
Tax & Spend	**–.037***	.049
Left/Right dist.	–.012	.543
Iraq	**–.127*****	.000
Macro economy pro	**.102*****	.000
Govt. crime	**.104*****	.000
Govt. asylum	–.004	.852
Govt. health	**.112*****	.000
Govt. terrorism	**.097*****	.000
Govt. Economy	**.107*****	.000
Govt. tax	**.090*****	.000
Efficacy Vol.	–.022	.229
Interest politics	**.132*****	.000
Knowledge	**–.084*****	.000
Group benefit	**.089*****	.000
Adj. R Square	.470	
N	1645	

are political interest (.132***) and disagreement with intervention in Iraq (–.127***). Satisfaction with government performance on the public policy areas of crime, health, terrorism, the economy and tax also prove to be relatively important, as well as general evaluations of the political parties. Note however that the distance measures on political issues (EU, tax and spend, Left/Right) prove to be of little importance. The cognitive variables of knowledge and perceived collective benefits of political activity have negative and positive impacts on trust respectively (–.084*** and .089***), and attention should also be given to the fact that social trust (.093***) and being active in voluntary organisations (.064***) also positively affect trust in government.

7.6 Models of social trust

Given that social trust has an impact on levels of trust in government, it is illustrative to also consider explanations for levels of social trust as well. This expands our understanding of the different social factors that determine levels of perceived trustworthiness of others and in part, evaluations of government.

To recall, the relevant explanatory factors for social trust derived in Chapter 3 were:

- Family background
- Education, Income and Wealth
- Social networks, Voluntary orgs and Perceptions of neighbourhood
- Group RD and Egoistic RD
- Crime
- Media effects
- Individual values including religious values

This gives the following framework for explaining individual's perceptions of the trustworthiness of others:

Analytical framework for explaining the trustworthiness of society

	Endogenous to social relations	**Exogenous to social relations**
Societal		Wealth
Individual socialisation	Social networks; Voluntary orgs; Neighbourhood	Ideology; Religion; Group RD
Individual evaluations	Crime; Values	Media effects; Egoistic RD

Putting these factors into separate regression models yields the following:

1. Societal model:

Trust = a + Wealth + e

where,
Family Background = highest educational qualification attained by mother and father
See Family/Friends = 'how often see close family and friends'.

2. Endogenous individual socialisation model:

Trust = a + Neighbourhood + Voluntary Associations + Talk + e

where,
Neighbourhood = Satisfied with neighbourhood
Voluntary associations = Active in voluntary associations
Talk = talk to other local community members.

3. Exogenous individual socialisation model:

Trust = a + Ideology + Group RD + Religion + SocStat + e

where,
Group RD = (1) Student/Retired/Unemployed
(2) Ordinary people get fair share of wealth (low income earners only)
Religion = Protestant/Catholic
SocStat = Perceived position on social ladder (least or best well off).

4. Endogenous individual evaluations model:

Trust = a + Crime + Values + Ideology + e

where,
Crime = General perception of crime
Individualism = People should take responsibility for their own life
Ideology = Self Left-Right ideological position.

5. Exogenous individual evaluations model:

Trust = a + Media + Egoistic Relative Deprivation

where,
Media = Read papers/Listen to radio/Watch television
Egoistic Relative Deprivation = Satisfied with life.

7.7 Results

Table 7.6 presents the results for the social trust models. The societal model demonstrates that one wealth item is significant (.067*) which indicates that owning property (and thereby being more wealthy) is associated with higher trust. The endogenous individual socialisation model proves to be relatively strong, in particular attachment to local neighbour is positively correlated with social trust (.171***) as well as inclination to talk to other community members (.198***) and being active in voluntary organisations (.061**). Of the exogenous socialisation factors, perceptions of social status proves to be a strong positive predictor of social trust (.181***).

Table 7.6 Explaining social trust

Variables	Societal		Endogenous individual socialisation		Exogenous individual socialisation		Endogenous individual evaluations		Exogenous individual evaluations	
	Beta	**Sig.**	**Beta**	**Sig.**	**Beta**	**Sig.**	**Beta**	**Sig.**	**Beta**	**Sig.**
Age	**.160*****	.000	**.097*****	.000	**.193*****	.000	**.196*****	.000	**.156*****	.000
Gender	**–.060****	.004	–.024	.220	**–.067*****	.001	**–.060****	.003	**–.059****	.004
Education	**.192*****	.000	**.248*****	.000	**.189*****	.000	**.198*****	.000	**.162*****	.000
Income levels	**.100*****	.000	**.109*****	.000	**.074***	.012	**.142*****	.000	**.105*****	.000
Ethnicity	.015	.484	.010	.602	.026	.213	.010	.630	.015	.455
Occupation	.028	.284								
Own/Rent	**.067****	.004								
Neighbourhood			**.171*****	.000						
Talk local			**.198*****	.000						
Voluntary			**.061****	.003						

Protestant					**–.052***	.015				
Catholic					.015	.490				
Wealth share					–.015	.545				
Student					**.056****	.009				
Unemployed					–.014	.506				
Retired					–.009	.770				
Social status					**.181*****	.000				
Crime							**–.057****	.005		
Individualism							–.022	.282		
Left/right							**–.104*****	.000		
Tabloid									–.014	.523
Broadsheet									**.059****	.008
Ego RD									**–.160*****	.000
R Square	.087		.195		.144		.116		.122	
N	2201		2219		2101		2212		2221	

Table 7.7 Composite social trust model

Variables	Beta	Sig
Age	**.083*** **	.000
Gender	–.027	.167
Highest education	**.161*** **	.000
Income levels	.047	.058
Own/Rent	.031	.156
Neighbourhood	**.159*** **	.000
Talk local	**.204*** **	.000
Voluntary	**.063** **	.002
Protestant	**–.077*** **	.000
Student	**.050* **	.012
Social status	**.129*** **	.000
Crime	**.056** **	.003
Left/right	**–.118*** **	.000
Broadsheet	**.072*** **	.000
Ego RD	**–.141*** **	.000
R Square	.298	
N	2090	

A perception of relatively high crime in society seems to reduce levels of social trust (–.057**), although this negative effect is not as strong as holding right-wing tendencies (–.104***). Readers of broadsheet newspapers are more trusting of others (.059**), supporting Newton's (1999a) contention that *some* forms of the media are civic mobilisers, and finally, feelings of ego RD have a relatively strong negative effect on reducing social trust (–.160***).

Evaluating the relative importance of each variable can be ascertained by placing them in a composite model. Table 7.7 presents the results. Predictably, the 'contextualised' variables of neighbourhood satisfaction and propensity to talk to local people are the biggest predictors of social trust (.159*** and .204*** respectively), followed by feelings of ego RD (–.141***), social status (.129***), and right-wing beliefs (–.118***). The positive effect that education levels has on social trust is demonstrated yet again as well (.161***).

7.8 Conclusion

The introduction of party system variables has made an advance on understanding differences in levels of trust in government. The British public have become more aware of the instrumental electoral strategies of the main parties, and this in turn has hindered trust. As part of this political landscape, citizens will be sensitive to whether or not party representatives are indeed speaking and acting from conviction when addressing public policy issues, or whether they are merely 'making the right noises'.

Summarising the statistical results, a list of important endogenous and exogenous factors for explaining trust of government in Britain can be provided. Cognitive engagement in politics is the important starting point, where interest promotes trust but higher levels of knowledge allows people to either raise their expectations of government (and hence lower trust) or simply puts them in a position where government can be seen for all its faults. Second, that the job of government above all else is to implement successful public policies, especially policies that effect economic outcomes. What this suggests is that trust in government is primarily influenced by individual evaluations that are endogenous to the political system. Third, as mentioned, Britain in having a party system must have political parties that are motivated to truly represent public interests and opinions. Finally, and supporting research in the United States, the impact that political events such as the invasion Iraq can have on trust need to be taken into account.

Despite the strong implications that all of the above have for trust in government, room is still leftover for the social capital variables of trust in society and voluntary associations to also have an effect. Social trust itself seems to be primarily the product of highly contextual and localised variables, especially levels of satisfaction and interactions with fellow community members. The role of individual values should also not be underestimated, where self-ideological positions and expectations regarding one's own life have an influential role in affecting levels of social trust. As such, social trust seems to be an expression of both social context *and* individual level character traits.

8
Trust and Political Behaviour

8.1 Introduction

As demonstrated, concomitant with falling trust in government is the falling popularity of political parties. But what changes has this had on voting in general elections? To what extent citizens are inclined to take part in politics and the political process provides a vital test for the 'health' of democracies. Not only is participation an empirical problem in terms of legitimating governments through the ballot box and articulating interests through non-conventional mechanisms; participation is also a normative problem, where each individual as part of a political community has a duty to invest some time and energy in the political process if the benefits of collective actions are to be reaped (Weale 1999). So while attitudes such as trust in government might be on the decline in Britain, this might mean very little if people's political behaviour hasn't actually changed.

The aim of this chapter is to shed light on a possible nexus between trust in people and institutions and wider civic behaviour. Initially, it is illustrative to consider the different channels of participation on offer to citizens. Once established, this chapter goes on to (1) track the trends of such behaviours to see whether they co-vary with declining trust in government, and (2) uses regression models to test the hypothesis that levels of trust are associated with more or less levels of political participation.

It should be noted that the there is no a priori reason to believe that the presence of trust or distrust of government alone will be a sufficient motivating factor to act. For example, should the perceived unjust invasion of Iraq create mass demonstrations or a feeling of powerlessness amongst the British public? Obviously, both occurred, but the important point is that neither is a necessary response for a mistrusting public. Apathy and outrage are two plausible yet completely different responses, even when individuals have very similar belief systems (Lenski 1954). It will also be hypothesised, therefore, that political trust will only affect voting behaviour when interacting with other variables. In particular, it will be demonstrated that levels of trust in government mediate between levels of political knowledge and vote choice.

Despite demonstrating that trust is indeed associated with some forms of participation, simply analysing the 'main effects' of trust variables would be to ignore the potential utility of using trust items as multiplicative terms with levels of political knowledge. Furthermore, using clustering techniques, greater analytical leverage can be gained in relation to social trust variables to identify different types of social trusters. In both instances, the application of these techniques uncovers further results regarding the relationship between trust and political behaviour.

1. Types and trends
2. Explanatory models
3. Heterogeneity
4. Further results

8.2 Types of political participation

Empirical analyses have demonstrated that citizen participation clusters around different dimensions. For example, Parry et al. (1992: 50–62) devise an empirical framework that identifies five different types of political participation: (1) voting; (2) party campaigning; (3) collective action; (4) contacting public officials and authorities; and (5) direct action. Other researchers have made use of a simple dichtomy between conventional forms of participation, for example voting, and unconventional forms such as protesting. Given the obvious importance of voting in elections for democratic politics, as well as the vital role that voluntary organisations play and 'elite challenging' activities, the following questions from the BES 2005 have been targeted as potentially useful.

Voting

Talking with people about the general election on May 5th, we have found that a lot of people didn't manage to vote. How about you, did you manage to vote in the general election?

Conventional acts

Using a scale from 0 to 10, where 0 means very unlikely and 10 means very likely, how likely is it that you will vote in the next local government election?

Now a few questions about how active you are in politics and community affairs. Let's think about the next few years.

Using a scale from 0 to 10, where 0 means very unlikely and 10 means very likely, how likely is it that you will be active in a voluntary organisation, like a community association, a charity group or a sports club?

Using a scale from 0 to 10, where 0 means very unlikely and 10 means very likely, how likely is it that you will work actively with a group of people to address a public issue or solve a problem?

Over the past few years, have you volunteered to get involved in politics or community affairs?

Unconventional acts

Using a scale from 0 to 10, where 0 means very unlikely and 10 means very likely, how likely is it that you will participate in a protest, like a rally or a demonstration, to show your concern about a public issue or problem?

Using a scale from 0 to 10, where 0 means very unlikely and 10 means very likely, how likely is it that you will join a boycott, that is, refuse to buy a particular product or to shop at a particular store?

Table 8.1 Factor analysis, types of political behaviour, Bes 2005

	Rotated component		
	1. Collective	**2. Vote**	**3. Party orientated**
Likelihood of protesting	.808		
Boycott	.795		
Work with a group on an issue	.603		
Involved in community affairs		.844	
Active in voluntary organisation		.718	
Voted in last general election			.884
Likelihood of voting in next local election			.851
Eigenvalue	2.556	1.406	.996
% variance explained	36.5	20.1	12.7

Performing a factor analysis on the above items reveals three dimensions to political participation – vote, 'conventional' voluntary organisation acts, and the more unconventional acts of protesting, demonstrating and boycotting products (Table 8.1).

Given these results the protesting, boycott and work with a group items will be added together to form an unconventional participation index, while the community affairs and voluntary organisation items will form a conventional participation index. The two vote items will likewise form a vote index measure.

8.3 Trends in political participation

The next task is to establish what has happened to these three different types of political participation across time in Britain. Figure 8.1 demonstrates that despite marginal increases in general, European, and local election turnouts during the 1980s, by the end of the 1990s,

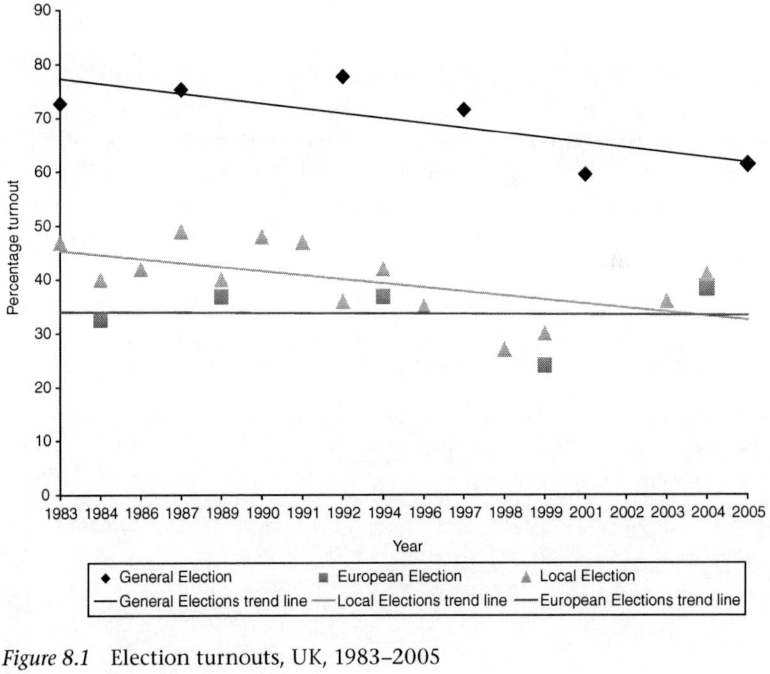

Figure 8.1 Election turnouts, UK, 1983–2005

Source: The Electoral Commission.

turnout in general elections had fallen by 18 per cent since 1992, and by 11 per cent since 1983. For local elections, the 1999 turnout was down by 19 per cent on its 1990 figure, 18 per cent in comparison to 1983. For European elections, turnout declined by 14 per cent since 1989, although this figure recovered to its trend average level in 2004.

Further to changes in vote turnout are changes in vote choice. Between 1987 and 2005 the third party – the Liberal Democrats – has managed to maintain its overall share of the vote at around 20 per cent, and other minority parties have actually increased their share from 4.3 per cent in 1987 to over 10 per cent in 2005 (Table 8.2). One could argue that this is a product of devolution to Wales and Scotland and merely reflects the greater significance of minority parties. However, further analyses demonstrate that the figures are almost identical when only considering vote share in England.

What these statistics do not show is results for council elections and European elections. An analysis of these elections and elections to the devolved regions would demonstrate recent success for minority parties. For example, the British National Party and the Green Party in 2002 and 2004 enjoyed surprising success in local elections, and the UK Independence Party (UKIP) became the United Kingdom's third largest party in the European Parliament. Similarly, since 1987, Plaid Cymru has gained at the expense of both Labour and the Conservatives in Wales, whereas the Scottish National Party and the Liberal Democrats in Scotland have likewise made gains on the two main parties. So regardless of which type of election and where it is held, one description fits all for the past two decades – that the two main parties are increasingly losing votes to minority parties.

Table 8.2 British general election turnouts and share of the vote, 1987–2005

	% Share of vote			
Year	**Cons**	**Lab**	**Lib**	**Other**
1987	42.2	30.8	22.6	4.3
1992	41.9	34.4	17.8	5.8
1997	30.7	43.2	16.8	9.3
2001	31.7	40.7	18.3	9.3
2005	32.3	35.3	22.1	10.3

Despite a long-term declining trend in voting, other forms of civic participation in Britain have remained strong. In fact, since 1987, overall participation – which includes joining a local club, boycotting goods, or attending a demonstration – has tended to increase (Bromley et al. 2001: 202; Maloney 2006: 99). So Britons are not opting out of civic life in general; they are simply opting out of the traditional forms of political activities.

8.4 Explaining differences in participation

A wealth of literature exists that attempts to explain why people participate in politically orientated acts. Drawing on general models used to account for political activity in the United States and electoral turnout in the United Kingdom, it is possible to test a trust model of engagement alongside the most familiar and favoured explanations for why citizens participate.

The first model to consider, and perhaps the most famous, is the *Civic voluntarism* model. Developed by Verba, Schlozman and Brady (1995), the basic tenets behind the approach are that citizens require both 'psychological engagement' and opportunities to participate through 'recruitment networks' (Verba, Schlozman and Brady 1995: 269). Together, they provide resources that trigger political engagement. Specifically, formal educational attainment is seen as the foremost resource as it correlates with people's ability to process information, which in itself correlates with higher levels of political interest and partisanship towards political parties. Implicit in this model then is Milner's (2002) notion of civic literacy – the stock of political interest and knowledge that individuals possess. Furthermore, it also makes sense to treat the *Social capital* model as implicit within the civic voluntarism model in so far as:

> people who trust their fellow citizens volunteer more often... participate more often in politics and community organizations, serve more readily on juries, give blood more frequently, comply more fully with their tax obligations, are more tolerant of minority views, and display many other forms of civic virtue. (Putnam 2000: 137)

In this sense local community ties act as a psychological engagement towards political participation. Indeed, social capital is often considered as a resource that individuals can draw upon (Bordieu 1997: 51).

A defining aspect of the civic voluntarism model is that it emphasises internal motivational postulates. Their presence combined with opportunity to participate is deemed as sufficient for participation. The next model, *Relative Deprivation*, assumes that citizens are motivated into political action for negative reasons. This approach assumes that individuals are concerned with issues of equity relative to their expectations. Such expectations are derived either from individual rationality, that is egoistic concerns, or from social norms derived from an individual's primary reference group (see Runciman 1966). When a gap opens up between such expectations and reality, feelings of injustice, perhaps even anger with resulting violence can occur (see Gurr 1970). Of course, less caustic reactions are just as likely, such as protesting or less trust in government.

Theories of cognitive mobilisation argue that education, media exposure and political awareness have vastly expanded since the 1950s contributing to a 'growth in the public's overall level of political sophistication through a process of cognitive mobilisation' (Phelps 2006: 25). Citizens are now capable of processing large amounts of politically relevant information due to enhanced access to higher education resources. Secondly, it is now easier and less costly for citizens to find information through print and electronic forms. These developments have meant that people are now more interested and knowledgeable about social and political issues and are more aware and concerned about politics and a functioning democracy. As a result of these developments citizens are more likely to be critical of governments and their policies and are more likely to be dissatisfied. Crucially, dissatisfaction may lead to abstention from electoral politics. The core ideas of the cognitive mobilisation model are education, media use, political interest, political knowledge and policy (dis)satisfaction (Clarke et al. 2004).

A second set of theories drawing on the work of Downs (1957) argue that an individual's choice to participate will result from weighing up the benefits of an action or activity in relation to the costs. If the costs are too great, or the benefits too few, then they are less likely to participate. As such, this model represents a rational choice explanation. Advancing on this is the notion of *General incentives* (see Whiteley and Seyd 2002: 51 and also Clarke et al. 2004: ch. 8). The core idea is that individuals need incentives and cues in order to vote. It supplements rational choice accounts of political behaviour by arguing that individuals take into account a wide range of incentives when they are considering to vote. The incentives in this decision are individual, group and system. Group benefits are not just those that flow to one's family but to people who are viewed as similar to oneself in need of help. System benefits are benefits that accrue to a political system when citizens vote. The recognition that a healthy democracy requires citizen involvement makes people vote. The model suggests that social norms are parts of the socio-political context in which people make choices about whether to vote, or not to vote. If other people in one's social environment think that voting is important then you are also more likely to.

The final model to consider is of course the *Trust in government* model. The first set of results will consider the dimensions of trust separately, that is, trust in incumbent government, trust in the two main opposition parties, feelings of efficacy towards politics, and finally satisfaction with the system. Under this model trust in government as a single item will be an attitudinal variable which will be tested separately.

8.5 Specifying the models

Given the above theoretical models to test, the following regression equations are specified. For reasons of clarity and brevity, the control variables of age, gender, education, income and ethnicity are not specified but ultimately included in each equation.

Relative deprivation model:

PolBeh = a + EgoRD + GovFair + Unemp + Student + Retired + PerFin + GovPer + Iraq + e

where,
a = constant
e = error term
PolBeh = Political behaviour (vote/conventional acts/unconventional acts)
EgoRD = Egoistic RD (individual expectations gap)
GovFair = Government treats people like me fairly
Unemp = Unemployed?
Student = In fulltime education?
Retired = Retired?
PerFin = Satisfaction with personal finances (when attributed to the actions of government)
GovPer = Overall satisfaction with government performance
Iraq = Agree/disagree with intervention.

Civic voluntarism model:

PolBeh = a + SocTru + VolOrg + DisPol + PolInt + ParBest + e

where,
SocTrus = Generalised trust in others
VolOrg = Active in voluntary organisations
DisPol = Propensity to discuss politics with others
PolInt = Interest in politics
ParBest = Is there a party that is best on most important issue.

Cognitive mobilisation model:

PolBeh = a + PolKno + ParChoi + Tabloid + Broadsh + e

where,
PolKno = Level of political knowledge (sum of right answers on political quiz)
ParChoi = Do the main parties offer a choice
Tabloid = Read a tabloid newspaper
Broadsh = Read a broadsheet newspaper.

General incentives model:

PolBeh = a + SelBen + ColBen + VotChg + VotNorm + e

where,
SelBen = Personal benefits from political activity
ColBen = Collective benefits from political activity
VotChg = Voting can change Britain*
VotNorm = Most people around here voted*

* Only included for vote model.

Trust in government model:

PolBeh = a + TrusInc + TrusOpp + Influe + System + e

where,
TrustInc = Trust in incumbent party
TrusOpp = Trust in two main opposition parties
Influe = Feelings of influence on politics and political process
System = Satisfaction with overall political system.

8.6 Results

Table 8.3 presents the results for predicting vote turnout. The relative-deprivation model suggests that being unemployed and dissatisfaction with personal finances (attributed to the actions of government) reduce the likelihood of voting (–.038* and–.048* respectively). However, these effects are marginal. The civic voluntarism model provides a slightly better prediction for turnout, with political interest (.124***) and discussion (.098***). Further to this, vote turnout is also partially determined by mobilisation factors, in particular knowledge (.145***) and the degree to which the main parties offer a real electoral choice (.085***).

In terms of general incentives to vote, the rational calculation that voting in general actually makes a difference represents the main incentive (.213***), whilst a prevailing norm of voting also has a positive though lesser effect (.092***). Finally, the trust model demonstrates that above all else it is feelings of efficacy that promote voting (.233***). The negative coefficient for trust incumbent (–.053*) demonstrates that the incumbent Labour failed to mobilise its supporters, while trust in the two main opposition parties and satisfaction with the political system all increased the likelihood of voting. We can also see that trust in government as a single attitudinal item has a strong positive association with voting (.243***). What is more, no other variable in all of the other models has a stronger effect; this variable alone accounts for over 13 per cent of the variation in voting (figure noted in brackets).

Table 8.4 evaluates the relative explanatory importance of the significant variables. The most important predictor of vote turnout is the attitude of trust in government (.189***) followed by feelings of efficacy (.140***), knowledge (.085**) and the prevalence of a norm of voting (.082***). Levels of political interest (.069*) and trust in opposition parties (.052*) likewise have a positive impact on vote, and so too does the belief that voting is collectively rational (.080*).

Turning attention to the second type of political behaviour, conventional acts of voluntary associations, Table 8.5 presents the results. According to the relative deprivation model, being retired and dissatisfied with personal finances (attributed to the actions of government) reduces the likelihood of conventional activities (–.069** and –.052** respectively). A key predictor in the civic voluntarism model is that of discussing politics (.202***), while interest and social trust demonstrate significant but marginal effects (.074* and .041* respectively). Like voting, levels of political knowledge also prove to be a positive correlate for conventional political acts (.109***) whereas parties offering a choice and reading a broadsheet have similar but marginal effects (.042* and .043* respectively).

Table 8.3 Voting

Variables	Relative deprivation		Civic voluntarism		Cognitive mobilisation		General incentives		Trust model	
	Beta	**Sig.**	**Beta**	**Sig.**	**Beta**	**Sig.**	**Beta**	**Sig.**	**Beta**	**Sig.**
Age	**.317*** **	.000	**.251*** **	.000	**.249*** **	.000	**.291*** **	.000	**.207*** **	.000
Gender	**–.046***	.011	**–.061** **	.003	**–.062** **	.002	–.033	.067	–.021	.322
Education	**.156*** **	.000	**.078*** **	.001	**.106*** **	.000	**.148*** **	.000	**.127*** **	.000
Income	**.109*** **	.000	**.097*** **	.000	**.097*** **	.000	**.131*** **	.000	**.115*** **	.000
Ethnicity	**–.055** **	.002	**–.076**** **	.000	**–.063** **	.002	**–.067*** **	.000	**–.074*** **	.000
Ego RD	.012	.518								
Govt. fair	.005	.821								
Unemployed	**–.038***	.038								
Student	–.002	.919								
Retired	.008	.769								
R's finances	**–.048***	.009								
Govt. perf.	.038	.074								
Iraq	.031	.098								
Social trust			**.058** **	.006						
Vol Org			.019	.373						

Discuss politics			**.098*** **	.000						
Interest			**.124*** **	.000						
Party best			**.044***	.030						
Knowledge					**.145*** **	.000				
Parties choice					**.085*** **	.000				
Tabloid					.012	.552				
Broadsheet					.022	.316				
Self-benefits							–.019	.312		
Group benefits							.004	.818		
Vote change							**.213*** **	.000		
Vote norm							**.092*** **	.000		
Trust Incumbent									**–.053***	.028
Trust Opposition									**.081*** **	.000
Influence									**.233*** **	.000
System									**.075*** **	.001
Trust Attitude									**.243*** **	.000
R Square	.127		.140		.129		.183		.159(.131)	
N	2750		2164		2311		2952		1950	

Table 8.4 Composite model of voting

Variable	Beta	Sig.
Age	**.170*****	.000
Gender	–.056	.019
Highest education	**.073****	.008
Income	**.097*****	.000
Ethnicity	**–.085*****	.000
Unemployed	.009	.692
Personal finances retro	–.001	.965
Social trust	.014	.576
Discuss politics	.037	.170
Interest	**.069***	.014
Which party is best on most important issue	–.012	.618
Knowledge	**.085*****	.001
Parties offer no choice	.033	.170
Voting can change Britain	**.080***	.017
Vote norm	**.082*****	.000
Trust incumbent govt.	–.027	.332
Trust opposition parties	**.052***	.029
Influence on politics	**.140*****	.000
Satisfied with democracy	.044	.086
Trust attitude	**.189*****	.000
Adj R Square	.230	
N	1624	

The general incentives model in effect becomes a simple rational choice model when predicting non-voting political behaviours. Of significance is the beliefs that political activity brings collective benefits (.072***). Finally, the trust in government model demonstrates the benefit of keeping the four dimensions of trust separate. While feelings of influence (.209***) and to a lesser degree trust in opposition parties (.046*) promote conventional political acts, satisfaction with the overall political system (–.046*) reduces the likelihood of such acts. Not surprisingly, given the different impact that the different dimensions of trust in government have on conventional political acts, trust in government as an attitude does not have a significant impact.

Table 8.6 presents the composite model for conventional acts. Two variables prove to be of particular importance – discussing politics (.151***) and influence on politics (.146***), suggesting that wider voluntary activities require both mobilisation and rational incentives precursors. Satisfaction with the overall system again proves to be

Table 8.5 Conventional acts

Variables	Relative deprivation		Civic voluntarism		Cognitive mobilisation		General incentives		Trust in government	
	Beta	Sig.	Beta	Sig.	Beta	Sig.	Beta	Sig.	Beta	Sig.
Age	–.016	.536	**–.087*** **	.000	**–.104*** **	.000	**–.086*** **	.000	**–.087*** **	.000
Gender	**–.053** **	.004	**–.056** **	.006	**–.065** **	.002	**–.050** **	.005	–.039	.069
Education	**.208*** **	.000	**.141*** **	.000	**.185*** **	.000	**.223*** **	.000	**.205*** **	.000
Income	**.069*** **	.001	**.062** **	.007	**.076*** **	.001	**.094*** **	.000	**.095*** **	.000
Ethnicity	–.001	.943	.003	.872	.011	.583	.000	.999	.003	.875
Ego RD	.028	.146								
Govt. fair	–.014	.495								
Unemployed	–.010	.587								
Student	.036	.062								
Retired	**–.069** **	.009								
R's finances	**–.052** **	.005								
Govt. perf.	.005	.829								
Iraq	.011	.558								
Social trust			**.041* **	.049						
Discuss			**.202*** **	.000						

(Continued)

Table 8.5 Continued

Variables	Relative deprivation		Civic voluntarism		Cognitive mobilisation		General incentives		Trust in government	
	Beta	**Sig.**	**Beta**	**Sig.**	**Beta**	**Sig.**	**Beta**	**Sig.**	**Beta**	**Sig.**
Interest			**.074****	.002						
Party best			–.008	.710						
Knowledge					**.109*****	.000				
Parties choice					**.042***	.033				
Tabloid					.024	.248				
Broadsheet					**.043***	.049				
Self benefits							.027	.153		
Group benefits							**.072*****	.000		
Trust govt.									–.032	.169
Trust opposition									**.046***	.036
Influence									**.209*****	.000
System									**–.046***	.049
Trust attitude									.054	.059
R Square	.090		.147		.107		.101		.146(.040)	
N	2939		2224		2857		1908		2952	

Table 8.6 Composite model of conventional acts

Variable	Beta	Sig.
Age	–.049	.110
Gender	**–.062****	.005
Highest education	**.144*****	.000
Income	**.052***	.041
Ethnicity	–.005	.820
Retired	**–.034***	.029
Personal finances retro	.005	.834
Social trust	.025	.262
Discuss politics	**.151*****	.000
Interest	.025	.364
Knowledge	.042	.082
Parties offer no choice	.000	.989
Broadsheet readers	.016	.492
Political activity – get collective benefits	.040	.068
Trust opposition	.027	.218
Influence on politics total	**.146*****	.000
Satisfied with democracy	**–.079***	.019
Adj R Square	.191	
N	1905	

negatively associated with conventional acts, suggesting that dissatisfaction with the system can promote wider civic activities, perhaps with a view to changing it.

Moving onto predicting the more unconventional acts of protesting and demonstrating, mobilisation and trust factors appear to be dominant (Table 8.7). Various feelings of relative deprivation also play a marginal role, with the perception that (1) government treats an individual's reference group unfairly (.093***); (2) government is responsible for worsening personal finances (.092***); and (3) the government's decision to intervene in Iraq is increasing the likelihood of protesting/demonstrating. As the mobilisation and incentives models suggest, the same is true for levels of political knowledge (.149***) and the perception that political activity brings group benefits (.099***).

Greatest explanatory utility however is found with the voluntarism model. Discussing and being interested in politics promotes unconventional acts (.243*** and .141*** respectively), while in the trust model a similar effect is found for influence (.210***). *Dis*satisfaction with the incumbent government and the political system also promotes unconventional acts as demonstrated by the negative coefficients (–.078**

Table 8.7 Unconventional acts

	Relative deprivation		Civic voluntarism		Cognitive mobilisation		General incentives		Trust in government	
Variables	**Beta**	**Sig.**	**Beta**	**Sig.**	**Beta**	**Sig.**	**Beta**	**Sig.**	**Beta**	**Sig.**
Age	**.079****	.003	–.031	.155	**–.047***	.041	.001	.973	–.024	.313
Gender	–.014	.467	**–.053*****	.009	**–.051***	.014	–.021	.234	–.022	.315
Education	**.174*****	.000	**.104*****	.000	**.155*****	.000	**.204*****	.000	**.180*****	.000
Income	.035	.110	.017	.448	.036	.125	**.068*****	.001	**.076****	.002
Ethnicity	.029	.127	.008	.707	.025	.215	.026	.148	.017	.429
Ego RD	.029	.132								
Govt. unfair	**.093*****	.000								
Unemployed	–.021	.264								
Student	**.040***	.038								
Retired	**–.079****	.003								
R's finances	**.092*****	.000								
Govt. perf.	.024	.277								
Iraq	**.068*****	.000								

Social trust			**.031***	.050						
Discuss			**.243*****	.000						
Interest			**.141*****	.000						
Party best			.010	.603						
Knowledge					**.149*****	.000				
Parties choice					.020	.335				
Tabloid					.014	.528				
Broadsheet					.042	.059				
Self benefits							.028	.140		
Group benefits							**.099*****	.000		
Trust govt.									**–.078****	.002
Trust opposition									.008	.716
Influence									**.210*****	.000
System									**–.112*****	.000
Trust Attitude									.051	.072
R Square	.070		.159		.076		.069		.101(.042)	
N	2750		2164		2311		2952		1950	

and –.122***). Finally, and again much like predicting conventional acts, trust in government as an attitude fails to be significant due to the different impacts that different dimensions of trust have on this type of participation.

Summarising these results in a composite model demonstrates that discussing politics is by far the best predictor of unconventional activities (.213***), followed by political interest (.109***) and influence on politics (.098***). The significant coefficient for the perception that government is unfair towards 'people like me' (.075**) also suggests that an element of relative deprivation promotes unconventional acts. Finally, Table 8.8 confirms that dissatisfaction with the overall system does indeed promote protesting/demonstrating (–.073**).

One feature of the previous results is that trust in government as an attitude strongly predicts the most conventional type of political participation, namely voting in the 2005 general election. A further notable feature in relation to the trust in government model is that different dimensions produced different results for both conventional and unconventional acts. A final observation relevant to the

Table 8.8 Composite model of unconventional acts

Variable	Beta	Sig.
Age	.003	.910
Gender	**–.042***	.040
Highest education	**.090*****	.000
Income	.006	.803
Ethnicity	.003	.881
Government unfair	**.075****	.002
In full time education	–.012	.553
Retired	**–.071***	.011
Personal finances retro	**.044***	.033
Social Trust	.033	.057
Iraq – success or failure?	**–.072*****	.001
Discuss politics	**.213*****	.000
Interest	**.109*****	.000
Knowledge	.029	.217
Political activity – get collective benefits	**.071*****	.001
Trust government	–.028	.289
Influence on politics	**.098*****	.000
Satisfied with democracy	**–.073*****	.001
Adj R Square	.211	
N	2203	

exogenous/endogenous explanatory divide is that despite social trust proving to be significant in the separate models for all three types of behaviours, it ultimately proves to be insignificant in all of the composite models once the most important endogenous factors are controlled for.

8.7 Citizen heterogeneity

One of the implications of viewing trust as a cognitive belief is that the role of information and knowledge regarding objects of trust are instrumental in the formation of such beliefs. Indeed, research into political behaviour in the United States and Canada (Basinger and Lavine 2005; Roy 2007) and in the United Kingdom (Bartle 2005), demonstrates how including different levels of political information and knowledge into explanatory models can help researchers to account for citizen heterogeneity and move beyond the 'one model fits all' type approach. Before this is considered, it is illustrative to begin by acknowledging that knowledge and information, despite dictionary definitions, are in fact two separate concepts that could well lead to different outcomes.

8.7.1 Information versus knowledge

According to the Oxford English Dictionary, 'information' is the 'knowledge communicated or received concerning a particular fact or circumstance gained through study, communication, research, instruction, etc.' 'Knowledge', on the other hand, is defined as 'acquaintance with facts, truths, or principles, as from study or investigation; general erudition'. A problem stems from the first definition in so far as information is defined as a function of knowledge which is in turn an expression of facts or truths. A simple move of syllogistic logic would conclude that information must therefore contain facts/truths.

Of course we know this to be false; information could in fact be misinformation. What we can say of information then is that it contains observations and messages regarding a particular event or object. In short, it is the content which informs our minds (whether it is based on facts/truths or not). Knowledge, in contrast, is the human experience of information – it's what our minds do with all that content. Knowledge is therefore present and instrumental in our deliberations as it is believed as useful or factual/truthful; information is merely the message that is received.

8.7.2 Different cognitive orientations towards government

Using the BES 2005, it is possible to measure political knowledge. The survey contains items that measure cognitive awareness of politics and the political process by asking eight questions relating to contemporary political facts. These include questions such as whether it is true or false that the Liberal Democrats policy position is to favour PR as well as other questions such as whether the Chancellor of the Exchequer sets levels of interest rates. By separating the sample into two groups – those with low levels of knowledge (scoring 0 to 2) and those with high (scoring 7 or 8) – the factor analysis in Chapter 6 was re-run to see if people's belief and attitudinal orientation towards government takes on a different structure depending on people's level of political information and knowledge.

Tables 8.9 and 8.10 present the results. As the results demonstrate, for individuals with low levels of political knowledge the nature of the dimensions change. Instead of trust in the Conservative Party and trust in the Liberal Democrat Party representing separate dimensions, it seems that individuals with low political knowledge do not differentiate between the two opposition parties but judge the opposition leaders separately from the two parties. It should also be noted that the 'trust politicians' and 'government is fair' items also load onto the trust opposition leaders dimension.

Performing the same analysis for those with high levels of political knowledge produces a more coherent cognitive map. Table 8.10 shows that such individuals make clear distinctions between the incumbent party in government, the two main opposition parties, and an overall sense of efficacy towards politics.

The above analyses were also performed by creating two separate groups from levels of media usage. Contrasting those who read newspapers and/or use the Internet to search for political information with those who don't or seldom do demonstrates no difference between the structure of trust in government variables. Therefore it seems that is *knowledge* that is the crucial intervening factor.

By combining attitudinal trust scores with levels of political knowledge to create a multiplicative term seems to potentially provide an improved measure to capture heterogeneity within political communities. To test this claim, the following graph presents aggregate levels of voting by different levels of trust and knowledge. It demonstrates how citizen heterogeneity in terms of behaviour is better captured by (1) combining beliefs to gauge latent constructs, that is attitudes, and (2) how interactions of knowledge and attitudes can make a further advance on the former.

Table 8.9 Factor analysis of beliefs in government, Britain 2005 – low political knowledge

	Rotated component			
	1. Trust government	**2. Trust opposition leaders**	**3. Trust opposition parties**	**4. Influence**
Trust Tony Blair	.699			
Trust current government	.854			
Trust Labour Party	.799			
Trust parliament	.734			
Trust politicians	.506	.517		
Trust Michael Howard		.863		
Trust Conservative Party			.883	
Trust Charles Kennedy		.842	.815	
Trust Liberal Democrats			.856	
Democracy satisfaction	.743			
Government is fair	.634	.421		
Influence on politics				.930
Eigenvalue	5.186	1.519	1.165	1.011
% variance explained	43.2	12.7	9.7	8.4

Table 8.10 Factor analysis of beliefs in government, Britain 2005 – high political knowledge

	Rotated Component			
	1. Trust 'Government'	**2. Trust Conservatives**	**3. Trust Lib Dems**	**4. Influence**
Trust Tony Blair	.856			
Trust current government	.832			
Trust Labour Party	.812			
Trust parliament	.740			
Trust politicians	.765			
Trust Michael Howard		.877		
Trust Conservative Party		.851		
Trust Charles Kennedy			.856	
Trust Liberal Democrats			.876	
Democracy satisfaction	.584			
Government is fair	.647			
Influence on politics				.974
Eigenvalue	4.425	1.923	1.293	1.014
% variance explained	36.9	16	10.8	7.5

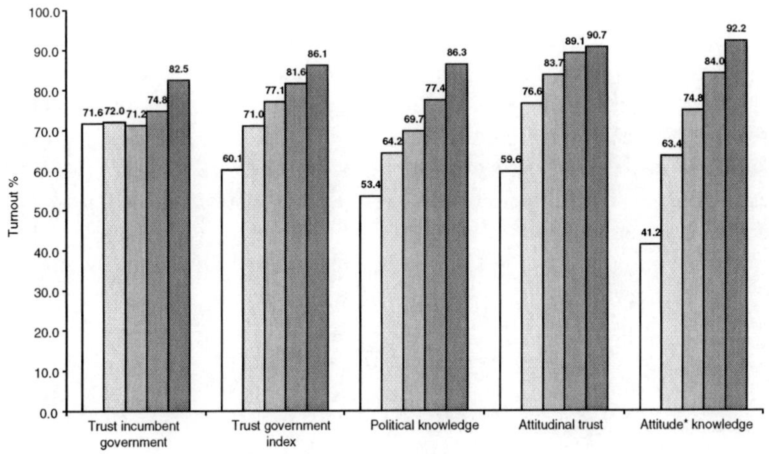

Figure 8.2 General election turnout 2005 by trust and knowledge

Note: * denotes interaction term.

Figure 8.2 outlines turnout levels at the UK general election 2005 by 5-point scale ratings of (1) trust in present government; (2) trust in government index (trust parliament + trust politicians); (3) political knowledge; (4) attitudinal trust; and finally (5) attitudinal trust * knowledge. The obvious feature is that as the trust items move towards more attitudinal scores and finally attitudinal * knowledge, at every step of the way greater heterogeneity within the population is captured. For example, in terms of vote turnout, analysing this outcome by different levels of trust in the incumbent government captures 10.9 per cent variation between the lowest and highest group. Using the multiplicative score of attitudinal trust * knowledge means that 51 per cent of variation can be uncovered in vote turnout, meaning that the politically disengaged can be separated from the very engaged.

Given such results, and given the suggested strong linear impact that trust in government as an attitude has on voting from the previous section, it seems difficult to ignore the potential utility of including such multiplicative scores in models to predict voting turnout at the level of the individual.

8.8 Results – trust and knowledge interactions

A common strategy in quantitative political science is to use regression to test the effects of interaction terms alongside the main effects variables in a model despite reservations about collinearity (Brambor et al. 2005; Bartle 2005). To make the interpretation of the interaction term easier, political knowledge is coded as a binary variable where 0 = low political information and 1 = high political information. Table 8.11 presents the results for the composite model of voting which now includes the interaction of attitudinal trust and knowledge. The main effects of political knowledge and attitudinal trust were significant and positive in the original model, but by adding the interaction term, knowledge has no significant main effects although attitudinal trust still does. The interaction term itself proves to be the strongest indicator in the model, with the positive coefficient suggesting that it is both high levels of knowledge *and* trust in government that promotes higher turnout. This updated model also shows a slight increase in the adjusted R square value (+.014).

Table 8.11 Composite models of political participation + interaction

	Voting	
Variable	**Beta**	**Sig.**
Age	**.166*** **	.000
Gender	**–.057***	.017
Highest education	**.070****	.010
Income	**.096*** **	.000
Ethnicity	**–.083*** **	.000
Unemployed	.008	.717
Personal finances retro	–.002	.947
Social trust	.011	.645
Discuss politics	.035	.198
Interest	**.066***	.019
Which party is best on most important issue	–.013	.610
Parties offer no choice	.031	.198
Voting can change Britain	**.080***	.017
Vote norm	**.083*** **	.000
Political activity – get collective benefits		
Trust Opposition Parties	**.052***	.027
Influence on politics	**.139*** **	.000
Satisfied with democracy	–.042	.095
Knowledge	–.047	.518
Trust govt. attitude	**.145***	.031
Trust * knowledge	**.180***	.043
Adj R Square	.244	
N	1624	

8.9 Different types of social trusters

To recall, social trust is identified through four components: trust in current neighbour, trust in those different from us, a sense of generalised trust, and finally a general perception that people act appropriately. Despite representing underlying attitudes, individuals are also a mixture of these different components of trust. For example, Citizen A might be trusting towards local community members, but be more sceptical about the wider general public. Citizen B however might live in an area that doesn't contain people like himself, but is quite trusting of those from different backgrounds. By employing a statistical clustering technique[1] it is possible to uncover a typology of trusters based on the four dimensions of trust for social orientations.

Table 8.12 presents the results for performing this procedure on the social trust dimensions, and the technique derived three distinct clusters. The first items by which groups are differentiated are the trust neighbourhood and generalised trust scores. As Table 8.12 demonstrates, clusters 1 and 2 highlight predominantly trusting groups as opposed to cluster 3 which is sceptical of others in general.

The next dimension to consider is the extent to which the groups trust others different from themselves. This captures the extent to which individuals are likely to 'bridge' their networks across social differences. As the mean scores suggest, only cluster number 1 contains such individuals. Finally, the appropriate behaviour dimension gauges how often people interact and perceive others to follow basic social rules. Only cluster number 1 contains individuals that perceive this to be the case more often than not.

Taking all of the above information into account, Table 8.13 outlines the different nature of the above clusters. Two groups of trusting clusters exists and one predominantly distrusting group, where the former can be separated into 'bridgers' and 'bonders'. This accords with much of

Table 8.12 Clusters based on social trust items

	1.00	2.00	3.00
Trust neighbourhood (mean)	3.33	4.21	2.51
Generalised trust (mean)	4.11	3.58	1.91
Trust those different (mean)	3.87	2.11	2.39
Appropriate behaviour (mean)	3.44	2.14	2.74
N	942	1134	990

Table 8.13 Typology of social trusters

Cluster Number	Typology
1	Bridging trusters
2	Bonding trusters
3	Distrusters

the conceptual developments in the social capital literature (Putnam 2000: 22–24; Halpern 2005).

The utility of generating typologies of trusters is that a deeper understanding of each individual's orientation towards government and society is provided. Saving each of the clusters as regression variables, it can be tested whether including these nuanced derivations of types of trusters can improve predictions of political behaviour. So in terms of testing whether civic participation has social origins, explanations can be couched in terms of different mixes of levels of social trust in different objects, as opposed to relying on variation of just one trust variable.

8.10 Results – typologies of social trusters

Unlike the knowledge interaction terms, the utility of providing a typology of trusters proved to be of use with both conventional and unconventional acts but not voting.

Table 8.14 presents the results for conventional acts. As the results demonstrate, isolating 'bonding' type trusters improves any predictions on levels of conventional activities (.078*). This represents an improvement on the original model where the attitudinal social trust variable proved to be insignificant. Furthermore, the value of the adjusted R square has improved from the original composite model.

Table 8.15 repeats the model but with unconventional acts as the dependent variable. This time, it is the social 'bridgers' that are more likely to engage (.061*).

These two sets of results highlight the fact that different types of trusters find different types of civic activities to pursue. Whereas the bonders prefer to engage in probably more localised voluntary acts, bridgers seek out less conventional and more wide-reaching political acts that encompass more national and international concerns than local.

Table 8.14 Conventional acts

Variable	**Beta**	**Sig.**
Age	**–.066***	.035
Gender	**–.059****	.008
Highest education	**.156*****	.000
Income	**.050***	.046
Ethnicity	–.004	.867
Retired	**–.074***	.013
Personal finances retro	.006	.790
Bridgers	.036	.169
Bonders	**.078****	.004
Discuss politics	**.146*****	.000
Interest	.025	.350
Knowledge	.042	.083
Parties offer no choice	.002	.945
Broadsheet readers	.019	.409
Political activity – get collective benefits	**.044***	.046
Trust opposition	.021	.349
Influence on politics total	**.143*****	.000
Satisfied with democracy	–.050	.024
Adj R Square	.196	
N	1905	

Table 8.15 Composite model of unconventional acts

Variable	**Beta**	**Sig.**
Age	.004	.990
Gender	–.041	.051
Highest education	**.093*****	.000
Income	.007	.766
Ethnicity	.004	.842
Government treats people like me fairly	**–.072****	.002
In full-time education	–.013	.529
Retired	**–.069***	.014
Personal finances retro	**.043***	.035
Bridgers	**.061***	.014
Bonders	.026	.302
Iraq – success or failure?	**–.074*****	.000
Discuss politics	**.213*****	.000
Interest	**.108*****	.000
Knowledge	.029	.210
Political activity – get collective benefits	**.072*****	.000
Trust government	–.029	.276
Influence on politics	**.099*****	.000
Satisfied with democracy	**–.072*****	.001
Adj R Square	.216	
N	2122	

8.11 Conclusion

This chapter has demonstrated that trust variables have a significant and direct effect on patterns of political behaviour. Indeed, the first set of results highlighted how individual trust items do not always affect behaviour in the same way. Feelings of influence, for example, promotes participation in all three forms of the political behaviours highlighted, whereas increased satisfaction with the political system reduces the likelihood of participating in conventional and unconventional acts. In contrast to political trust variables, social trust was an insignificant predictor of all behaviours.

Following the lead of recent research in North America and Britain, it was possible to highlight heterogeneity amongst the population by separating people by low and high political knowledge. Specifically, the meaning of government changes between the two groups, where the former adopts a general interpretation of government while the latter interprets this to mean the 'government of the day'. Indicating potential interaction effects between knowledge and trust variables, it was deemed useful to explore whether models of political behaviour could be improved using such terms. The results suggest they can. In particular, knowledge interacting with trust variables provides a relatively powerful predictor of vote turnout in Britain.

However, levels of the other two forms of political behaviour outlined in this chapter – conventional and unconventional acts – did not appear to be affected by knowledge and trust interaction terms. Instead, it was demonstrated that heterogeneity at a social as opposed to political level improved predictions of such acts. By employing clustering techniques such heterogeneity was isolated, most notably the difference between social bonders and social bridgers. As an extension of this, localised trust bonders were more inclined to engage in voluntary activities, whereas social bridgers were more likely to engage in the more issue orientated acts of protesting and demonstrating.

9
The Challenge to Political Institutions

Trust is prevalent in our lives but not everywhere. Where incentives are present for people not to harm the interests of others (e.g., driving a car safely), the inductive belief of confidence will guide us through such situations of risk safely. Nonetheless, the moral of this story has been that, all things being equal, cooperating with others on the basis of trust provides more assurances than cooperating without it. Acting as a heuristic in situations of risk, trust subsuming the concept of confidence informs us of the likelihood that our interests will be satisfied and not harmed. Where trust moves beyond confidence is that it also considers information regarding the motives and intentions of relevant others. However, the playing field is not level – human psychology dictates that distrust is presumed more often than it should be, partially a product of what Hollis (1998) labels 'psychological egoism'. The implication is that the idea of 'strong fences making for good neighbours' might reduce risk but it also wastes possibilities for fruitful cooperation.

The unique status of trust relationships is that they possess a moral flavour. In such a context, it is never enough to simply believe that a person or organisation acts in a way that is beneficial to us; we must also believe that they are acting that way *because* it is of benefit to us. This is what makes trust a central concept for some of our most important relationships, such as the bond between friends, partners, business associates, and as we have seen, the governed and government. When trust is missing, such relationships fail to fulfil their full potential.

9.1 Creating trust

In September 1996, only months away from their triumphant general election victory, New Labour produced a document entitled 'Labour

Party: New Politics, New Britain – Restoring trust in the way we are governed'. In the same month, Tony Blair published an article calling for widespread constitutional reform in order to reinvigorate the relationship between the governed and government.[1] Constitutions define the relationship between citizens and political authority and so, in theory, appropriate constitutional changes should promote more trust in government. Pertinent examples of such changes under New Labour include the decentralisation of power and the widespread use of public participation initiatives.[2]

The question of whether political institutions can engineer trust and cultural practices is a prevalent concern for social and political scientists (e.g., see Jackman and Miller 2005). The crux is whether or not public policy can effectively change people's behaviour by overpowering cultural habits, with some arguing that it rarely can (Fukuyama 1995). However, there are numerous instances where public policy does change people's behaviour, in the form of tax incentives for example, so the question is to what *degree* political institutions can be effective.

A caveat is that government policies can sometimes have a negative effect on trust and civic life. For example, Western democracies have embraced globalisation trends and multinational companies, perhaps a form of 'post hoc rationalisation' for pursuing policies designed to stimulate economic growth (see Watson 2004). This seems sensible given that economic growth and social capital reinforce each other (Fukuyama 1995; Whiteley 2000), but scholars argue that a trade-off can exist – the ease by which multinational companies can now locate and open stores can across time actually destroy social capital and civic participation within communities by undermining local and family businesses (Goetz and Rupasingha 2007). It has also been recently demonstrated that in the short term, increasing immigration and social heterogeneity actually reduce levels of social trust and networks, an effect referred to as 'hunkering down' (Putnam 2007).

A further caveat is that the reforms that are the most appropriate to invigorate trust and participation within a society depend on the nature of the society's political culture. Britain is a representative democracy in the sense that representatives are elected by citizens to make decisions on behalf of the public (Held 1996: 7–11). However, by handing to members of parliament (MPs) the right to participate in decision-making, the electorate removes itself from the process of decision-making. As such, the electorate plays no part in the mechanism of decision-making – that process has been handed to MPs and the government.

The forthcoming sections will argue that the challenge to political institutions is to stimulate the precursors of trust as opposed to dangling incentives in front of citizens that encourage trustworthy behaviour only. One of the consistent themes across the empirical results in previous chapters is the association of education, political interest and political knowledge with trust and participation. These represent civic skills, building blocks for civic engagement, and do not directly tackle participation per se. Indeed, the positive cognitive mobilisation effect that these factors have on democratic politics have been most famously emphasised by Verba et al. (1995) and Milner's (2002) notion of civic literacy.

Nonetheless, such factors only represent one-third of the precursors that generate trust and civic engagement. Another crucial area demonstrated by the empirical results are the importance of perceptions of national political parties. Understanding politics through the idiom of a rational choice approach, parties provide a 'general incentive' to engage in conventional forms of politics (Whiteley and Seyd 2002). The problem is that

> declining public confidence in, and respect for, conventional political institutions and procedures has provided a stimulus to alternative forms of politics. Recent well-publicised exercises in protest, particularly against road and airport runway developments, fuel taxes, a ban on fox hunting, and the US-led war in Iraq suggest a greater public willingness to engage in direct action or street demonstrations. Riots in 2001 in Bradford and Oldham provided additional evidence of public disenchantment, particularly among young ethnic minorities, with traditional methods of political participation. (Pattie et al. 2004: preface, xvii)

In other words, citizens are increasingly by-passing the party system as a way of influencing public policy. Indeed, according to data from the BES 2005, 67.3 per cent believe that political parties are either less or no more influential than outside interest groups. If more conventional forms of participation, such as voting and interest in party politics, are to be boosted, then parties need to find ways to provide general incentives to citizens.

Further to this, a society also needs a tight social-psychological base, that is, a widespread common understanding and respect for prevalent social norms promoting collective intentions and civic engagement,

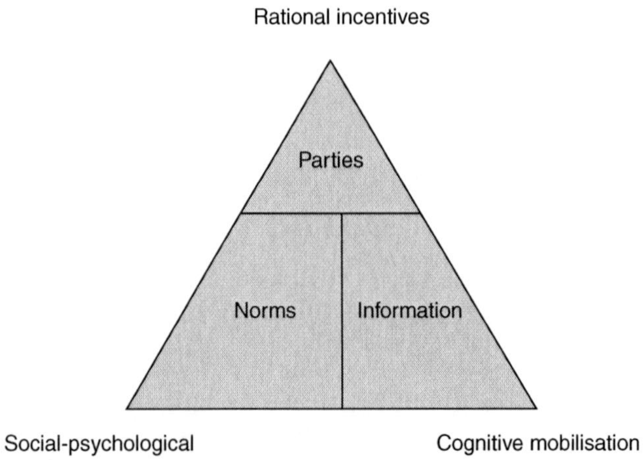

Figure 9.1 Mobilising trust and civic engagement

what Putnam would refer to as the formation of 'we' intentions (2000: 43). We can think of this and the previous two conditions as satisfying social-psychological, cognitive and rational reasons for participating in civic society, as Figure 9.1 illustrates.

A significant proportion of strategies attempting to resolve the trust and participation problem, however, seem to focus far too much on the incentives part, and in ways that only provide specific localised incentives for engagement, not general. Two of these strategies in particular is to bolster the notion of 'e-Democracy' and to use more direct consultation methods.

9.1.1 e-Democracy and direct democracy

The strategies of e-Democracy and direct forms of consultation methods attempt to tackle democratic problems by easing the process of existing political participation channels or by creating new ones. Simply getting more people involved in politics is the overriding aim. Pertinent examples are the various trials that have taken place for different methods of registering a vote. The United Kingdom in recent local and general elections trialled postal balloting as a way of boosting turnout, and the Electoral Reform Society (ERS) recommended that forms of 'e-voting' (via text messaging or the Internet) should be considered if experimentation studies prove them to be effective ways of improving electoral participation (ERS 2003).

If seen as truly effective ways of overcoming low voter turnout then the implication is that citizens are simply too busy or too lazy to vote; convenience is the key to civic engagement. Coupled with making participation in existing channels easier in Britain are clear attempts to also introduce more overt participatory mechanisms into the political process. Since 1997, localised participatory mechanisms such as citizens' juries and deliberative panels have been widely used to test opinion on proposals and provide legitimacy for elected and unelected local policy actors (see Leach 2003 for an extensive overview). At the national level, it was promised that the issues of a European Constitution and Electoral Reform were put to a national referendum.

While direct consultation of the public by government is increasing, these are usually restricted to local governance. In 1999, for example, the council district of Milton Keynes held a referendum of the levels of tax in the area.[3] Even then, more consultation is not the same as more control or even greater influence, and the local nature of such consultation will do little for trust in national political institutions anyway. So despite reforms to enhance direct public consultation since 1997, the political process in Britain still requires an increase in the level of unmediated or direct forms of democracy, particularly for issues that are currently controlled nationally. This seems particularly desirable given the increase in issue-orientated politics,[4] a style of politics that is possibly the result of falling trust in parties and government. But reservations exist over the feasibility of direct democracy at a national level amongst a large population with diverse interests. As Dalton et al. (2004: 150) note:

> On the negative side, one of the greatest problems with direct democracy is that it must reduce all decisions to simple yes-or-no alternatives. Given the complexity of political circumstances in modern societies and the necessity for compromise, expanding the use of such decision making could strain the fabric of democracy. In addition, the structure of direct democracy is deceptively simple, and there are few options for amendment and revision once the public has spoken. *The loss of these deliberative aspects of democracy may lessen the wisdom of democratic decisions.* [italics added]

It is the final point that is crucial. The e-Democracy and direct strategies for participation are not conducive to the democratic virtue of encouraging *considered* and *informed* political judgements and acts. For this to happen, citizens first need the 'resources' to develop trust and a civic inclination (Verba et al. 1995; Milner 2002).

9.2 Mobilising trust, interest and knowledge

In *Voice and Equality*, Verba, Schlozman and Brady (1995) highlight the importance of such 'civic skills' and their development as the crux for civic engagement. One of the defining features of civic skills is that they are generally developed through activities that have no political content, and thus are not simply the *effect* of a predisposition towards political engagement. These skills are the product of certain social resources, particularly education, which enables individuals to ease their way into associational activities. As such, a ubiquitous concern for the authors is an individual's Socio-economic Status (SES). For educated, white-collar workers, civic skills of effective communication and cooperative exchanges are often second nature. Individuals with lower SES, however, are often intimidated by such associational activities. Without developing a habit of attending and participating in g roup meetings, for example, the basic processes of developing an opinion on a public issue and then sharing and evaluating this with others are not automatic.

This suggests that political institutions can confront the problems of trust and civic engagement with a two-pronged strategy: first, creating a predisposition towards civic engagement by stimulating awareness and interest in public matters through formal education structures; second, making sure that the structure of society facilitates as much associational activities as possible so that individuals develop collective 'we' intentions and enhance the civic skills of effective communication (a precursor of trust relationships) and cooperative behaviour.

9.2.1 Education systems

Civic socialisation theories – constructed in terms of providing a civic education in schools – have emerged en-masse in the light of Verba et al.'s (1995) findings (see for example Campbell 2006; Milner 2002; Plutzer 2002; Riedel 2002). One of the reasons that Scandinavian exceptionalism exists is because this group of countries demonstrates comparatively high spending on social services and education, paving the way for civic socialisation effects. Bastions of the 'social democracy' approach to governing society, government policies and institutions are often designed to facilitate levels of civic engagement, and part of this framework is treating education as a common good, as a part of each individual's social citizenship.

A key indication of this is the way public goods such as education are funded in Scandinavia, and the level to which they are funded. Further and Higher Education is funded through general taxation, where students are not charged tuition fees and are offered generous loans and grants. This is reflected in above average spending on education. For example, spending in the EU on Higher Education is on average 1.2 per cent of national income, whereas the same figure in Scandinavia is 1.8 per cent; and this higher than average investment doesn't go to waste. The Programme for International Student Assessment (PISA) run by the OECD collects comparative information on the proficiency of students across the world. One domain of interest is 'reading literacy', defined as an 'understanding, using and reflecting on written texts, in order to achieve one's goals, to develop one's knowledge and potential and to participate in society'. According to their data from 2003, Finland, Sweden and Norway rank far in excess of the OECD average, in comparison to Italy and Spain who lag somewhat behind (data not available for UK).[5] Finland in particular consistently ranks as one of the highest scorers. Further data from 2003 suggests that in world terms, Finnish 15-year-olds are top in mathematics and science as well as reading literacy, and second in 'problem solving'.

Milner (1989) also notes that for countries like Sweden, further measures such as mobile libraries and a subsidised national press are also part of Scandinavian exceptionalism:

> An informed, educated populace...means a significant reduction in uncertainty. Sweden achieves this notably through free public education at all levels, a major effort at adult education, publicly owned communications media, and heavy expenditures on libraries, museums and popular culture. (Milner 1989: 42)

However, the goal of creating greater awareness and interest in public issues isn't merely restricted to the adult population. In Sweden, it has been demonstrated with the use of longitudinal data that social studies courses within secondary schools increase pupils' knowledge of public issues and events (Westholm, Lindquist and Niemi 1990). Esping-Anderson (2002) has also noted that day care institutions in Scandinavian countries are essential for lone parents in avoiding the risks of poverty (by freeing up their time to facilitate employment opportunities) and to also maximise children's possibilities for learning. A 'spill-over' effect of such institutions is that they provide a focal point for children and parents to form local social networks, particularly desirable if such interactions bring together people from different backgrounds.

The UK government, recognising that in relation to Scandinavian countries British society is somewhat lacking in trust and civic engagement, has initiated schemes to address the problem. An increasing concern amongst policy makers in the UK is that the National Curriculum (a framework for educating 5 to 16 year olds) neglects promoting the *virtues* of character that promote good citizenship, which goes beyond merely teaching children political facts. As Crick explains,

> In the 1970s some of us tried to promote programmes in schools with the object of enhancing what was cleverly called 'political literacy' – the knowledge, skills and values need[ed] to be an informed, active and responsible citizens. But, in hindsight, the idea on its own of 'political literacy' was always too narrowly political – or could encourage a narrowing sense of what counted as political, only the activities of the parties, the government and the proceedings in Parliament. However, 'political literacy' is needed in almost any form of group activity; even the skills needed for party or pressure group activity may best be learned in local voluntary groups or, indeed, in free discussions of issues that are real to the pupils and the exercise by them of real responsibilities in school. This is far more important than force-feeding with safe and objective knowledge about the constitution and the machinery of government. (Crick 2002: 496)

The efficacy of such a move is not only reinforced by the obvious benefits of the Scandinavian model, but also by research in Political Science that supports the logical implications of such a policy. Utilising longitudinal data from the United Kingdom, Whiteley (2005) suggests that models of civic participation are significantly shaped by political knowledge and interest as well as exposure to citizenship education, and that in line with 'civic voluntarism' models, these factors are shaped by political interest and educational attainment of parents. Combining both models, Whiteley claims that 'citizenship education appears to have a direct impact on ... rather different forms of participation, even when many other factors are taken into account' (Whiteley 2005: 51). Indeed, the results presented in Chapters 7 and 8 only add to the growing weight of support that encourages attention towards mechanisms that stimulate political interest and knowledge.

Government led programmes designed around the notion of civic literacy then can actually create a disposition towards interest and participation in public affairs in the first place. Some might call it the development of 'habits of the heart' (Bellah et al. 1985). But apart from developing a civic-minded disposition in individuals and giving them access to information required for active citizenship, public policy designed to increase levels of civic literacy will only work if individuals actually feel part of a civic community. This leads us to concerns over social capital and the development of trust and the norm of reciprocity. The next section will demonstrate that the ability to develop these preconditions for active citizens competes with certain economic considerations.

9.2.2 The structure of society

It is often said that the defining characteristic of Scandinavian countries are their commitment to universal welfare programmes (Einhorn and Logue 2004). Equality to all citizens is the guiding principle, and despite some recent departures from this principle, for example supplementary benefits that give greater benefits to those who are in the labour market, the Scandinavian model is still by far the most generous and closest welfare systems there are to being 'universal' (see Bergh 2004; Greve 2004). A corollary of this is that Scandinavian countries are 'exceptional' in terms of their high levels of trust in people and institutions (Delhey and Newton 2005).

Broadly speaking, there are three types of social welfare systems:

- *Conservative* – Average taxes. Security for all at given levels of income. Selective nature means the model is more social insurance than social welfare. (Italy, Spain, France, Germany)
- *Liberal* – Low taxes. Security for the most needy. Selective, means-tested benefits. (Great Britain)
- *Social Democratic* – High taxes. Universal public welfare programmes, with the aims of full employment and generous family support. Focus on equality, not just reducing poverty. (Scandinavia)

(Esping-Anderson 1990)[6]

One notable feature of the above differences in the types of welfare systems is that such divergence has only occurred over the last 40 years. Rothstein points out that 'if we go back to the early 1960s, we can see that these countries [USA and the rest of Western Europe] spent almost the same as a percentage of GDP on welfare policies' (Rothstein 2001: 213–14). The difference in Scandinavian welfare policies then reflect recent changes in institutional practices and are not simply a by-product of cultural underpinnings.

The main reason why countries with universal welfare state programmes have greater levels of civic engagement is that such an approach creates societies with less wealth inequality, compared to the selective liberal and conservative approaches. Prima facie, it seems plausible that redistributive policies specifically targeting the most needy in society would be the most efficient way to reduce poverty. The contrasting approach of providing universal welfare offers all citizens the same benefits, which limits (in relative terms to liberal systems) any direct redistributive effects to poorest in society.

The empirical evidence suggests that this is not the case – societies covered by universal welfare programmes are far less likely to suffer from poverty (Swank 2002). The important element here is adherence to the principle of equality. Universal programmes treat everyone in the same situation as equals. Benefit claimants are not treated differently based on whether a threshold is met that identifies them as sufficiently poor enough to require financial assistance from the state. By treating them differently as in selective programmes, this can reinforce the view that the least privileged in society are being looked after by the privileged. This can have the effect of either categorising the poor as simply incapable of looking after themselves, which promotes a sense of social superiority amongst the privileged, or even worse, they are categorised as free-riders – people who live off the efforts of others. Indeed, there is evidence to suggest that means-tested programmes reflect a lack of trust and social cohesion within populations, where an in-group (privileged class) and out-group (least privileged) status exists, leading to the latter sometimes being classed as 'lazy' (Gilens 1999). So by employing selective measures in terms of welfare programmes, public institutions are effectively stigmatising welfare benefits (Kumlin and Rothstein 2005).

This is why universal welfare programmes are more likely to be condoned by the middle classes (Svallfors 1997). The state by not making selective distinctions between the poor and the 'deserving' poor, and instead working from the premise of welfare as a right of citizenship, constructs benefit systems in terms that appeal to a broad coalition across the social spectrum. For example, during when the more conservative and right-wing parties have been in power in Scandinavia, these governments did not alter the universal nature of their welfare systems, and at no point did their voting publics demand they do so (Huber and Stephens 2001).

Apart from reinforcing divisions between the 'haves' and 'have nots', the actual experience of claimants on means-tested benefits compared to those on universal programmes can be somewhat degrading. In order for discretionary decisions to be made in selective systems, officials are required to decide which deprived groups are the most deserving of help, a process that often intrudes on the private lives and personal integrity of claimants when being interviewed (Rothstein 1998). This has a significant negative effect on people's ability to trust others in general. A survey conducted in Sweden asked respondents about their experience of the few selective welfare programmes, for example housing benefits (see Bengtsson 2001). The results suggest that controlling for education, social class, income, civic engagement, interest in politics, general happiness, political ideology (left-right), and job market status (employed or unemployed), the minority of Swedes with experience of selective programmes had significantly lower social trust in comparison to the rest of the population (Kumlin and Rothstein 2005).

This issue is further compounded by the fact that ethnic minorities, especially in relatively unequal countries like Britain and the United States, are usually over represented in terms of measures of deprivation and as recipients of welfare benefits (Modood et al. 1997; Ratcliffe et al. 2001). This means that for some sections of the population, the stigmatising effects of selective welfare systems only make it harder for such groups to successfully integrate into a political community.

9.2.3 Creating general incentives through the party system

While in theory Britons elect individual candidates to represent their constituencies, the de facto situation in Britain has been that the *party* provides individual candidates with a moral resource for governance. Furthermore, within the political process, factors such as the whip system make MPs subordinate to parties in relation to agenda setting and parliament less effective in scrutinising government policy (Holzhacker 2002: 24–6). But the empirical chapters suggest that this style of governance is at odds with a public deeply sceptical of the motives of political parties and a party system that constrains political choice. So if trust in government is to be restored, and parties are to provide general incentives, then a period of party realignment has to take place in order to boost party competition and improve the representation of the spectrum of interests.

As was highlighted in Chapter 8, the increasingly instrumental rationality of parties has meant that the three main parties in Britain have converged, ideologically speaking, on centre ground politics (Dalton 1996: 149–56). And the British public have responding accordingly. Figure 9.2 demonstrates that the public have increasingly perceived Labour and the Conservatives to be less and less different. The trend suggests that 1992 was the last election that any significant difference

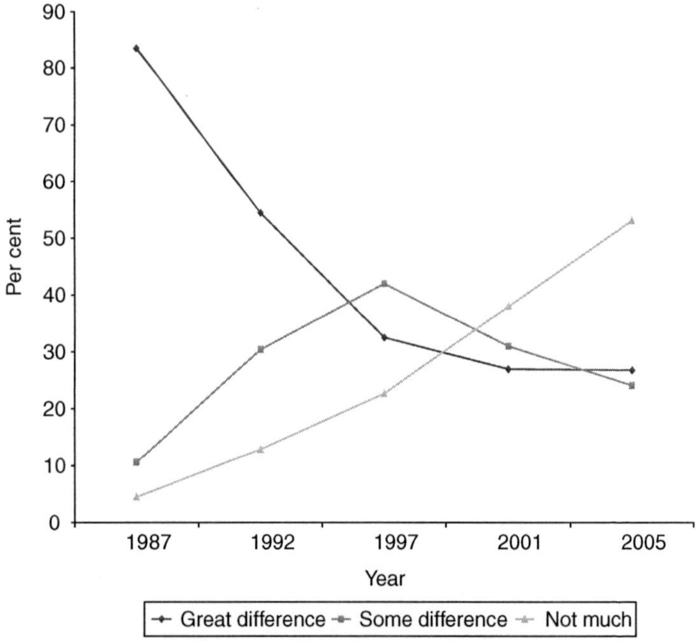

Figure 9.2 Perceived difference between the two main parties
Sources: BES cross-section surveys 1987, 1992, 1997, 2001, 2005.

was perceived to exist between the two main parties. By 1997, the modal response was 'only some difference' as opposed to 'a great deal of difference' in 1987 and 1992, and by 2001, the modal response was 'not much difference at all' which has continued to increase to the point where in 2005, over 50 per cent of the electorate believe this to be the case.

Accommodating the opinions of the majority of the public (as opposed to representing ideas and interests) has led to a concern of 'populist' governance by parties and an increasing reliance on 'spin' to put over a good message. As the public has become more aware of this party political strategy, trust in the institution of government fell.

But while accommodating views ostensibly appears more democratic, the effect is to stifle political interest in elections. Indeed, the relatively low turnouts of 59 per cent and 62 per cent in 2001 and 2005 suggests that voters actually have less incentive to vote in general elections. This can be gauged by asking whether or not individuals 'care who wins the general election'. Figure 9.3 demonstrates that between 1992 and 1997

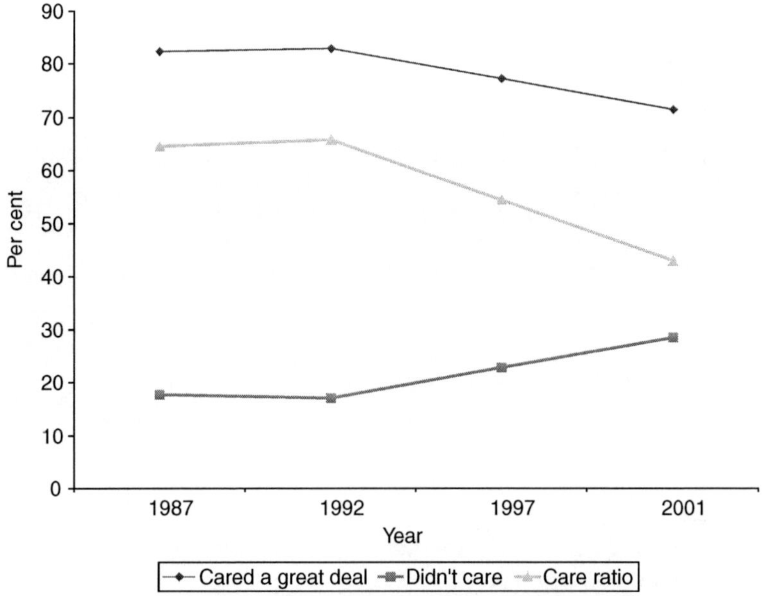

Figure 9.3 Do respondents care which party wins the next general election?

and 1997 and 2001, a clear trend of increasing indifference to election outcomes exists. By 2001, nearly a third of the voting public didn't care who won the general election (unfortunately the same question was not asked in the 2005 BES).

Equally as alarming is the data presented in Figure 9.4. The current disaffection with parties and voting coupled with Britain's single member, simple plurality voting system has led to government's being elected with record low percentages of the vote. So, in the 1997 general election for example, around 31 per cent of all eligible voters had voted for a New Labour candidate. The same figure in 2005 was barely 22 per cent – a scenario where not even a quarter of the electorate actually voted for the party that formed the government. Even if we present the same figure for 2005 by all of those who actually voted (as opposed to all of those *eligible* to vote), New Labour's mandate for government is on the basis of only 35.2 per cent share of the vote in the United Kingdom. A further concern is that in England, Labour acquired 286 English seats, while the Conservative acquired 193 – this despite the fact that the Conservatives actually won 35.7 per cent of the vote, compared to Labour's 35.4 per cent. One can therefore rightfully question whether

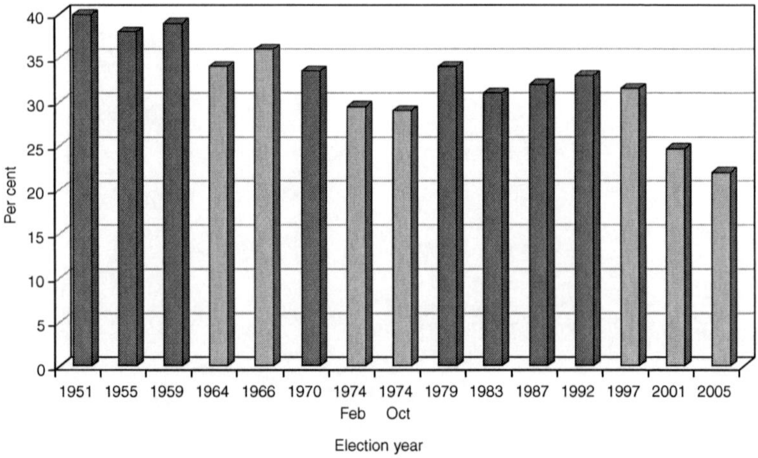

Figure 9.4 Percentage of eligible electorate that voted for winning party

under such circumstances the government of the day actually has a meaningful mandate to govern on.

As such, the rationality of party competition and the nature of the voting system then has led British politics to a situation where (1) little difference is perceived between the two main parties and (2) governments end up governing on a minority share of the vote.

Given the nature of party competition, it seems unlikely that the main parties will realign in order to create greater party competition. Tailoring party policy to accommodate the opinions of floating voters is by far the preferred strategy as there are 'few grounds for supposing that a rational party leadership would view preference-shaping strategies as...less certain or less effective than equivalent accommodative strategies' (Dunleavy and Ward 1981: 377). Party realignment then needs to be externally imposed on the political system. An effective way of doing so is to change the electoral system to alter the way votes are transferred into number of seats in Parliament. Furthermore, it can be changed in a way to reflect more fairly the opinions of voters and to reduce the problem of a lack of democratic mandate given to government.

A possible corrective is to introduce a proportionally representative (PR) electoral system. Opinion polls indicate that 'arrogance' was one characteristic consistently attributed to Margaret Thatcher, likewise Tony Blair.[7] The large majorities that the current electoral system handed to the Tory governments of 1983 and 1987 as well as the New Labour governments of 1997 and 2001 undoubtedly allowed for this criticism as the two leaders were able to push through record levels of legislation. But increasingly, the public have expressed reservations about the current electoral system. According to BES data, those in favour of the current electoral system in 1987 stood at 58 per cent, a figure which more than halved to 25.2 per cent in 2005. Of the remaining 74.8 per cent, over 62 per cent were in favour of introducing a proportional electoral system.

9.2.4 Disengaged and critical citizens

The introduction of this book posed three possibilities regarding declining trust of government in Britain:

- Citizens want to be politically aware and participate but feel it is not worth the effort.
- Lower trust reflects nothing more than a healthy increase of critical citizens.
- Falling trust in government is within the context of general political apathy.

The evidence presented in previous chapters overwhelmingly suggests that the first characterisation is the most accurate. It is entirely plausible that citizens in Britain are also 'critical' of government; more information is available on public matters and the previous empirical analyses demonstrated that higher levels of political information and knowledge actually promote less trust in government. The final characterisation that general political apathy is on the rise finds no support. Trust in other public institutions like the police and the media have remained stable across time. Only government demonstrates falling trust.

Abstention at the 2001 general election was generally regarded as a rational response to the fact that another Labour victory was as good as guaranteed. As one commentator noted, 'just provide the voters with a closely fought election at which a great deal is at stake and, make no mistake, they will again turn out in their droves' (King 2001). A similar scenario provided the backdrop for the 2005 general election with an equally low turnout (see Bartle and King (eds) 2006, for an overview). But while it seems future elections in Britain will be more closely fought as New Labour's popularity wanes, it is not yet clear that the main political parties will be able to convince the British public that a great deal is actually at stake. The permanent campaign for the median voter guarantees this and guarantees that government is unworthy of the public's trust.

Notes

Introduction

1. '"Trust me" says Blair over funding row', *The Daily Telegraph*, Monday 17 November 1997.
2. 'Tony Blair: A mandate for change', Election 2001 Special Report, *The Guardian*, Tuesday 8 May 2001.
3. A Guardian and ICM survey 18 August 2004: 52 per cent trust neither the government nor the BBC to tell the truth over its position on the war in Iraq.
4. Speech given in Sedgefield. See http://www.number-10.gov.uk/output/Page5461.asp
5. See www.mori.com/sri/pdf/final.pdf
6. Known as Clause IV within the Labour Party's constitution, originally adopted in 1918 and amended in 1929.
7. See Hollis (1998) for an exposition of how a presumption of 'psychological egoism' undermines the perceived trustworthiness of others thus denying cooperative behaviour.
8. See Evans (1999) for a discussion on the topic, especially chapters 3, 5, and 12.
9. See www.mori.com/sri/pdf/final.pdf

1 The Meaning of Trust

1. Inglehart (1999) uses trust, confidence and respect interchangeably.
2. An important question is whether 'we' rationalities develop because of an irreducible cultural aspect (Ostrom 1990), iterated interaction (Axelrod 1984), or through a mixture of both (Putnam 1993).
3. Specifically, the potential for opportunism and the assumption of bounded rationality form the premise of Transaction Cost Economics, an influential theory designed to explain the behaviour of firms and organisations within Neo-Institutional Economics. See O.E. Williamson, (1979), 'Transaction-Cost Economics: The Governance of Contractual Relations', in *Journal of Law and Economics*, 22: 233–62.
4. And it seems the public doesn't. See Felicity Lawrence, *The Guardian*, 10 May 2003, '82% back clampdown on child food advertisements'. According to ICM polls, only 38% of the public trust government vis-à-vis advice on food safety.
5. A recent survey suggests that 90% of Britons do not trust government with personal data. See: 'Love All, Trust a Few', Data Encryption Systems, February 2008. Electronic copy: www.deslock.com/downloads/DES_Research_love_all_trust_a_few_Feb_08.pdf

6. Or, to use Hardin's (2002) characterisation, it is 'cognitive knowledge'. This is not to argue that emotions are not involved, but they are either prior to, or a consequence of, a belief of trust. For an analysis of trust as an emotion, see J.M. Barbalet, 'Social Emotions: Confidence, Trust and Loyalty', *International Journal of Sociology and Social Policy* 16, 1996, pp. 75–96.
7. That is, an individual acts from an intention that has taken the relevant other's interests into consideration.
8. This is to acknowledge that trust always has a 'moral flavour'. For the actors involved, the trusted has a duty to fulfil the trust placed in them simply because a promise has been made. See Hollis (1998: 5–8).
9. For example, Gambetta (1988: 217) defines trust as 'a particular level of subjective probability with which an agent assesses that another agent or group of agents will perform a particular action'. Assigning probabilities to an agent – perhaps important in the logic of trust – does not actually capture the essence of trust.
10. Default strategies involve the adoption of a presumption, and we do so in the absence of sufficient information but under the pressure of a choice.
11. Putnam (1993) would argue that individuals in Northern Italy are predisposed to employing trusting strategies while those of the South are pre-disposed to employing distrusting strategies.

2 The Role and Maintenance of Trust

1. The distinction refers to the analytic separation Herbert Simon made between substantive and procedural rationality. The former assesses whether an individual has achieved his goals/objectives (agents as satisficers), whereas the latter takes into account an 'interrupt mechanism' that emphasises the state of an individual's mind. See Herbert Simon (1967). See also Marcus et al. (2000) for advancements in procedural accounts of rationality with the introduction of 'affective intelligence'.
2. Furthermore, we can question the nature of the agent itself as posited within rational choice accounts that emphasise social sanctions. Marcus et al. (2000: 53–8) question the ability of individuals to consciously calculate the co-occurrence of events and outcomes and their associated costs and benefits. Even if social sanctions do exist, agents invariably find it difficult to rationally evaluate their presence.
3. However, it seems plausible that shame can be turned into guilt, a point not discussed here.
4. Kohlberg (1976) argues that all human beings pass through three major levels in our intellectual development: (1) the pre-conventional level, where individuals obey rules out of fear of punishment or some similar self-interest; (2) the conventional level, in which individuals are able to grasp basic ethical concepts like the Golden Rule; and finally (3) the post-conventional level, where individuals reason in terms of abstract notions like individual rights.
5. A maxim is an internalised rule of conduct.

6. This is to say that a truster must believe a trusted to possess a 'good will', a point originally made by Aristotle in Book II of *Rhetoric* (translation from Barnes 1984: 2194).
7. See Hollis (1998) for a rejection of such an assumption in social and political theory.
8. The mean trust score presented is the aggregated average of trust in politicians and trust in parliament combined from a ten-point scale. Turnout out figures are based on the most recent elections for legislative assemblies between 2003 and 2007.

3 Frameworks of Trust

1. The Statistics for Canada website is particularly good for compiling comparative immigration statistics. See www.statcan.ca/english/census96/nov4/imm2b.htm
2. Adams's theory of inequity (1963) states that a sense of injustice arises through job-related comparisons (for example, between office colleagues) where a discrepancy exists between the individuals perceived job inputs (time, effort, skill application) and job outputs (wages and worth to the company). Homans' concept of distributive justice (1961) expands the notion of comparisons between individuals (and only individuals) beyond merely the workplace where the rewards received by an individual should be proportional to his/her costs.
3. See table 2.1 in Dalton (1996: 24) for evidence of the widespread reliance on television for political information.
4. A theory central to this proposition is the 'Political Business Cycle' (PBC; see Nordhaus 1975; Alesina, Roubini and Cohen 1997). It states that in the run-up to an election governments manipulate the economy so as to acquire a greater percentage of votes. Essentially, they want the electorate to remember as they walk into their voting booths that, above all, the current government can 'deliver' – that it has a record of performing well.

4 Comparative Overview: Trust and Civic Cultures

1. This Schumpeterian style of democracy is also referred to as a 'procedural' view (Talisse 2005: 2).
2. For the non-specialist reader, regression analysis is a statistical technique that analyses the correlation between a set of explanatory variables (e.g., age, gender, education) and a dependent variable (e.g., trust in government). Tables are produced listing a series of correlations between each explanatory variable and the dependent variable. Its main strength is that the list of correlations represent the negative or positive impact for each of the explanatory variables whilst controlling for the impact of all the others in the model. The technique thereby isolates the 'pure' statistical relationship between each explanatory variable and the dependent variable.

5 Exploring Trust: A Critique

1. As Hardin notes (1998: 35): 'Varied conceptions of trust – if they are explanatory or grounded in explanatory theory – are what we probably want at this stage of research'.
2. Primarily determined by an individual's level of *anxiety* towards objects and stimuli. See Marcus et al. (2000: 5–12).
3. For example, Andrew Grice, 'Blair's Bloody Legacy: Iraq', *The Independent* Newspaper, 1 May 2007.

7 Explaining Trust in Britain

1. See: http://news.bbc.co.uk/1/hi/uk_politics/3121512.stm
2. This figure doesn't include those affiliated, which is why the membership levels for Labour in Figure 7.1 look underestimated in comparison to Conservative Party figures.

8 Trust and Political Behaviour

1. The 'Two-Step' Clustering technique in SPSS 12 employed here uses a sequential clustering approach. It scans the data records one by one and decides if the current record should be merged with the previously formed clusters or start a new cluster based on a distance criterion.

9 The Challenge to Political Institutions

1. See 'Tony Blair: Blair on the Constitution', *The Economist*, 14 September 1996.
2. See New Labour Manifesto for the 1997 General Election, which states that New Labour 'will clean up politics, decentralise political power throughout the United Kingdom and put the funding of political parties on a proper and accountable basis'. Electronic copy available at: http://www.labour-party.org.uk/manifestos/1997/
3. See http://www.local.odpm.gov.uk/research/council/08.htm
4. A consequence (or possibly a contributing factor) of the decline in political parties is that single issue politics offers the most direct route into political activities. See Edwards, L. (2001), 'Politics not Parties', paper for the *Institute for Public Policy Research*: *Young People and Political Engagement*, March 2001. Electronic copy. http://www.ippr.org.uk/research/files/team22/project46/politic.pdf
5. See http://pisacountry.acer.edu.au/
6. Others have developed four types of welfare systems, see Leibfried (1993).
7. ICM polls indicate that between October 1997 and October 2000 the number of people believing Blair to be arrogant rose from 21 per cent to 42 per cent. For the same time period, the number agreeing that Blair 'understands people like me' fell from 65 per cent to 27 per cent.

Bibliography

Abramson, P. R. and Inglehart, R. (1995), *Value Change in Global Perspective*, Ann Arbor, MI: University of Michigan Press.

Ackerlof, George A. (1997), 'Social Distance and Social Decisions', in *Econometrica* LXV: pp. 1005–27.

Adams, J. S. (1963), 'Toward an Understanding of Inequity', *Journal of Abnormal and Social Psychology* 67: pp. 422–36.

Ahn, T. K. (2002), 'Trust and Collective Action: Concepts and Causalities', paper presented at the 2002 meeting of the American Political Science Association, Boston, MA, 28 August–1 September.

Akcomak, S. (2008), 'The Impact of Social Capital on Crime: Evidence from the Netherlands', paper presented at the JESS seminar, ISER, University of Essex, 7 May 2008.

Alesina, A., Roubini, N. and Cohen, G. (1997), *Political Cycles and the Macroeconomy*, Cambridge, MA: MIT Press.

——. and La Ferrara, E. (2002), 'Who Trusts Others?' *Journal of Public Economics* 85(2): pp. 207–34.

Allison, G. T. (1971), *Essence of Decision: Explaining the Cuban Missile Crisis*, Boston, MA: Little, Brown and Company.

Allison, S. T. and Messick, D. M. (1990), 'Social Decision Heuristics in the Use of Shared Resources', *Journal of Behavioral Decision Making* 3: pp. 195–204.

Allport, G. W. (1954), *The Nature of Prejudice*, Cambridge, MA: Addison-Wesley.

Almond, G. A. and Verba, S. (1963), *The Civic Culture: Political Attitudes and Democracy in Five Nations*, Princeton, NJ: Princeton University Press.

Aronson, E. (1999), 'Adventures in Experimental Social Psychology: Roots, Branches, and Sticky New Leaves', in Rodrigues, A. and Levine, O. V. (eds), *Reflections on 100 years of Experimental Social Psychology*, New York: Basic Books.

Arrow, K. J. (1972), 'Gifts and Exchanges', *Philosophy and Public Affairs* 1(4): pp. 343–67.

——. (1974), *The Limits of Organization*, New York: W. W. Norton and Co.

Aust, R. (2003), 'Ethnicity and Drug Use: Key Findings From the 2001/2002 British Crime Survey', UK Home Office Report, 209. Electronic copy. Available at: http://www.homeoffice.gov.uk/rds/pdfs2/r209.pdf

Axelrod, R. (1984), *The Evolution of Cooperation*, New York: Basic Books.

——. (1997), *The Complexity of Cooperation*, Princeton, NJ: Princeton University Press.

Bacharach, M. and Gambetta, D. (2001), 'Trust in Signs', in Cook, K. S. (ed.), *Trust in Society*, New York: Russell Sage Foundation.

Baier, A. (1986), 'Trust and Antitrust', *Ethics* 96: pp. 231–60.

Barber, B. (1983), *The Logic and Limits of Trust*, New Brunswick, NJ: Rutgers University Press.

Barbalet, J. M. (1996), 'Social Emotions: Confidence, Trust and Loyalty', *International Journal of Sociology and Social Policy* 16: pp. 75–96.

Barnes, J. (ed.) (1984), *The Complete Works of Aristotle: The Revised Oxford Translation*. 2 vols. The Jowett Copyright Trustees. Princeton, NJ: Princeton University Press.

Baron, A. and Byrne, D. (1984), *Social Psychology: Understanding Human Interaction*, 4th edition, Boston: Allyn and Bacon.

Barrett C. (1997), 'Idea Gaps, Object Gaps, and Trust Gaps in Economic Development', *Journal of Developing Areas* 31: pp. 553–68.

Barro, R. J. (1991), 'Economic Growth in a Cross Section of Countries', *Quarterly Journal of Economics* 106: pp. 407–33.

Barry, B. (1970), *Economists, Sociologists, and Democracy*, London: Collier-Macmillan.

Bartels, L. (2003), 'Economic Inequality and Political Representation', paper for the Russell Sage Foundation Project on the Social Dimensions of Inequality, Princeton, NJ: Princeton University.

Bartle, J. (1998), Models of the 1992 British General Election, PhD Thesis, Department of Government, University of Essex.

——. (2001), 'The Measurement of Party Identification in Britain: Where Do We Stand Now?' in Jon Tonge et al. (eds), *British Elections and Parties Review*, Vol. 11. London: Frank Cass.

——. (2004), 'Not All Voters Are the Same: The Impact of Knowledge in the 2001 General Election', paper presented at the Elections, Public Opinion, and Parties (EPOP) Conference, 2004.

——. (2005), 'Homogeneous Models and Heterogeneous Voters', *Political Studies* 53(4): pp. 653–75.

——. and Griffiths, D. (2001), *Political Communication Transformed: From Morrison to Mandelson*, London: Palgrave.

——. and King, A. (eds) (2006), Britain at the Polls, 2005, Washington DC: CQ Press.

Basinger, S. J. and Lavine, H. (2005), 'Ambivalence, Information, and Electoral Choice', *American Political Science Review* 99: pp. 169–84.

Beck, U. (1992), *Risk Society: Towards a New Modernity*, London: Sage.

Bellah, R. N. (1985), *Habits of the Heart: Individualism and Commitment in American Life*, Berkeley: University of California Press.

Bengtsson, Bo (2001), 'Solving the Tenants' Dilemma: Collective Action and Norms of Co-operation in Housing', *Housing, Theory and Society* 17(1): pp. 175–87.

Berg, J., Dickhaut, J. and McCabe, K. (1995), 'Trust, Reciprocity and Social History', *Games and Economic Behavior* 10: pp. 122–42.

Bergh, Andreas. (2004), 'The Universal Welfare State: Theory and the Case of Sweden', *Political Studies* 52: pp. 745–66.

Berkman, L. F. and Glass, T. (2000), 'Social Integration, Social Networks, Social Support, and Health', in Berkman, L. F. and Kawachi, I. (eds), *Social Epidemiology*, New York: Oxford University Press, pp. 137–73.

Birch, A. H. (1993), *The Concepts and Theories of Modern Democracy*, London: Routledge.

Blackburn, S. (1998), 'Trust, Cooperation, and Human Psychology', in Braithwaite, V. and Levi, M. (eds), *Trust and Governance*, New York: Russell Sage Foundation.

Blau, M. (1964), *Exchange and Power in Social Life*, New York: John Wiley & Sons.

Bok, D. (1997), 'Measuring the Performance of Government', in Nye, J., Zelikow, P. and King, D. (eds), *Why People Don't Trust Government*, Cambridge, MA: Harvard University Press.

Bourdieu, P. (1997), 'The Forms of Capital', in Halsey, A., Lauder, H., Brown, P. and Stuart Wells, A. (eds), *Education: Culture, Economy and Society*, Oxford: Oxford University Press.

Braithwaite, Valerie. (1998), 'Communal and Exchange Trust Norms, Their Value Base and Relevance to Institutional Trust', in Braithwaite, V. and Levi, M. (eds), *Trust and Governance*, New York: Russell Sage, pp. 46–74.

Brambor T., Clark, W.R. and Golder, M. (2005). 'Understanding Interaction Models: Improving Empirical Analyses', *Political Analysis* 14: pp. 63–82.

Bromiley, P. and Cummings, L. L. (1996), 'The Organisational Trust Inventory', in Kramer, R. M. and Tyler, T. R. (eds), *Trust in Organisations: Frontiers of Theory and Research*, Thousand Oaks, CA: Sage Publications, pp. 302–30.

Bromley, C., Curtice, J. and Seyd, B. (2001), 'Political Engagement, Trust and Constitutional Reform', in Park, A., Curtice, J., Thomson, K., Jarvis, L. and Bromley, C. (eds), *British Social Attitudes – the 18th Report: Public Policy, Social Ties*, London: Sage.

Budge, I., Crewe, I. and Farlie, D. (eds) (1976), *Party Identification and Beyond: Representations of Voting and Party Competition*, New York: Wiley.

Burt, R. S. and Knez, M. (1995), 'Kinds of Third-Party Effects on Trust', *Rationality & Society* 7(3): pp. 255–92.

Campbell, A., Converse, P. E., Miller, W. E. and Stokes, D. E. (1960), *The American Voter*, New York: John Wiley.

Campbell, D. E. (2006), *Why We Vote: How Schools and Communities Shape Our Civic Life*, Princeton, NJ: Princeton University Press.

Carens, J. (2000), *Culture, Citizenship and Community, A Contextual Exploration of Justice as Evenhandedness*, New York: Oxford University Press.

Child, D. (1990), *The Essentials of Factor Analysis*, 2nd edition, London: Cassel Educational.

——. (2006), *The Essentials of Factor Analysis*, 3rd edition, London: Continuum.

Chong, D. (2000), *Rational Lives*, Chicago: University of Chicago Press.

Citrin, J. (1974), 'The Political Relevance of Trust in Government', *American Political Science Review* 68: pp. 973–88.

——. and Green, D. P. (1986), 'Political Leadership and the Resurgence of Trust in Government', *British Journal of Political Science* 16: pp. 431–53.

Clarke, H., Sanders, D., Stewart, M. and Whiteley, P. (2003), 'Britain (not) at the Polls, 2001', *PS: Political Science and Politics* XXXVI: pp. 59–64.

Clarke, H. D., Sanders, D., Stewart, M. C. and Whiteley, P. (2004), *Political Choice in Britain*, Oxford: Oxford University Press.

Coleman, J. (1990), *Foundations of Social Theory*, Cambridge, MA: Harvard University Press.

Cook, K. S. (2004), 'Networks, Norms and Trust: The Social Psychology of Social Capital', *Social Psychology Quarterly* 68(1): pp. 4–14.

Crewe, I., Särlvik, B. and Alt, J. (1977), 'Partisan Dealignment in Britain 1964–1974', *British Journal of Political Science* 7: pp. 129–90.

——. and Thomson, K. (1999), 'Party Loyalties: Dealignment or Realignment?' in Evans, G. and Norris, P. (eds), *Critical Elections: British Parties and Voters in Long-Term Perspective*, London: Sage, pp. 64–86.

Crick, B. (2002), 'Education for Citizenship: The Citizenship Order', *Parliamentary Affairs*, 55.

Crozier, M., Huntington, S. P. and Watanuki, J. (1975), *The Crisis of Democracy*, New York: New York University Press.

Culver, K. (2003), 'Calling All Citizens: The Challenges of Public Consultation', paper presented at the Annual Conference of the Canadian Political Science Association, Halifax, 30 May–1 June 2003.

Curran, J. and Seaton, J. (1985), *Power Without Responsibility*, 2nd edition, London: Routledge

Curtice, J., Seyd, B., Park, A. and Thomson, K. (2000), 'Fond Hearts and Wise Heads? Attitudes to Proportional Representation Following the 1999 Scottish and Welsh Elections', Centre for Research into Elections and Social Trends (CREST), Working Paper Number 80.

Dahl, R. A. (1982), *Dilemmas of Pluralist Democracy: Autonomy vs. Control*, New Haven, CT: Yale University Press.

Dalton, R. J. (1996), *Citizen Politics: Public Opinion and Political Parties in Advanced Western Democracies*, Chatham, NJ: Chatham House.

——. (1999), 'Political Support in Advanced Industrial Democracies', in Norris, P. (ed.), *Critical Citizens*, Oxford: Oxford University Press.

——. (2002), *Citizen Politics: Public Opinion and Political Parties in Advanced Industrial Democracies*, 3rd edition, Chatham, NJ: Chatham House.

——., Burklin, W. and Drummond, A. (2001), 'Public Opinion and Direct Democracy', *Journal of Democracy* 12(4): pp. 141–53.

——., Scarrow, S. and Cain, B. (2004), 'Advanced Democracies and the New Politics', *Journal of Democracy* 15(1): pp. 124–38.

Dasgupta, P. (1988), 'Trust as a Commodity', in Gambetta, D. (ed.), *Trust: Making and Breaking Cooperative Relations*, New York: B. Blackwell, pp. 49–72.

Davis, R. and Owen, D. (1999), *New Media and American Politics*, Oxford: Oxford University Press.

Delhey, J. and Newton, K. (2003), 'Who Trusts? The Origins of Social Trust in Seven Societies', *European Societies* 5(2): pp. 93–137.

——. and Newton, K. (2005), 'Predicting Cross-national Levels of Social Trust: Global Pattern or Nordic Exceptionalism?' *European Sociological Review* 21: pp.311–27.

Deutsch, M. (1958), 'Trust and Suspicion', *Journal of Conflict Resolution* 2: pp. 265–79.

Di Palma, G. (1970), *Apathy and Participation: Mass Politics in Western Societies*, New York: The Free Press.

Diener, E. (2000), 'Subjective Well-Being: The Science of Happiness and a Proposal for a National Index', *American Psychologist* 55(1): pp. 34–43.

Dionne, E. J. (1991), *Why Americans Hate Politics*, New York: Simon and Schuster.

Dobel, P. J. (1990), 'Integrity in the Public Service', *Public Administration Review* 50(3): pp. 354–66.

Douglas, M. (1992), *Risk and Blame: Essays in Cultural Theory*, London: Routledge.

Downes, B. T. (1968), 'Social and Political Characteristics of Riot Cities: A Comparative Study', *Social Science Quarterly* 49(3) (December), pp. 504–20.

Downs, A. (1957), *An Economic Theory of Democracy*, Boston: Addison WesleyDowns.

Dryzek, J. (2000), *Deliberative Democracy and Beyond. Liberals, Critics and Contestations*, Oxford: Oxford University Press.
Dunleavy, P. and Ward, H. (1981), 'Exogenous Voter Preferences and Parties with State Power: Some Internal Problems of Economic Theories of Party Competitio', *British Journal of Political Science* 11: pp. 351–80.
Durkheim, E. (1933), *The Division of Labor in Society*, New York: The Free Press.
Easton, D. (1965), *A Systems Analysis of Political Life*, New York: John Wiley and Sons.
Eckstein, H., Fleron, F. J., Hoffmann, E. P. and Reisinger, W. M. (1998), *Can Democracy Take Root in Post-Soviet Russia? Explorations in State-Society Relations*, Lanham, MD: Rowman & Littlefield.
Edwards, B., Foley, M. and Diani, M. (2001), *Beyond Tocqueville: Civil Society and the Social Capital Debate in Comparative Perspective*, Hanover, New Hampshire: University Press of New England.
Einhorn, E. S. and Logue, J. (2004), 'Can the Scandinavian Model Adapt to Globalization?' *Scandinavian Studies* 76 (Winter): pp. 501–34.
Electoral Reform Society (ERS) (2003), *Piloting Alternative Voting Methods in the 2003 Local Elections in England*, a report by the Electoral Reform Society (June 2003). Available online http://www.electoral-reform.org.uk/publications/briefings/pilotingalternativevotingmethods.htm. Last accessed 01/06/07.
Elster, J. (1983), *Explaining Technical Change*, Cambridge: Cambridge University Press.
——. (1989), *The Cement of Society: a Study of Social Order*, Cambridge: Cambridge University Press.
——. (1999), *Alchemies of the Mind: Rationality and the Emotions*, Cambridge: Cambridge University Press.
——. and Hylland, A. (eds) (1986), *Foundations of Social Choice Theory*, Cambridge: Cambridge University Press.
Erikson, R. S., MacKuen, M. B. and Stimson, J. A. (2002), *The Macro Polity*, New York: Cambridge University Press.
Esping-Anderson, G. (1990), *The Three Worlds of Welfare Capitalism*, Princeton, NJ: Princeton University Press.
——. (2002), 'Towards the Good Society Once Again', in Esping-Anderson, G., Gallie, D., Hemerijck, A. and Myles, J. (eds), *Why we Need a New Welfare State*, Oxford: Oxford University Press.
Etzioni, A. (2000), 'Social Norms: Internalization, Persuasion, and History', *Law & Society Review*, 34: pp. 157–78.
Evans, G. (ed.) (1999), *The End of Class Politics*, Oxford: Oxford University Press.
Feierabend, I. K., Feierabend, R. L. and Nesvold, B. A. (1969), 'Social Change and Political Violence', in Graham H. D. and Gurr T. (eds), *Violence in America: Historical and Comparative Perspectives*, New York: Frederick A. Praeger.
Finkel, S. E. (1995), 'Causal Analysis with Panel Data', Sage University Paper Series on Quantitative Applications in the Social Sciences, Beverly Hills: Sage Publications.
Flanagan, C. and Sherrod, L. (1998), 'Youth Political Development: an Introduction', *Journal of Social Issues* 54: pp. 447–56.
Foley, M. W. and Edwards, R. (1999), 'Is It Time to Disinvest in Social Capital?' *Journal of Public Policy* 19(2): pp. 199–231.
Ford, W. F. and Moore, J. H. (1970), 'Additional Evidence on the Social Characteristics of Riot Cities', *Social Science Quarterly* 51(2) (September): pp. 339–48.

Friedrich, R. J. (1982), 'In Defense of Multiplicative Terms in Multiple Regression Equations', *American Journal of Political Science* 26: pp. 797– 834.

Fukuyama, F. (1995), *Trust: the Social Virtues and the Creation of Prosperity*, London: Hamish Hamilton.

——. (1999), *The Great Disruption: Human Nature and the Reconstitution of Social Order*, New York: The Free Press.

Gabriel, O. W. (1995), 'Political Efficacy and Trust', in van Deth, J. W. and Scarbrough, E. (eds), *The Impact of Values*, New York: Oxford University Press.

Gallup International (2005), International Voice of the People Survey Results Available online: http://www.voice-of-the-people.net/. Last accessed 03/09/08.

Gambetta, D. (1988), *Trust: Making and Breaking Cooperative Relationships*, New York: Blackwell.

Gamson, W. A. (1968), *Power and Discontent*, Homewood, IL: The Dorsey Press.

Geschwender, J. (1964), 'Social Structure and the Negro Revolt', *Social Forces* 43: pp. 248–56.

Giddens, A. (1990), *The Consequences of Modernity*, Cambridge: Polity.

Gilbert, D. T. and Hixon, J. G. (1991), 'The Trouble of Thinking: Activation and Application of Stereotypic Beliefs', *Journal of Personality and Social Psychology* 60: pp. 509–17.

Gilens, Martin. (1999), *Why Americans Hate Welfare: Race, Media, and the Politics of Antipoverty Policy*, Chicago: University of Chicago.

Gilovich, T., Griffin, D. and Kahneman D. (eds) (2002), *Heuristics and Biases: the Psychology of Intuitive Judgement*, Cambridge: Cambridge University Press.

Glaeser, E., Laibson, D., Scheinkman, J. and Soutter, C. (2000), 'Measuring Trust', *Quarterly Journal of Economics* 115 (August): pp. 811–46.

Goetz, Stephan J. and Anil Rupasingha. (2007), 'Determinants and Implications of Growth in Non-Farm Proprietor Densities in the U.S.: 1990–2000', *Small Business Economics*, Springer Netherlands. Available online: http://www.springerlink.com/content/n0758p8637n46x15/fulltext.pdf. Last accessed 03/09/08.

Green, D. P. and Palmquist, B. (1994), 'How Stable is Party Identification?' *Political Behavior* 16(4): pp. 437–65.

——. and Shapiro, I. (1994), *Pathologies of Rational Choice Theory*, New Haven, CT: Yale University Press.

Greve, B. (2004), 'Denmark: Universal or Not so Universal Welfare State?' *Social Policy and Administration* 38: pp. 156–69.

Grindstaff, C. F. (1968), 'The Negro, Urbanization, and Relative Deprivation in the Deep South', *Social Problems* 15(3) (Winter): pp. 342–52.

Guinnane, T. W. (2005), 'Trust: A Concept Too Many', Central Discussion Paper no. 907, Economic Growth Center, Yale University.

Gurr, T. (1970), *Why Men Rebel*, Princeton, NJ: Princeton University Press.

Habermas, J. (1981), *The Theory of Communicative Action*, Cambridge: Polity.

Hall, P. A. (1999), 'Social Capital in Britain', *British Journal of Political Science* 29: pp. 417–61.

Halpern, D. (2005), *Social Capital*, Cambridge: Polity Press.

Hansard Society and Electoral Commission Report (2004), 'An Audit on Political Engagement'. Electronic copy. Available at: http://www.electoralcommission.org.uk/templates/search/document.cfm/9273.

Hardin, R. (1998), 'Trust in Government', in Braithwaite, V. and Levi, M. (eds), *Trust and Governance*, New York: Russell Sage Foundation.

——. (1999), 'Do We Want Trust in Government?' in Warren, M. (ed.), *Democracy and Trust*, Cambridge University Press, pp. 22–41.

——. (2000), 'The Public Trust,' in Pharr, S. J. and Putnam, R. D. (eds), *Disaffected Democracies: What's Troubling the Trilateral Democracies*, Princeton, NJ: Princeton University Press, pp. 31–51.

——. (2001), 'Conceptions and Explanations of Trust', in Cook, K. S. (ed.), *Trust in Society*, New York: Russell, pp. 3–39.

——. (2002), *Trust and Trustworthiness*, New York: Russell Sage Foundation.

Hay, C. (1995), 'Structure and Agency', in Marsh, D. and Stoker, G. (eds), *Theory and Methods in Political Science*, Hampshire: Macmillan Press.

Held, D. (1996), *Models of Democracy*, 2nd Edition, Stanford: Stanford University Press.

Helliwell, J. F. (1996a), 'Do Borders Matter for Social Capital? Economic Growth and Civic Culture in U.S. States and Canadian Provinces', National Bureau of Economic Research, NBER Working Paper Number 5863. Cambridge, MA: National Bureau of Economic Research.

——. (1996b), 'Economic Growth and Social Capital in Asia', NBER Working Paper Number 5470, Cambridge, MA: National Bureau of Economic Research.

Hetherington, M. (2004), *Why Trust Matters: Declining Political Trust and the Demise of American Liberalism*, Princeton, NJ: Princeton University Press.

Hibbing, J. R. and Theiss-Morse, E. (eds) (2001), *What Is It About Government That Americans Dislike?* Cambridge: Cambridge University Press.

Hoffman, E., McCabe, K. and Smith, V. (1996) 'Social Distance and Other Regarding Behavior in Dictator Games', *American Economic Review* 86: pp. 653–60.

Hollis, M. (1994), *The Philosophy of Social Science*, Cambridge: Cambridge University Press.

——. (1998), *Trust Within Reason*, Cambridge: Cambridge University Press.

Holmberg, Sören. (1999), 'Down and down We Go: Political Trust in Sweden', in Norris, P. (ed.), *Critical Citizens*, Oxford: Oxford University Press.

Holzhacker, R. (2002), 'Europeanization and National Political Institutions: A Model to Comparatively Assess the Power to Scrutinize: Rules, Institutions, and Party Behavior', paper presented at the European Consortium for Political Research conference on Europeanization and National Political Institutions, Turin, Italy, March 2002. Electronic Copy. Available at: http://www.essex.ac.uk/ecpr/events/jointsessions/paperarchive/turin/ws19/Holzhacker.pdf.

Homans, G. C. (1961), *Social Behaviour: Its Elementary Forms*, New York: Harcourt, Brace and World.

Huber, E. and Stephens, J. D. (2001), *Development and Crisis of the Welfare State*, Chicago: The University of Chicago Press.

Hume, D. (1751), *An Enquiry Concerning the Principles of Morals*, Oxford: Clarendon Press.

Hursthouse, R. (1999), *On Virtue Ethics*, Oxford: Oxford University Press.

Inglehart, R. (1997), 'Postmaterialist Values and the Erosion of Institutional Authority', in Nye, J. S. Jr., Zelikow, P. D. and King, D. C. (eds), *Why People Don't Trust Government*, Cambridge, MA: Harvard University Press.

——. (1999), 'Postmodernization Erodes Respect for Authority, but Increases Support for Democracy', in Norris, P. (ed.), *Critical Citizens*, Oxford: Oxford University Press.

——., Basañez, M. and Moreno, A. (1998), *Human Values and Beliefs: A Cross-Cultural Sourcebook: Political, Religious, Sexual, and Economic Norms in 43 Societies: Findings from the 1990–1993 World Values Survey*, Ann Arbor: The University of Michigan Press.

Iyengar, S. (1991), *Is Anyone Responsible? How Television Frames Political Issues*. Chicago, IL: University of Chicago Press.

——. (1996), 'Framing Responsibility for Political Issues', *Annals of the American Academy of Political and Social Science* 546: pp. 59–70.

Jackman, R. W. and Miller, R. A. (1996), 'A Renaissance of Political Culture', *American Journal of Political Science* 40: pp. 632–59.

——. (2005) *Before Norms: Institutions and Civic Culture*, Ann Arbor, MI: University of Michigan Press.

Jagodzinski, W. and Dobbelaere. K. (1995), 'Secularization and Church Religiosity', in van Deth, J. W. and Scarbrough, E. (eds), *The Impact of Values*, Oxford: Oxford University Press.

Kaase, M. (1999), 'Interpersonal Trust, Political Trust and Non-institutionalized Political Participation in Western Europe', *West European Politics* 22 (3): pp. 1–21.

——. and Newton, K. (1995), *Beliefs in Government*, Oxford: Oxford University Press.

Kahneman, D. and Tversky, A. (1973), 'On the Psychology of Prediction', *Psychological Review* 80: pp. 237–51.

Kane, J. (2001), *The Politics of Moral Capital*, Cambridge: Cambridge University Press.

Kant, I. (1964), *Groundwork of the Metaphysic of Morals*, translated and analysed by Paton, H. J., New York: Harper Torchbooks.

Keane, J. (1991), *The Media and Democracy*, Cambridge: Polity Press.

Keele, L (2004), 'Social Capital, Government Performance, and Dynamics of Trust in Government': pp. 1–34. Available online: http://polmeth.wustl.edu/retrieve.php?id=463. Last accessed 05/08/08.

Kim, B. (2007), 'Increasing Trust in Government Leadership through more Participatory and Transparent Government', paper presented at the 7th Global Forum on Reinventing Government: Building Trust in Government 26–29 June 2007, Vienna, Austria.

King, A. (2000), 'Distrust of Government: Explaining American Exceptionalism', in Pharr, S. and Putnam, R. (eds), *Disaffected Democracies: What is Troubling the Trilateral Countries?*, Princeton, NJ: Princeton University Press, pp. 74–98.

——. (2001), 'Why A Poor Turnout Points To a Democracy in Good Health', *The Daily Telegraph* 17 May 2001.

——. (2002), 'Do Leaders' Personalities Really matter?', in King, A. (ed.), *Leaders' Personalities and the Outcomes of Democratic Elections*, Oxford: Oxford University Press.

——. (ed.) (1998), *New Labour Triumphs: Britain at the Polls, 1997*, Chatham, NJ: Chatham House.

Knack. S. (2003), 'Groups, Growth and Trust: Cross-Country Evidence on the Olson and Putnam Hypotheses', *Public Choice* 117 (304, December): pp. 341–55.

Knack. S. and Keefer, P. (1997), 'Does Social Capital Have an Economic Payoff? A Cross-Country Investigation,' *Quarterly Journal of Economics*, 72(4): pp. 1251–88.

Kohlberg, L. (1976), 'Moral Stages and Moralization', *Moral Development and Behavior*, 31: pp. 32–5.

——. (1981), *The Philosophy of Moral Development: Moral Stages and the Idea of Justice*, San Francisco: Harper.

Kreps, D. (1997), 'Intrinsic Motivation and Extrinsic Incentives', *American Economic Review* 87(2): pp. 359–64.

Kriesi, H. (2002), 'How Direct-Democratic Decisions Are Made – Towards a Realistic Theory of Direct Democracy', paper presented at the ECPR Joint Sessions of Workshop, Turin, 22–27 March 2002. Electronic copy.

Kumlin, S. and Rothstein, B. (2005), 'Making and Breaking Social Capital', *Comparative Political Studies* 38: pp. 339–65.

La Porta, R., Lopez-de-Silane, F., Shleifer, A. and Vishny, R. W. (1997), 'Trust in Large Organizations', AEA Papers and Proceedings, Vol. 87, No. 2 (Interaction of Economic Institutions and Theory), May.

Landman, T. (2003), *Issues and Methods in Comparative Politics: An Introduction*, 2nd edition, London: Routledge.

Lane, R. E. (1962), *Political Ideology: Why the American Common Man Believes What He Does*, New York, Free Press.

——. (1972), *Political Man*, New York: Free Press.

Laver, M. (1997), *Private Desires, Political Action*, London: Sage Publications.

Lawrence, R. Z. (1997), 'Is It Really the Economy, Stupid?', in Nye, J., Zelikow, P. and King, D. (eds), *Why People Don't Trust Government*, Cambridge, MA: Harvard University Press.

Leach, S. (2003), 'Strengthening Local Democracy: Making the Most of the Constitution'. Electronic copy. Available at: Office of the Deputy Prime Minister website, http://www.local.odpm.gov.uk/research/strength/rprt.pdf.

Lederman, Daniel, Loayza, N. and Menéndez, A. M. (2002), 'Violent Crime: Does Social Capital Matter?', *Economic Development and Cultural Change* 50(3): pp. 509–39.

Lees-Marshment, J. (2004), *The Political Marketing Revolution*, Manchester: Manchester University Press.

Leibfried, S. (1993), 'Towards a European Welfare State? On Integrating Poverty Regimes in the European Community', in Jones, C. (ed.), *New Perspectives on the Welfare State in Europe*, London and New York: Routledge, pp. 133–56.

Lenski, G. E. (1954), 'Status Crystallisation: A Non-Vertical Dimension of Social Status', *American Sociological Review* 19: pp. 405–13.

Letki, N. and Evans, G. (2005), 'Endogenizing Social Trust: Democratisation in East-Central Europe', *British Journal of Political Science* 35: 515–29.

Levi, M. (1996), 'Social and Unsocial Capital. A Review Essay of Robert Putnam's Making Democracy Work', *Politics and Society* 24: pp. 45–55.

——. (1998), 'A State of Trust', in Braithwaite, V. and Levi, M. (eds), *Trust and Governance*, New York: Russell Sage Foundation.

——. (1999), 'When Good Defences Make Good Neighbors. A Transaction Cost Approach to Trust and Distrust', New York: Russell Sage Foundation, Working Paper Number 140. Electronic copy.

Levin, J. (2003), 'Relational Incentive Contracts', *American Economic Review* 93: pp. 835–57.

Lewis-Beck, M. S. (1994), *Factor Analysis & Related Techniques*, SAGE Publications, Toppan Publishing.

Lieske, J. A. (1978), 'The Conditions of Racial Violence in American Cities: A Developmental Thesis', *American Political Science Review* 72(4) (December): pp. 1324–40.

Locke, J. (1988), *Two Treatises of Government*, edited by Peter Laslett, Cambridge: Cambridge University Press.

Lubell, M. and Scholz, J. T. (2001), 'Cooperation, Reciprocity, and the Collective Action Heuristic', *American Journal of Political Science* 45: pp. 160–78.

Luhmann, N. (1979), *Trust and Power: Two Works*, Chichester: Wiley.

Lupia, A. and McCubbins, M. D. (1998), *The Democratic Dilemma: Can Citizens Learn What They Need to Know?*, Cambridge: Cambridge University Press.

Mair, P. and van Biezen, I. (2001), 'Party Membership in Twenty European Democracies, 1980–2000', *Party Politics* 7: pp. 5–22.

Maloney, W. A. (2006), 'Political Participation: Beyond the Electoral Arena', in Dunleavy, P., Heffernan, R., Cowley, P. and Hay, C. (eds), *Developments in British Politics* vol. 8, London: Palgrave Macmillan.

Mansbridge, J. (ed.) (1990), *Beyond Self-Interest*, Chicago: University of Chicago Press.

March, J. G. and Olsen, J. P. (1989), *Rediscovering Institutions: The Organizational Basis of Politics*, New York: The Free Press.

Marcus, G. E., Neuman, W. R. and Mackuen, M. (2000), *Affective Intelligence and Political Judgement*, Chicago: The University of Chicago Press.

Margetts, H., van Heerde, J. and Dunleavy, P. (2005), 'Explaining Voters' Choices in the 2004 London Elections', paper presented at the 55th annual conference of the Political Studies Association of the United Kingdom (PSA), 5 April 2005, University of Leeds.

Marshall, T. H. (1992), 'Citizenship and Social Class', in Marshall, T. H. and Bottomore, T. (eds), *Citizenship and Social Class*, London: Pluto Press, pp. 3–51.

McAdams, Richard (1997), 'The Origin, Development, and Regulation of Norms', *Michigan Law Review* 96: pp. 338–81.

McAllister, D. J. (1995), 'Affect and Cognition Based Trust as a Foundation for Interpersonal Cooperation in Organisations', *Academy of Management Review* 38(1): pp. 24–59.

McAllister, I. (1999), 'The Economic Performance of Governments', in Norris, P. (ed.), *Critical Citizens*, Oxford: Oxford University Press.

McConnell, G. (1966), *Private Power and American Democracy*, New York: Knopf.

McDonald, M. D. and Budge, I. (2005), *Elections, Parties, Democracy: Conferring the Median Mandate*, Oxford: Oxford University Press.

McNair, B. (2003), *An Introduction to Political Communication*, 3rd edition, London: Routledge.

McNally, R. J. (1987), 'Preparedness and Phobias: A Review', *Psychological Bulletin* 101: pp. 283–303.

Messick, D. M. and Kramer, R. M. (2001), 'Trust as a Form of Shallow Morality', in Cook, K. S. (ed.), *Trust in Society*, New York: Russell Sage Foundation.

Mill, J. S. (1859), *On Liberty and Other Essays*, edited with an introduction by John Gray, Oxford: Oxford University Press.

Miller, A. H. (1974), 'Political Issues and Trust in Government: 1964–1970', *American Political Science Review* 68(3): pp. 951–72.
——. and Listhaug, O. (1998), 'Policy Preferences and Political Distrust', *Scandinavian Political Studies* 21(2): 161–87.
——. and Listhaug, O. (1999), 'Political Performance and Institutional Trust', in Norris, P. (ed.), *Critical Citizens*, Oxford: Oxford University Press.
Milner, H. (1989), *Sweden: Social Democracy in Practice*, Oxford: Oxford University Press.
——. (2002), *Civic Literacy: How Informed Citizens Make Democracy Work*, Hanover: University Press of New England.
Mishler, W. and Rose, R. (1996), 'Trajectories of Fear and Hope: Support for Democracy in Post-Communist Europe', *Comparative Political Studies* 28 (January): pp. 553–81.
——. (2001), 'What are the Origins of Political Trust: Testing Institutional and Cultural Theories in Post-Communist Societies.' *Comparative Political Studies* 34: pp. 30–62.
——. (2005), 'What are the Political Consequences of Trust? A Test of Cultural and Institutional Theories in Russia', *Comparative Political Studies* 38(9, November): pp. 1050–78.
Misovich, S. J., Fisher, J. D. and Fisher, W. A. (1997), 'Close Relationships and Elevated HIV Risk Behavior: Evidence and Possible Underlying Psychological Processes', *Review of General Psychology* 1: pp. 72–107.
Misztal, B. A. (1996), *Trust in Modern Societies*, Cambridge: Polity Press.
Modood, T., Berthoud, R., Lakey, J., Nazroo, J., Smith, P., Virdee, S. and Beishon, S. (1997), *Ethnic Minorities in Britain: Diversity and Disadvantage. The Fourth National Survey of Ethnic Minorities*, London: Policy Studies Institute.
Moorman, C., Zaltman, G. and Deshpande, R. (1992), 'Relationships between Providers and Users of Market Research: the Dynamics of Trust within and between Organisations', *Journal of Marketing Research* 29 August: pp. 314–28.
Morrow, J. D. (1994), *Game Theory for Political Scientists*, Princeton, NJ: Princeton University Press.
Morton, R. (1999), *Methods and Models: A Guide to the Empirical Analysis of Formal Models in Political Science*, New York: Cambridge University Press.
Mudde, C. (2007), *Populist Radical Right Parties in Europe*, Cambridge: Cambridge University Press.
Muller, E. N. and Seligson, M. A. (1994), 'Civic Culture and Democracy: the Question of Causal Relationships', *American Political Science Review* 88: pp. 635–52.
Mutz, D. C. (1998), *Impersonal Influence: How Perceptions of Mass Collectives Affect Political Attitudes*, Cambridge: Cambridge University Press.
Nannestad, P. and Svendsen, G. T. (2005), *Institutions, Culture and Trust*, Göteborg: The Quality of Government Institute, Göteborg University.
Nelson, Barbara J. (1984), *Making an Issue of Child Abuse*, Chicago: University of Chicago Press.
Newton, K. (1997), 'Politics and the News Media: Mobilisation or Videomalaise?', in Roger Jowell et al. (eds), *British Social Attitudes: the 14th Report*, Aldershot: Ashgate, pp. 151–65.
——. (1999a), 'Mass Media Effects: Mobilization or Media Malaise?', *British Journal of Political Science*, 29: pp. 577–99.

——. (1999b), 'Social and Political Trust in Established Democracies', in Norris, P. (ed.), *Critical Citizens*, Oxford: Oxford University Press, pp. 169–87.

——. and Norris, P. (2000), 'Confidence in Public Institutions', in Pharr, S. J. and Putnam, R. D. (eds), *Disaffected Democracies: What's Troubling the Trilateral Countries*, Princeton, NJ: Princeton University Press.

Nordhaus, W. (1975), 'The Political Business Cycle', *Review of Economic Studies* 42 (April): pp. 169–90.

Norris, P. (ed.) (1999), *Critical Citizens*, Oxford: Oxford University Press.

——. (2000), *A Virtuous Circle: Political communications in Post-industrial Societies*, Cambridge: Cambridge University Press.

——. (2002), *Rising Phoenix: Democratic Participation Worldwide*, Cambridge: Cambridge University Press.

North, D. C. (1990), *Institutions, Institutional Change, and Economic Performance*, Cambridge: Cambridge University Press.

Nye, J., Zelikow, P. and King, D. (eds) (1997), *Why People Don't Trust Government*, Cambridge, MA: Harvard University Press.

Offe, C. (1999), 'How Can We Trust Our Fellow Citizens?' in Warren, M. E. (ed.), *Democracy and Trust*, Cambridge, Cambridge University Press.

Olson, M. (1965), *The Logic of Collective Action: Public Goods and the Theory of Groups*, Cambridge, MA: Harvard University Press.

Orbell, J., Dawes, R. and Schwartz-Shea, P. (1994), 'Trust, Social Categories, and Individuals: the Case of Gender', *Motivation and Emotion* 18(2): pp. 109–28.

Orren, G. (1997), 'Fall from Grace: The Public's Loss of Faith in Government', in Nye, J., Zelikow, P. and King, D. (eds), *Why People Don't Trust Government*, Cambridge, MA: Harvard University Press.

Orren, K. and Skowronek, S. (1995), 'Order and Time in Institutional Studies', in Farr, J. et al. (eds), *Political Science in History*, New York: Cambridge University Press, pp. 296–317.

Ostrom, E. (1990), *Governing the Commons: The Evolution of Institutions for Collective Action*, Cambridge: Cambridge University Press.

——. (1998), 'A Behavioral Approach to the Rational Choice Theory of Collective Action', *The American Political Science Review* 92(1): pp. 1–22.

——. (2003), 'Toward a Behavioral Theory Linking Trust, Reciprocity, and Reputation', in *Trust and Reciprocity*, New York: Russell Sage Foundation, pp. 19–79.

Parkinson, John. (2003), 'Legitimacy Problems in Deliberative Democracy', *Political Studies* 51: pp. 180–96.

Parry, G., Moyser, M. and Day, N. (1992), *Political Participation and Democracy in Britain*, Cambridge: Cambridge University Press.

Pattie, C. J. and Johnston, R. J. (2001), 'Losing the Voters' Trust: Evaluations of the Political System and Voting at the 1997 British General Election', in *British Journal of Politics and International Relations* 3: pp. 191–222.

——., Seyd, P. and Whiteley, P. (2004), *Citizenship in Britain: Values, Participation and Democracy*, Cambridge: Cambridge University Press.

Pharr, S. and Putnam, R. (eds) (2000), *Disaffected Democracies*, Princeton, NJ: Princeton University Press.

Phelps, E. (2006), 'Young Adults and Electoral Turnout in Britain: Towards a Generational Model of Political Participation', Sussex European Institute (SEI) Working Paper no. 92. Available online http://www.sussex.ac.uk/sei/documents/sei_working_paper_92_.pdf. Last accessed 05/09/08.

Pilisuk, M. and Skolnick, P. (1968), 'Inducing Trust: a Test of the Osgood Proposal', *Journal of Personality and Social Psychology* 8: pp. 121–33.

Plutzer, E. (2002), 'Becoming a Habitual Voter: Inertia, Resources and Growth in Young Adulthood', *American Political Science Review* 96(1): pp. 41–56.

Postman, N. (1987), *Amusing Ourselves to Death*, London: Methuen.

Pratkanis, A. R. (1989), 'The Cognitive Representation of Attitudes', in Pratkanis, A. R., Breckler, S. and Greenwald, S. (eds), *Attitude Structure and Function*, Hillsdale, NJ: Erlbaum, pp. 70–98.

Putnam, R. D. (1993), *Making Democracy Work*, Princeton, NJ: Princeton University Press.

——. (1995), 'Tuning In, Tuning Out: The Strange Disappearance of Social Capital in America', *Political Science Review* 28(4): pp. 664–83.

——. (2000), *Bowling Alone*, New York: Simon & Schuster.

——. (2007), 'E Pluribus Unum: Diversity and Community in the TwentyFirst Century'. The 2006 Johan Skytte prize lecture, *Scandinavian Political Studies* 30(2): pp. 137–74.

Raiser, M., Haerpfer, C., Nowotny, Th. and Wallace, C. (2001), 'Social Capital in Transition: a First Look at the Evidence', EBRD Working Paper Number 61, London: EBRD.

Rawls, J. (1972), *A Theory of Justice*, Oxford: Clarendon Press.

Rapley, M. (2003), *Quality of Life Research: A Critical Introduction*, London: Sage Publications.

Ratcliffe P., Harrison, M., Hogg, R., Line, R., Phillips, D., Tomlins, R. and Power, A. (2001), *Breaking the Barriers: Improving Asian Access to Social Rented Housing*, London: Chartered Institute of Housing.

Reeskens, T. and Hooghe, M. (2008), 'Cross-Cultural Measurement Equivalence of Generalized Trust. Evidence from the European Social Survey, 2002 and 2004'. *Social Indicators Research* 85(3): pp. 515–32.

Ricci, D. M. (2004), *Good Citizenship in America*, Cambridge: Cambridge University Press.

Riedel, E. (2002), 'The Impact of High School Community Service Programs on Students' Feelings of Civic Obligation', *American Politics Research* 30(5): pp. 499–527.

Rose, R. (1999), 'Politics in England', in Almond, G., and Powell, B., Strøm, K. and Dalton, R. (eds), *Comparative Politics*, 7th Edition, New York: Harpers, pp. 161–209.

Rothstein, B. (1998), *Just Institutions Matter: The Moral and Political Logic of the Universal Welfare State,* Cambridge: Cambridge University Press.

——. (2001), 'Social Capital in the Social Democratic Welfare State', *Politics & Society* 29(2): pp. 207–41.

——. and Stolle, D. (2003), 'Social Capital, Impartiality and the Welfare State: An Institutional Approach', in Hooghe, M. and Stolle, D. (eds), *Generating Social Capital: Civil Society and Institutions in Comparative Perspective*, New York: Palgrave Macmillan.

——. and Uslaner, E. M. (2005), 'All for All: Equality, Corruption, and Social Trust', *World Politics* 58: pp. 41–72.

Roy, J. (2007), 'Voter Heterogeneity: The Direct and Indirect Effect of Information', paper presented at the CPSA Annual Conference 2007.

Runciman, W. G. (1966), *Relative Deprivation and Social Justice : A Study of Attitudes to Social Inequality in Twentieth-Century England*, London: Routledge & K. Paul.

Sanders, D. and Tanenbaum, E. (1983), 'Direct Action and Political Culture: The Changing Political Conciousness of the British Public', *European Journal of Political Research* 11: pp. 45–61.

Sapiro, V. (2004), 'Not Your Parent's Political Socialization: Introduction for a New Generation', *Annual Review of Political Science* 7 (2004): pp. 1–23.

Scheufele, D. A. (1999), 'Framing as a Theory of Media Effects', *Journal of Communication* 49 (4): pp. 103–22.

Scheufele, D. A. and Shah, D. V. (2000), 'Personality Strength and Social Capital. The Role of Dispositional and Informational Variables in the Production of Civic Participation', *Communication Research* 27(2): pp. 107–31.

Schmitt, H. and Ohr, D. (2000), 'Are Party Leaders Becoming More Important in German Elections? Leader Effect on the Vote in Germany, 1961–1999', paper presented at the Annual Meeting of The American Political Science Association, Washington, DC, 31 August–3 September.

Schudson, M. (1995), *The Power of News*, Cambridge, MA: Harvard University Press.

Schumpeter, J. A. (1942) *Capitalism, Socialism and Democracy*. New York: Harper & Brothers.

Sennett, R. (1999), *The Corrosion of Character: The Personal Consequences of Work in the New Captialism*, New York: W. W. Norton.

Shapiro, S. P. (1987), 'The Social Control of Impersonal Trust', *American Journal of Sociology* 93(3): pp. 623–58.

Sidgwick, H. (1890), *The Methods of Ethics*, 4th edition, London: Macmillan.

Simon, H. A. (1967), 'Motivational and Emotional Controls of Cognition', *Psychological Review* 74: pp. 29–39, reprinted in *Models of Thought*, Vol 1, New Haven: Yale University Press.

——. (1982), 'A Behavioral Model of Rational Choice', in Simon, H. A. (ed.), *Models of Bounded Rationality. Behavioral Economics and Business Organization*, Vol 2, Cambridge, MA: MIT Press, pp. 239–58.

——. (1983), *Reason in Human Affairs*, Oxford: Basil Blackwell.

Sitkin, S. B. (1995), 'On the Positive Effect of Legalization on Trust', *Research on Negotiation in Organizations* 5: pp. 185–217.

Slovic, P. (1987), 'Perception of Risk', *Science* 236: pp. 280–5.

——. (ed.) (2000), *The Perception of Risk*, London: Earthscan.

Smith, K. W. and Kinsey, K. A. (1987), 'Understanding Taxpayer Behavior: A Conceptual Framework with Implications for Research', *Law and Society Review* 21: pp. 639–63.

Sniderman, P. M., Brody, R. A. and Tetlock, P. E. (1991), *Reasoning and Choice: Explorations in Political Psychology*, New York: Cambridge University Press.

Solomon, L. (1960), 'The Influence of Some Types of Power Relationships and Game Strategies upon the Development of Interpersonal Trust', *Journal of Abnormal and Social Psychology* 61(2): pp. 223–30.

Stark, D. (1995), 'Not by Design: The Myth of Designer Capitalism in Eastern Europe', in Hausner, J., Jessop, B. and Nielsen, K. (eds), *Strategic Choice and Path-Dependency in Post-Socialism*, Aldershot: Edward Elgar, pp. 67–83.

Stimson, J. A. (1999), *Public Opinion in America: Moods, Cycles, and Swings*, 2nd edition, Boulder, CO: Westview Press.

Stokes, D. and DiIulio, J. (1993), 'The Setting: Valence Politics in Modern Elections', in Nelson, M. (ed.), *The Elections of 1992*, Washington, DC: Congressional Quarterly Press, pp. 1–20.

Stolle, D. and Hooghe, M. (2004), 'The Roots of Social Capital. Attitudinal and Network Mechanisms in the Relation between Youth and Adult Indicators of Social Capital', *Acta Politica* 39(4): pp. 422–41.

Stone, W. (2003), 'Bonding, Bridging and Linking with Social Capital', *Stronger Families Learning Exchange Bulletin* 4: 13–16.

Sturgis, P., Patulny, R. and Allum, N. (2007), 'Re-evaluating the Individual Level Causes of Trust: a Panel Data Analysis', paper presented at the European Survey Research Association conference, Prague, June. Available online: http://staff.soc.surrey.ac.uk/psturgis/papers/trustpanel.pdf. Last accessed 04/09/08.

Sturgis, P. and Smith, P. (2008), 'Assessing the Validity of Generalized Trust Questions: What Kind of Trust Are We Measuring?' paper presented at the 'Conference on Composite Scores' ESADE, Barcelona, 14–15 February 2008.

Suls, J. and Wills, T. A. (eds) (1991), *Social Comparison*, Hillsdale, NJ: Lawrence Erlbaum Associates.

Sundquist, J. L. (1980), 'The Crisis of Competence in Our National Government', *Political Science Quarterly* 95: pp. 183–208.

Svallfors, S. (1997), 'Words of Welfare and Attitudes to Redistribution: A Comparison of Eight Western Nations', *European Sociological Review* 13: pp. 283–304.

Swank, D. (2002), *Global Capital, Political Institutions, and Policy Change in Developed Welfare States*, New York: Cambridge University Press.

Szreter, S. (2002), 'The State of Social Capital: Bringing Back in Power, Politics and History', *Theory and Society* 31(5): pp. 573–621.

Talisse, R. B. (2005), *Democracy After Liberalism: Pragmatism and Deliberative Politics*, New York: Routledge.

Taylor, C. (1989), *Sources of the Self: The Making of the Modern Identity*, Cambridge, MA: Harvard University Press.

Tolchin, S. J. (1996), *The Angry American: How Voter Rage is Changing the Nation*, Boulder, CO: Westview Press.

Tse, W. S. and Bond, A. J. (2002), 'Serotonergic Intervention Affects Both Social Dominance and Affiliative Behaviour', *Psychopharmacology* 161(3, May): pp. 324–30.

Tyler, T. R. (1990), *Why People Obey the Law*, New Haven, CT: Yale University Press.

——. and Caine, A. (1981), 'The Influence of Outcomes and Procedures on Satisfaction with Formal Leaders', *Journal of Personality and Social Psychology* 41(4): pp. 642–55.

——., Rasinski, K. and McGraw, K. (1985), 'The Influence of Perceived Injustice Upon Support for the President, Political Authorities, and Government Institutions', *Journal of Applied Social Psychology* 15: pp. 700–25.

Ullmann-Margalit, E. (2002), 'Trust, Distrust, and in Between', in Hardin, R. (ed.), *Distrust*, New York: Russell Sage Foundation, pp. 46–73.

Useem, M. (1975), *Protest Movements in America*, Indianapolis: Bobbs-Merrill.

Uslaner, E. (1999), 'Democracy and Social Capital', in Warren, M. (ed.), Democracy and Trust, Cambridge: Cambridge University Press.

Uslaner, E. (2002), The Moral Foundations of Trust, Cambridge: Cambridge University Press

Uzzi, B. (1997), 'Social Structure and Competition in Interfirm Networks: The Paradox of Embeddedness', *Administrative Science Quarterly* 42(1): pp. 35– 47.

van Deth, J. W. and Scarbrough, E. (eds) (1995), *The Impact of Values*, Oxford: Oxford University Press.

——., Maraffi, M., Newton, K. and Whiteley, P. (1998), *Social Capital and European Democracy*, London: Routledge.

Verba, S., Schlozman, K. and Brady, H. (1995), *Voice and Equality: Civic Voluntarism in American Politics*, Cambridge, MA: Harvard University Press.

Veenstra, G. (2002), 'Explicating Social Capital: Trust and Participation in the Civil Space', *Canadian Journal of Sociology* 27 (4): pp. 547–72.

Vetter, A. and Gabriel, O. W. (1998), 'Candidate Evaluations and Party Choice in Germany, 1972–94: Do Candidates Matter?' in J. Anderson Christopher and Zelle Carsten (eds), *Stability and Change in German Elections. How Electorates Merge, Converge, or Collide*, Westport: Praeger, pp. 71–98.

von Neumann, J. and Morgenstern, O. (1944), *Theory of Games and Economic Behavior*, New York: John Wiley and Sons.

von Wright, G. (1971), *Explanation and Understanding*, Ithaca, NY: Cornell University Press.

Walker, I. and Pettigrew, T. F. (1984), 'Relative Deprivation Theory: An Overview and Conceptual Critique', *British Journal of Social Psychology* 33: pp. 301–10.

Ward, H. (2002), 'Rational Choice', in Marsh, D. and Stoker, G. (eds), *Theory and Methods in Political Science*, Second Edition, New York: Palgrave Macmillan, pp. 65–89.

Ware, A. (1996) *Political Parties and Party Systems*, Oxford: Oxford University Press.

Warren, M. (1999), 'Introduction', in Warren M. (ed.), *Democracy and Trust*, Cambridge: Cambridge University Press, pp. 1–21.

——. (2002), 'What Can Democratic Participation Mean Today?' *Political Theory* 30(5): pp. 677–701.

Watson, M. (2004) Endogenous Growth Theory: Explanation or Post Hoc Rationalisation for Policy?', *British Journal of Politics and International Relations* 6 (4): pp. 543–51.

Weale, A. (1999), *Democracy*, Houndmills, Basingstoke: Macmillan.

——. (2001), '*Explanation by Implicit Social Contract*', Department of Government Papers, University of Essex.

——. (ed.) (2002), *Risk, Democratic Citizenship and Public Policy*, Oxford: Oxford University Press.

Weatherford, S. M. (1984), 'Economic Stagflation and Public Support for the Political System', *British Journal of Political Science*, 14: pp. 187–205.

Weaver, R. K. and B. A. Rockman (eds) (1993), *Do Institutions Matter? Government Capabilities in the United States and Abroad*, Washington DC: Brookings.

Westholm, A., Lindquist, A. and Niemi, R.G. (1990), 'Education and the Making of the Informed Citizen: Political Literacy and the Outside World', in Ichilov, O. (ed.), *Political Socialisation, Citizenship Education, and Democracy*, New York: Teachers College Press, pp. 177–204.

White, R. W. (1959), 'Motivation Reconsidered: the Concept of Competence', *Psychological Review* 66: pp. 297–333.

Whiteley, P. (1999) 'The Origins of Social Capital', in Jan van Deth, Marco Maraffi, Kenneth Newton, and P. Whiteley (eds), *Social Capital and European Democracy*, London: Routledge.

Whiteley, P. (2005), 'Citizenship Education Longitudinal Study: Second Literature Review', *Citizenship Education: The Political Science Perspective Research Report RR631*. Available online: http://www.dfes.gov.uk/research/data/uploadfiles/RR631.pdf. Last accessed 03/09/08.

Whiteley, P. and Seyd, P. (2002), *High-Intensity Participation: The Dynamics of Party Activism in Britain*, Ann Arbor, MI: University of Michigan Press.

Whiteley, P. Clarke, H. Sanders, D. and Stewart, M. (2001), 'Turnout', in Norris, P. (ed.), *Britain Votes 2001*, Oxford, Oxford University Press.

Whiteley, P. F. (1997), *Economic Growth and Social Capital*, Sheffield: Blackwell.

——. (2000), 'Economic Growth and Social Capital', *Political Studies*, 48: pp. 443–66.

Williams, B. A. O. (1980), 'Internal and External Reasons', in Williams, B. A. O., *Moral Luck*, Cambridge: Cambridge University Press, pp. 101–13.

Williams, B. (1988), 'Formal Structures and Social Reality', in Gambetta, D. (ed.), *Trust: Making and Breaking Cooperative Relationships*, New York: Blackwell, pp. 3–13.

Williamson, O. E., (1979), 'Transaction-Cost Economics: The Governance of Contractual Relations', *Journal of Law and Economics* 22: 233–62.

——. (1981), 'The Economics of Organization: The Transaction Cost Approach' *American Journal of Sociology* 87(3, November): pp. 548–77.

——. (1993), 'Calculativeness, Trust, And Economic Organization', *Journal of Law and Economics* 36, April: pp. 453–86.

Wincott, D. (2004), 'Devolution and Social Democracy: Policy Diversity and Social Citizenship in the UK', paper presented at the Biennial Conference of Europeanists, 11–14 March, Palmer House Hilton, Chicago.

Yamagishi, T. and Kiyonari, T. (2000), 'The Group as the Container of Generalized Reciprocity', *Social Psychology Quarterly* 63(2): pp. 116–32.

Zak, P. J. and Knack, S. (1998), 'Trust and Growth', IRIS Working Paper Number 219, University of Maryland, College Park.

——. (2001), 'Trust and Economic Growth', *Economic Journal* 111 (470): pp. 295–321.

Zaller, J. (1992), *The Nature and Origins of Mass Opinion*, Cambridge: Cambridge University Press.

Zimmermann, E. (1983), *Political Violence, Crises, and Revolutions: Theories and Research*, Boston, MA.: G.K. Hall; Scheinkman Pub. Co.

Zmerli, S., and Newton, K. (2006), 'Social Trust and Attitudes Towards Democracy: A Close Association After All?', paper presented at the ESRC Research Methods Festival, Oxford.

——., Newton, K. and Montero, J. R. (2007), 'Trust in People, Confidence in Political Institutions, and Satisfaction with Democracy', in Maloney, W. A. and Rossteutscher, S. (eds), *Social Capital and Associations in European Democracies*, London: Routledge, pp. 153–77.

Name Index

Subject Index